Archetypal Figures in "The Snows of Kilimanjaro"

ARCHETYPAL FIGURES IN "THE SNOWS OF KILIMANJARO"

Hemingway on Flight and Hospitality

David L. Anderson

The Kent State University Press

Kent, Ohio

Library of Congress Catalog Card Number 2019013203
ISBN 978-1-60635-388-2
Manufactured in the United States of America

Library of Congress Cataloging-in-Publication Data
Names: Anderson, David L. (David Louis), author.
Title: Archetypal figures in the Snows of Kilimanjaro : Hemingway on flight and hospitality / David L. Anderson.
Description: Kent, Ohio : The Kent State University Press, [2019] | Includes bibliographical references and index.
Identifiers: LCCN 2019013203 | ISBN 9781606353882 (cloth)
Subjects: LCSH: Hemingway, Ernest, 1899-1961. Snows of Kilimanjaro. | Hospitality in literature. | Death in literature.
Classification: LCC PS3515.E37 Z555 2019 | DDC 813/.52--dc23
LC record available at https://lccn.loc.gov/2019013203

23 22 21 20 19   5 4 3 2 1

CONTENTS

INTRODUCTION

Great writers in their youth, undaunted by their limited experience and even their limited reading but trusting in their intuition, often seize upon iterations of the most universal characters and plots. Such a writer was Jack London. In the final year of his life, when he began to read the writings of Carl Gustav Jung, London had to have experienced a shock of recognition, finding in himself and in his own previous writings—the writings of his youth—evidence of Jung's theory of the collective unconscious. London's copy of Jung's *Psychology of the Unconscious* has hundreds of notations (see Hamilton 175–76).[1] Images from the collective unconscious, which Jung called archetypes, stem from the most primordial and recurrent experiences of the human race. What could be more primal than the anthropomorphized dog Buck of *The Call of the Wild?* The power of London's allegory of the struggle of life versus the hostile elements of this world was and remains so strong that the phrase "call of the wild" instantly assumed its place as a permanent part of our culture. In his first published work of fiction, a Klondike tale titled "To the Man on Trail," from which this volume took its working title, London intuited two archetypal figures that have recurred with notable regularity in literature throughout the millennia. The first is the man on trail, pursued by death and in need of shelter from both the literal and figurative storms of life. The second is the host who unhesitatingly offers him heartfelt hospitality.

An understanding of these figures, whose roots are pre-Homeric, will ultimately lead to the unraveling of one of the great literary enigmas of the twentieth century. Despite its enormous popularity and critical success, Ernest Hemingway's classic "The Snows of Kilimanjaro" remains a polarizing text, given to widely differing and irreconcilable interpretations. There is, to use the phrase popularized by Henry James, a "figure in the carpet" woven into the text of Hemingway's greatest short story. To make out that figure, readers must follow literary trails far from Mount Kilimanjaro, but they may rest assured that the path, in these pages at least, will always return there. These trails will lead the reader to works of literature from widely separated times and places and from different genres. Many are canonical. A few are obscure, but there is no work of literature discussed in these pages that I cannot heartily recommend as a pleasurable read.

Genesis of "The Snows of Kilimanjaro"

At the time Ernest Hemingway began to write "The Snows of Kilimanjaro," his career path and the course of world events had brought him to a crossroads. He often employed material derived from his wide-ranging travels—the places he had been to and the events he had witnessed. He incorporated in his fiction the effects that those places and events had on his characters and on their worlds. However, this by no means indicates that his fiction is little more than autobiography with the names changed. Nor does it validate as definitive a purely biographical interpretation of the story. As early as 1924, in the deleted ending of "Big Two-Hearted River," finally published in *The Nick Adams Stories* in 1972 as "On Writing," Hemingway insists on the importance of a writer's power of invention, the core of a writer's creativity. In this case, the writer is Nick Adams, the alter ego of the young Hemingway: "The only writing that was any good was what you made up, what you imagined. That made everything come true. . . . Everything good he'd ever written he'd made up" (237). Three and a half decades later, in his interview with George Plimpton for *The Paris Review,* he struck the same note several times. Of *For Whom the Bell Tolls,* he states that he "knew what was going to happen in principle. But I invented what happened each day as I wrote" (123). He once again mentions both experience and invention when he refers to his African stories, "The Snows of Kilimanjaro" and "The Short Happy Life of Francis Macomber," as "stories which I invented from the knowledge and experience acquired on the same long hunting trip" (123). *Green Hills of Africa* came from that same safari. The interview ends on the same note: "From things that have happened and from things as they exist and from all things that you know, you make something through your invention that is not a representation but a whole new thing truer than anything true and alive" (129). That is the formula that produced "The Snows of Kilimanjaro."

A young Ernest Hemingway, looking for action, left his home in Oak Park, Illinois, just outside Chicago, to join the Red Cross during World War I. His service as an ambulance driver for the Italian army ended on July 8, 1918, when an Austrian trench mortar seriously wounded him near the town of Fossalta, Italy. His love affair with one of the nurses who cared for him during his hospital stay in Italy ended badly. As will be discussed later, hospitals often serve as settings in his fiction, more so than in the fiction of his contemporaries. He completed his recuperation at home in Oak Park. He soon married and returned to Europe as a newspaper correspondent for *The Toronto Star*. When he eventually began his career as a serious creative writer, he had at his disposal the accumulated material from his war experiences, his experience as a journalist covering the appalling human tragedy of the Greco-Turkish War, summering at his family's cottage in Michigan, and attending bullfights in Spain.

The elements of travel, experience, and their effects come together, as Paul Smith has pointed out, in "Indian Camp," one of his early masterpieces from *In Our Time* (36–38). He had visited an Indian camp near his family's cottage in northern lower Michigan. During his coverage of the Greco-Turkish War, he saw a woman in a refugee procession, attended by only a frightened young girl, struggling to have a baby in the rain and in the back of a cart. Dr. Clarence Hemingway, Ernest's father, had delivered many babies during his career. Hemingway knew of an Indian suicide: Prudence Bolton, a childhood companion and likely his first lover. All of this experience he structured around his own invention, moving the Indian camp to upper Michigan, making an Indian woman the one experiencing the difficult delivery, including the suicide of the Indian woman's husband, and making his alter ego Nick Adams the frightened observer. If "Indian Camp" had been written purely as self-therapy over the traumas of his own life, Hemingway would not have needed his inventions and would not have needed to publish the story. But he did add the inventions—which he was most proud of. While there may be biographical relevance, the story was written primarily for readers. Hemingway's inventions for his readers are a key to understanding the aesthetic totality of "The Snows of Kilimanjaro."

Hemingway's first major story collection, *In Our Time* (1925), chronicled the epiphanies, disappointments, and traumas of Nick Adams's formative years and war experiences—based on Hemingway's own travels and experiences but to which Hemingway consistently added his own inventions, as he did in "Indian Camp." Like *In Our Time, Men without Women* (1927) included stories about Nick Adams as well as freestanding stories drawn from a similar mix of experience and invention. Both volumes achieved critical success.

In 1926, *The Sun Also Rises* brought critical as well as his initial popular success. His depiction of the festival of San Fermin in Pamplona, Spain, started a phenomenon that still thrives today in popular culture; it is common knowledge the world over what "running with the bulls" means and where it takes place. For the generation that fought it, World War I with its epic mechanized slaughter in the service of questionable national objectives resulted in a massive disillusionment with the values, traditions, institutions, and modes of expression that the wartime generation saw as responsible for their suffering. The wounds Jake Barnes suffered in the war rendered him incapable of sexual intercourse while leaving him with normal erotic desires—essentially, severe damage to the penis but not the testicles. Jake's suffering came to represent Hemingway's own generation's struggles with that massive disillusionment. Although many of the characters of that novel are drawn from life, as numerous Hemingway biographies have shown (most recently Lesley Blume's *Everybody Behaves Badly*), the character of Jake and the representative nature of his wound are largely Hemingway's invention. An entire generation responded to Jake, not to perceived connections between character and author. Hemingway's letters to Max Perkins, his editor at Scribner's, during this period often requested that biographical material on dust jackets and in promotional materials be kept to a bare minimum.

Success continued with *A Farewell to Arms,* which was based on the ill-fated love affair with his nurse in Italy, his war experience, and on historical research as well. It outsold all of his previous books combined and was also a critical success.[2] *A Farewell to Arms* is not about the aftermath of war, as is *The Sun Also Rises.* It places its characters firmly within actual events of the war, most notably the disorderly Italian retreat from the Austrians after the Battle of Caporetto in 1917. Like Hemingway, Frederic Henry, the narrator and protagonist of the novel, is wounded by the explosion of an Austrian trench mortar and falls in love with one of his nurses. However, Hemingway carefully researched the retreat from Caporetto, which actually occurred before he arrived in Italy. The novel's shattering conclusion, Hemingway's own invention, owes little to Hemingway's personal experience.

The Sun Also Rises, A Farewell to Arms, and many of his short stories from *In Our Time* and *Men without Women* focus on the suffering of the individual, "the one," in scenarios—often war-related—caused by "the many," in the form of countries finding lame pretexts to start wars, in the form of armies engaging in mechanized slaughter and in summary executions. The pretext for the Great War, as it was called, did not come close to justifying the slaughter required to resolve it, neither in the minds of the participants nor in the final judgment of history. The young man who left his home to seek the action of war ultimately condemned the appalling slaughter of millions but also depicted with extraordinary sensitivity the war's initial traumatic and later insidious effects on individuals both during and after the war. It is no incidental episode when Frederic and Catherine, the lovers of *A Farewell to Arms,* escape war-torn Italy to seek their own separate peace in Switzerland. Hemingway's stance in the postwar period was understandably antiwar in general and American isolationist in particular. His recoiling from the horrors of a thoroughly questionable war—which resulted in some of his greatest—indeed immortal—fiction constituted one of the trails that led Hemingway to the crossroads of "The Snows of Kilimanjaro."

By 1926 Hemingway's first marriage, which had produced a son, came to an end; in his posthumous memoir, *A Moveable Feast,* he depicted his life in Paris with his first wife as one of picturesque and romantic poverty; though his biographers have challenged that portrait, particularly the poverty, he would later make use of that material in "The Snows of Kilimanjaro" and in other works as well. His marriage to his second wife, from a wealthy family, changed his lifestyle dramatically and produced two more sons. He lived with his second wife's family in Arkansas for a time before taking up residence in a large house on Whitehead Street in Key West. Her uncle helped to finance the 1934 African safari that resulted in *Green Hills of Africa* and the African stories. Biographical consensus has it that Hemingway always regretted leaving his first wife and that Harry's unkind baiting of his wife, Helen, and her wealth in "The Snows of Kilimanjaro" reflects Hemingway's own growing resentment of his second wife, whom he would leave shortly.

On returning to the States, Hemingway ordered the *Pilar,* his deep-sea fishing boat, financed in part by his fiction and nonfiction contributions to the then nascent *Esquire* magazine. During the mid-1930s, he became a true pioneer of Atlantic deep-sea sport fishing. His efforts in actually establishing, popularizing, and organizing this sport are chronicled in detail in Ashley Oliphant's *Hemingway and Bimini: The Birth of Sport Fishing at "The End of the World."*

During his travels in Spain in the mid-1920s, he became a true aficionado of the *corrida,* better known in English as bullfighting. His had put his heart into the writing of *Death in the Afternoon* (1932), his book on bullfighting, still regarded by many as the most essential book written in English on the subject. Sales were modest, and some critics began to turn against him. Sales of the still underrated story collection *Winner Take Nothing* (1933) were also modest. Returning from his African safari, he began work in an experimental form, *Green Hills of Africa* (1935), a slightly fictionalized narrative of the hunts he had participated in while in Africa; disappointingly, sales and critical reactions failed to surpass even those of *Death in the Afternoon.*

Hemingway's awareness that he had come to a personal and aesthetic crossroads can be seen as early as the opening chapter of *Green Hills of Africa,* in which he depicts himself as a pompous drunk. In the ensuing chapters he comes across as an overly competitive trophy hunter. When he criticizes other American writers, he seems to be criticizing himself. (See chapter 9, note 2.)

European politics and the Great Depression of 1929, the same year in which *A Farewell to Arms* was published, were also markers on the trail that brought Hemingway to the crossroads of writing "The Snows of Kilimanjaro." Some of the criticism that targeted Hemingway during the early 1930s expressed disappointment over his focus on sporting interests of the wealthy—bullfighting, big-game sport fishing, and big-game hunting—instead of on world economic turmoil in the form of the Great Depression and political turmoil in the form of the rise of fascism.

Hemingway clearly had a strong social conscience. As early as 1923 in writing for *The Toronto Star* he warned his readers about Mussolini. In his short story "Che Ti Dice La Patria," included in 1927's *Men without Women,* he depicted fascism's corrupting influence on daily life in Italy. Though not a collectivist, he wrote one of his best journalistic pieces for *New Masses,* the voice of the Communist Party in America at the time. On Labor Day weekend of 1935, a hurricane swept through the Florida Keys, killing a thousand World War I veterans working in the Civilian Conservation Corps. In "Who Murdered the Vets? A First-Hand Report on the Florida Hurricane," published in *New Masses* on September 17, 1935, Hemingway described the carnage and tragic deaths of the veterans and placed blame on government bureaucrats who had placed them in danger. He would continue this focus on suffering humanity in "The Snows of Kilimanjaro," especially in the scenes from World War I and the Greco-Turkish War.

Hemingway turned back to fiction after *Green Hills of Africa,* not only to reestablish his reputation but also for purposes of self-examination and evaluation—which, as will be argued later, may have actually begun in the *Green Hills of Africa.* (Once again, see chapter 9, note 2.) Returning to the material of his African safaris, he produced two stories that his readers, the critics, and even Hemingway himself regarded as among his best, if not his very best: "The Short Happy Life of Francis Macomber," published in the September 1936 issue of *Cosmopolitan* and "The Snows of Kilimanjaro" published in the August 1936 issue of *Esquire.* Both would eventually be made into major motion pictures, both, incidentally, starring Gregory Peck. The biographical connections of these stories have proven irresistibly fascinating to both critics and biographers. Events from his entire life, not just his African sojourn, were used throughout "The Snows of Kilimanjaro," as were portraits of people he knew to greater or lesser degrees.

As critics and biographers too numerous to list here have shown, many of the experiences of Harry, the protagonist of "The Snows of Kilimanjaro," were based on Hemingway's own. But the key elements—Harry's fatal gangrene, his desertion of his writing talent and his duty to write, and his succumbing to the comforts of his wife's money—were Hemingway's inventions. Indeed, Harry's gangrenous wound thwarts his ambition to rekindle his writing career. At this crossroads, when Hemingway began to look over the trails leading in separate directions and to realize what he might have become had he succumbed to the attractions of the good life, he invented a story about a man who took the wrong path, realized he had done so, but tragically died as he was trying to find his way again. Hemingway turned from the pursuit of the good life to refocus on the challenges facing suffering and troubled humanity. The economic turmoil of the Great Depression and the evils of fascism outweighed his abhorrence of war and his tendency toward isolationism.

His new commitment to focusing his writing on humanity rather than just on individuals would surface very shortly after "The Snows of Kilimanjaro" in *To Have and Have Not* (1937), whose main character is also a man named Harry, a deep-sea fishing guide struggling to make a living to support his family during the Depression. *The Fifth Column* (1938) and the short stories of the Spanish Civil War (1938–39) address the rise of fascism. His commitment would come to a climax—and would magnificently still include plot lines focused on individuals as well as on entire peoples—in the iconic and hugely selling blockbuster *For Whom the Bell Tolls* (1940), about the Spanish Civil War, the prelude to World War II. In "The Snows of Kilimanjaro" Hemingway does not so much criticize his former positions as he does acknowledge the change of direction world events demanded of him.

Remarkably, however, nobody has ever published a book on "The Snows of Kilimanjaro." This, despite what Hemingway said about the story in "The Art of the Short Story," posthumously published in *The Paris Review* in 1981:

> and [I] put into one short story things you would use in, say, four novels if you were careful and not a spender. I throw everything I had been saving into the story and spend it all . . . and with all the load, the most load any short story ever carried, it still takes off and flies. This makes me very happy. So I thought that

> and the Macomber story are as good short stories as I can write for a while, so I lose interest and take up other forms of writing. (316–17)

The two stories were first published in book form in *The Fifth Column and the First Forty-Nine Stories* in 1938. As he claimed, Hemingway indeed seemed to lose interest in the form and never returned in those short stories that he did write to the heights that he had achieved in the African stories. He published stories from time to time in periodicals but never again another collection in book form, other than repackagings of previously published short stories. Thus, his African stories, as they are called, became Hemingway's self-proclaimed, as well as critically and popularly acclaimed, high-water mark in the short story form.

The Salient Feature

Italics are the salient feature of "The Snows of Kilimanjaro," a feature Hemingway occasionally employed.[3] In "The Snows of Kilimanjaro," italic print is used in the four-sentence epigraph—and is more famously used to present the five series of memories Harry, the story's writer/protagonist, runs through his mind as he awaits his death from gangrene on the plains of east Africa.

Hemingway had previously employed italics in the "interchapters" of the classic 1925 *In Our Time,* published by Boni & Liveright, his first major commercial publisher.[4] The interchapters were revised versions of the eighteen experimentally brief stories that made up the 1924 *in our time,* published in Paris by Three Mountains Press; six of these eighteen had been published previously in 1923 in the "Exiles" number of *The Little Review,* a small-press Paris literary magazine. The 1924 *in our time,* Hemingway's second small-press book, was printed in miniscule numbers but marked the entrance of Hemingway's genius-level talent onto the pages of the world's literature.[5] At Scribner's request, Hemingway added another story, later titled "On the Quai at Smyrna," to the 1930 edition.[6] Scribner's began as Hemingway's publisher in 1926 and continues in that role to this day, albeit as a Simon & Schuster imprint. One of the prospective titles Hemingway considered for the six stories he had sent to *The Little Review* was "Unwritten Stories Are Better" (Cohen 37). The same title might just as well have served for Harry's reminiscences in "The Snows of Kilimanjaro."

Although a lesser-known entry of the Hemingway canon, the 1924 *in our time* has generated significant critical attention, most notably Milton A. Cohen's 2005

Hemingway's Laboratory: The Paris in our time. Detailed and excellent as Cohen's analysis is, it is dwarfed by the volume of criticism the 1925/1930 *In Our Time* has and continues to engender. The relationships between the italicized interchapters (the entries reproduced from *in our time*) and the short stories they are interspersed among reveal the whole volume as a masterpiece of interrelated subtlety, irony, loss, tragedy, pity, and horror. What must be taken from the textual history of *In Our Time* as it relates to analysis of "The Snows of Kilimanjaro" is that at every stage of development, Hemingway revised the material—not because he planned to do so but because of the demands and opportunities of publishing. When he began "The Snows of Kilimanjaro," however, he could work with italics on a clean slate to get exactly the effects he wanted from the contrasts of the sections in italic and Roman type, all the while free of the baggage imposed by previous texts (happily, resulting in a case of *intratextuality* rather than the currently popular *intertextuality!*). Notably, *In Our Time* and "The Snows of Kilimanjaro" share not only the stylistic feature of italicized passages interspersed between narrative (Roman print) passages, they also both include events from World War I and the Greco-Turkish War of 1919–22.

The Scribner's *In Our Time* (1930 text) depicts the Greco-Turkish War in the following: "On the Quai at Smyrna," about the arrival of Greek refugees in Smyrna; chapter 2, on Greek refugees on the Karagatch Road between Adrianople and Karagatch; chapter 5, the execution of the Greek cabinet ministers; and "L'Envoi," an interview with the king and queen of Greece, both under house arrest.

In "The Snows of Kilimanjaro," the following are episodes from the same conflict: Harry's departure from Karagatch after witnessing the Greek retreat and flight of refugees; Nansen's mistake in exchange of populations operations leading to deaths of the secretaries in the snow, perhaps a parallel to the execution of the cabinet ministers of *In Our Time,* **IM I.1** (Italicized Memory. **I.1** refers to first group of memories, first paragraph. See the end of this chapter for an outline of the italicized passages from "The Snows of Kilimanjaro."); sex with the Armenian woman, likely a refugee from the Armenian holocaust perpetrated by the Turks in eastern Anatolia in 1915; and friendly fire of incompetent Constantine Greek officers leading to the advance of the Turks, and Harry's flight along with the retreat of Greek troops (**IM II.1–3**).

This conflict and the human tragedy these events generated make up part of the content of both "The Snows of Kilimanjaro" and *In Our Time* (as well as *in our time*). Further, both works present this content largely in the same way, in italicized passages that bear a structural and thematic relationship to the surrounding narratives. Very strangely, criticism of "The Snows of Kilimanjaro" often largely or entirely neglects the italicized passages.

Critical Scholarship

Serious, methodical scholarship of "The Snows of Kilimanjaro" begins with the coauthored essays of Robert W. Lewis and Max Westbrook. Together, their two insightful *Texas Quarterly* articles approach book length, although such a book never came to be. The first, "The Texas Manuscript of 'The Snows of Kilimanjaro'" (1966), is divided into three sections. "Part I: Text and Critic," by Lewis and Westbrook, is the definitive listing and analysis of the surprising number of textual variants. "Part II: Vivienne de Watteville, Hemingway's Companion on Kilimanjaro," by Lewis, investigates possible sources, notably Watteville's *Speak to the Earth.* "Part III: The Stewardship of Ernest Hemingway," by Westbrook, addresses the key interpretive questions already posed by such critics as Marion Montgomery, who asserted that the story was contrived and ultimately fails. In comparing "The Snows of Kilimanjaro" with *A Moveable Feast,* Westbrook discusses some of Harry's memories that have parallels in the posthumous memoir of his early life in Paris, such as the Tristan Tzara / American poet reference, which is discussed in relation to manuscript changes ("The Snows" 92). The defeat of the Greek Evzones is regarded as "ground-level realism" (96). However, Westbrook's thoughtful treatment of "remembered scenes in which good will is tripped by fate" notably includes the Nansen (**IM I.1**) and chore-boy (**IV III.3**) episodes, the misdelivered letter (**IM II.1–3**), and the death of Williamson (**IM V**) (96, 97–98). Westbrook makes a thoughtful interpretive statement about the italicized memories: "Redemption lies in purging one's self of the sickness of the temporal, in freezing one's self into an 'impersonal state'" (100). The Gulf Stream in *Green Hills of Africa* and Mount Kilimanjaro itself exemplify this impersonal state. "Harry's italicized reflections, unlike the thoughts which are closer to the surface and which are not in italics, are exercises in attaining this 'impersonal state.' They contain no self-pity, no viciousness, no sentimentality" (100). Lewis and Westbrook's sterling example of paying due attention to and analyzing close reading and interpretation of Harry's italicized memories has, unfortunately, not always been heeded by the critics who followed, among whom truly unfortunate monolithic treatments of the memories has been all too common.

Lewis and Westbrook's second article, "'The Snows of Kilimanjaro': Collated and Annotated" presents the story's five texts: first, the typescript held at the University of Texas at Austin, second, *Esquire* (1936), third, *The Fifth Column and the First Forty-Nine Stories* (Scribner's, 1938), fourth, *The Fifth Column and the First Forty-Nine Stories* (Jonathan Cape, 1939), and fifth, *Esquire* (1949). The article presents an entire collated text, including variant readings, along with well researched and insightful annotations.

More recently a typescript draft of the story, called "The Happy Ending," a brief page of material developed for the italicized memories, and a draft of the story's epigraph have been included in the Hemingway Library series edition of *The Short Stories of Ernest Hemingway,* edited by Seán Hemingway.

Problems Addressed in Literary Criticism

Many articles work well into the fifteen- to twenty-page range but typically end there, well short of a comprehensive interpretation, which is curious, especially for a story that, according to the author, uses up enough material to support as many as four novels. Critics often make a quick point and then get out before the leopard or the hyena catches up; this seems to have been the safest and one of the most common treatments. Many of the points made in such essays are worthy of note, but something has kept the authors from applying their theses to the italicized details of this four-novel-rich story.

Not surprisingly for a story that burns through material so lavishly, many scholars have produced useful findings by researching its many references and allusions, often in periodicals that publish useful "notes" rather than full-blown critical interpretations, such as *The Explicator, American Notes & Queries,* or the "Notes" section of *The Hemingway Review.* Representative examples include Peter Hays on the bicycle police (1981), Kenneth G. Johnston on the songs alluded to in the story ("Frog Who Would A-Wooing Go" and Cole Porter's "It's Bad for Me") (1984) or Johnston again on the Tristan Tzara reference (1988), Barney Childs on the leopard carcass (1993), and C. Harold Hurley on the story's pen/pencil/penis wordplay (2014). These and others are often individually useful because the story has more dark corners than many novels have. In the aggregate, they become essential for a comprehensive reading.

Entire monographs, as well as collections, of essays have been published on the stories about Nick Adams. Thus, it is strange that there has been no collection of essays, let alone a book-length monograph, dedicated to "The Snows of Kilimanjaro." John Howell's edited collection, *Hemingway's African Stories: The Stories, Their Sources, Their Critics* (1969), makes the most ambitious attempt, with half of the material being dedicated to "The Snows of Kilimanjaro" and half to "The Short Happy Life of Francis Macomber," although it is a casebook, consisting of texts of the stories and of material previously published in literary journals, not a monograph.

Hemingway was an innovator of the short-story form, and critics and anthologists have taken seriously his claim of "The Snows of Kilimanjaro" as his crowning achievement in the genre. While the existing corpus of critical articles focusing on "The Snows of Kilimanjaro" could probably form a multivolume study, the disagreements among the critics would reduce the volume to an introduction-to-the-critical-differences approach. Not even the biographical critics, of whom there are many, have attempted anything approaching book-length studies. A comprehensive interpretive study—one that includes analysis of Harry's memories, individually and as a whole—is the only means by which to properly appreciate the story's artistry and to satisfactorily address the interpretive controversies it poses. It is a magnificent and powerful story and deserves book-length analysis.

Critical analyses of "The Snows of Kilimanjaro" have always had to contend with two seemingly contrasting elements. First is the story's epigraph, which mentions the mountain's African name, its (incorrect) height, and the dried, frozen leopard carcass once found near its summit.[7] Second is the heavenly vision of Harry the protagonist's majestic death flight at the story's conclusion. The question that every critic and reader must contend with has been and continues to be whether it is appropriate or ironic that Harry, who has deserted his talent as a writer, truly earns such a soaring, beautiful death vision. For example, in the relatively recent critical literature on "The Snows of Kilimanjaro," Jennifer Riddle Harding, in her 2011 essay "'He Had Never Written a Word of That': Regret and Counterfactuals in Hemingway's 'The Snows of Kilimanjaro,'" makes a well-argued case for an unredeemed Harry who has not written what he "*should have written*" (32). Much earlier, Gennaro Santangelo, in his essay "The Dark Snows of Kilimanjaro" (1975), drew an uncompromising portrait of a thoroughly unredeemed Harry. Max Westbrook, however, after considerable weighing of the evidence, concludes: "And thus it is that Harry's corruption represents the failures other heroes have avoided but, like Hemingway himself, avoided by the narrowest of margins, avoided—at least in part—by luck. And it is this narrow margin between the temporal and the permanent, between rot and Kilimanjaro, which makes it possible for Harry's honest awareness of his failures to work as a proper grounds for his redemption" (Lewis and Westbrook, "The Texas Manuscript" 95). Also judging Harry less severely, Joseph Flora has observed that "[t]here is grace in Harry's death because he has been a stern judge of himself" (*Ernest Hemingway* 88). Flora also suggests that Harry's final attempt to write has a redeeming quality (88). Over the decades, other interpretations have followed along these lines. Harry redeemed and Harry unredeemed thus make up two of the three common critical theses regarding the story.

Through these analyses runs a strong tendency for critics who assert Harry's redemption to look more closely at the italicized memories and for those who assert Harry's lack of redemption to treat the italicized memories monolithically and/or minimally. Paul Smith has admirably and comprehensively summarized the state of criticism up to the late 1980s (355–59).

The third common thesis is that in presenting what has so often been regarded as an ambiguous ending, Hemingway has simply produced a faulty story—the ostensible proof of the ambiguity, of course, being the two irreconcilable critical theses. (These critics too tend to devote insufficient analysis to the italicized memories.) In the Howell casebook, for example, Marion Montgomery asserts that the ending of the story "seems void of any real meaning" (149). Even as early as 1966, Westbrook was able to summarize the cul-de-sac that the criticism had found itself in—and from which it has not emerged:

> The story has won high praise from numerous critics, and yet it has also been said to be a story which fails, which fails basically, as story. The critical dispute, furthermore, does not represent merely the differences between one school of criticism and another school of criticism. The point at issue with "The Snows" is based on a principle common to all reputable schools of criticism: the resolution of "The Snows"—Harry's imaginary flight to Kilimanjaro—is for some readers a failure in structure, a trick ending with no organic relation to the rest of the story. (Lewis and Westbrook, "Texas Manuscript" 89)

The riddle of "The Snows" must be solved by analysis of its insufficiently discussed salient feature: the italicized presentation of five series of reminiscences that the writer Harry makes on his death cot on the plains of east Africa. Indeed, the idea of focusing on "The Snows of Kilimanjaro" without giving due and comprehensive analysis to the italicized passages is the exact equivalent of attempting to come to terms with *In Our Time* without giving due and comprehensive analysis to both the interchapters and their relationship to the whole of *In Our*

Time. In either case, such an analysis must be regarded as incomplete. Attempts to classify all of the reminiscences monolithically under a general heading of "experiences Harry should have written about" bypass much of the story's artistry. James R. Mellow, for example, in his full-length Hemingway biography writes only that "[t]he italicized recollections run through the story like a great fugue" (454). In an early full-length monograph (1963) on Hemingway, Earl Rovit asserts that Harry's final "airplane ride was Hemingway's trick on the reader" (36). As such, he cites the natural choice of the story's literary source as Ambrose Bierce's "An Occurrence at Owl Creek Bridge," which uses the trick of placing its entire plot (of escape from a hanging) into the final seconds of the thoughts of a man experiencing death by hanging.[8] (Noted early Hemingway scholar and critic Philip Young mentioned the connection with Bierce in 1952.) The ending of Bierce's story constitutes a trick on the reader; ergo, Hemingway's ending constitutes a trick on the reader. Although Rovit does mention snow as appearing "in Harry's reminiscence," he makes no other specific reference to Harry's memories; his is the epitome of the monolithic approach: "Harry spends the afternoon and early evening . . . remembering sharp vignettes of the past that he had always intended to use in his writing but never did" (36). Judgments of Harry as unredeemed or of the story as a failure cannot be regarded as successful when they fail to confront the specifics of Harry's memories. Rovit was neither the first nor the only critic to fail to perceive an essential irony: that of entirely omitting analysis of Harry's italicized memories while simultaneously condemning Harry for not using in his writing those very same memories!

Two years later, in his full-length study, *Hemingway on Love,* Lewis focused on Eros and Agape in Harry's relationships. He refers to the italicized memories as "flashbacks," analyzing them more as groups rather than individually. The first Italicized Memory (**IM I**) "tells of death and suffering," with snow representing death and skiing "a type of the death flight . . . and a type of the sexual act" (101). Harry's experience before, during, and after his time in Anatolia (**IM II**) (101–03) develops "the combination of eros and death or violence" (101). Memories of life in Europe (**IM III**), treated monolithically, receive brief mention and focus on a younger, less cruel Harry who had not yet been corrupted by fame and Helen's money. **IM IV** and **V** are omitted.

Sheldon Norman Grebstein's often reliable *Hemingway's Craft* (1973) also exemplifies the monolithic approach. Grebstein's discussion of the italicized memories is reductivist: "He [Harry] cannot move except in his mind, which recalls a vigorous former life, one characterized by action, travel, involvement—intense even when unpleasant" (21–22). Harry's rotting leg mirrors his "corrupt moral condition." His "hallucinated flight over Kilimanjaro" is seen as "starkly ironic . . . sharpened by the portrayal of the death-moment itself as soaring and ecstatic" (22). This facile interpretation—omitting the leopard, the hyena, and all specifics regarding Harry's memories—supports Grebstein's thesis regarding Hemingway's characters' inner and outer worlds; however, in its disregard of the artistry of Harry's memories, this reading itself becomes ironic, especially in what purports to be an analysis of Hemingway's craft.

Equally inadequate is the time-honored critical tradition of cherry-picking the reminiscences, discussing only those that support the thesis at hand. As early as 1973, Ekaterini Georgoudaki noted how "each critic seems to have provided only a partial reading of the story, often ignoring elements that do not support a particular view of the story" (261). The connections between the reminiscences and the narrative must be found and accounted for.

Each of the five sections of italicized memories has value in itself, in its relationships with the other four sections of memories, and in its relationships with the narrative sections; indeed, only a comprehensive analysis of all five groups of italicized memories can reveal the full extent of Hemingway's artistry—the figure in the carpet. Only when that artistry is fully revealed can the unresolved interpretive questions of the leopard and the death flight be addressed with any degree of confidence.

Marion Montgomery's incomplete analysis (1976) finds the italicized segments exemplify the "heroic tone" of the "full-hearted deed" that contrasts with the "spiritual half-measures" that have brought Harry to the end of his road. While not fully monolithic in his use of italicized passages, neither is he specific. He includes in his analysis brief summaries of Harry's experience covering the Greco-Turkish War (**II.3**), the "snow group" (**I.1–5**), Harry's experiences just prior to covering that war (**II.1**), memories of his grandfather (**III.1**), Paris memories (**III.5**), and the chore-boy incident (**IV.3**). The death of Williamson (**V**) is omitted. He concludes that the story is faulty, with Hemingway making good symbolic use of the hyena but not of the mountain or the leopard. The story's end is "sentimental" rather than "metaphysical" and thus "void of any real meaning" (149). Actually, it is Montgomery's failure to adequately address the specifics of Harry's memories that voids his conclusions of any real meaning.

More recently, Harding's analysis of counterfactuals in the story takes a more purely monolithic approach. Although Harding includes a quotation from the cattle-herding description (**IV.2**), she discusses and interprets Harry's memories monolithically as "masterpieces that might have been" that "provide proof of Harry's [unrealized] promise" (30).

Approaches such as these imply that just about any tale that exhibits something Harry could well have written about but did not actually write about, could serve equally well as an appropriate inclusion. On the contrary, the italicized passages certainly do not constitute a Hemingway garage sale of material he could not use elsewhere. He chose these particular episodes because individually and collectively they are central and integral to the story's meaning and artistry.

When one considers Hemingway's artistic standards, the faulty-story thesis simply does not wash. In the "Scott Fitzgerald" chapter of *A Moveable Feast,* Hemingway writes that Fitzgerald revealed to him that when he submitted good stories to the *Saturday Evening Post,* he revised them in order to make "them into salable magazine stories. I had been shocked at this and I said I thought it was whoring. He said it was whoring but that he had to do it as he made money from the magazines to have money ahead to write decent books. I said that I did not believe anyone could write any way except the very best he could write without destroying his talent" (155–56). That passage says all one needs to know about Hemingway's aesthetic standards. The faulty-story critics would have us believe Hemingway operated at a level of aesthetic hypocrisy that would enable him to claim that the story he touted as his best was in reality based on a cheap commercial trick of the kind he claimed to have warned Fitzgerald about. The fault, dear Brutus, is not in the story but in our analysis. Not surprisingly, the faulty-story critics also tend to treat the italicized memories monolithically and/or minimally, as does Rovit.

Critics have routinely found material of biographical relevance in "The Snows of Kilimanjaro," sometimes citing a statement made to Hemingway's personal friend and biographer A. E. Hotchner: "Never wrote so directly about myself as in that story," which seems to open a Pandora's box of free-for-all biographical interpretation; a closer look at the statement, however, reveals it as more focused (162). Of his refusal of a wealthy woman's offer of a fully financed return trip to Africa, Hemingway tells Hotchner:

> By the time we got down here to Key West, I had given a lot of thought to her and the offer and how it might be if I accepted an offer like that. What it would do to a character like me whose failings I know and have taken so many soundings on. Never wrote so directly about myself as in that story. The man is dying, and I got that pretty good, complete with handles, because I had been breathed upon by the Grim Reaper more than once and could write about that from the inside out. (161–62)

Because the story focuses on death, the most relevant biographical material would be Hemingway's having been breathed upon by the Grim Reaper. In addition, biographical critics are attracted by Hemingway's many veiled allusions to his own works, probably more so than in any other story. Be that as it may, the story must ultimately stand on its own as a work of art. No artist, particularly one who created within standards as uncompromising as Hemingway's, would publish a story for which the readers' understanding must depend on knowledge of private (or even public) details of the author's life. Nor should a reader be expected to be familiar with an author's entire body of work. Biographical criticism of any Hemingway short story may certainly make valid points and add depth to our understanding of Hemingway the man. And the best biographies give insights into Hemingway the man that circle back around and also illuminate Hemingway's works. The objective here, however, is to better understand "The Snows of Kilimanjaro," the short story, on its own terms rather than as a biographical footnote.

Of critics being led astray by the siren song of biographical connections, Norman Friedman's essay "Harry or Ernest? The Unresolved Ambiguity in 'The Snows of Kilimanjaro'" (1997) stands as a notable example. While Friedman claims to address "the function—or functions—of the italicized reminiscences" as a significant "issue" in "The Snows of Kilimanjaro" and claims that he will examine "the story's structure itself," little such analysis takes place involving the memories (279). He offers only the briefest of summaries of the italicized memories' contents, buoyed by one brief quote each from the second and fourth of Harry's italicized memories, as well as two (one of which is misquoted: someone/some one) from the fifth. After minimally examining the actual content of the memory sections, and thus offering little insight, the article examines Hemingway's relationship with Scott Fitzgerald ("poor Julian" 283) and its reflection in "The Snows of Kilimanjaro." When Friedman addresses the problem of the leopard, he asserts that Hemingway "had difficulty . . . in sustaining that essential distance between Harry and Ernest upon which the meaning, integrity, and success of the story depends" (283). In short, he asserts that the story cannot be properly understood outside of the biographical context. Along the way, he speculates that Hemingway may have tried to write about the rich in order to placate his mother over his career choice and later perpetrates the tabloid-worthy hatchet job that "his knock-about career landed him in one too many plane crashes and he died by his own hand in despair over his vanishing ability to focus his mind on his writing" and finally the conclusion that the "story resists a unified hypothesis" (281, 283, 284). This conclusion comes after the disclaimer that his purpose is "to clarify the formal problems of this story rather than to analyze its author's psychology" (284). Whenever an analysis of Hemingway's life and professional relationships is substituted for a specific analysis of Harry's memories, "The Snows of Kilimanjaro" will always resist a unified hypothesis.

Too often, literary biography becomes its own end and loses its connection with the author's works. A recent biography of Jack London devotes more pages to London's discovery of surfing in Hawaii than it does to discussing the genesis of great works such as *The Call of the Wild* or *Martin Eden*. Nicholas Reynolds's *Writer, Sailor, Soldier, Spy: Ernest Hemingway's Secret Adventures, 1935–1961* (2017) emerges as one of the many useful niche or focused Hemingway biographies produced in recent years. Painstakingly researched and well written, it delves into Hemingway's experiences in espionage and related activities. The biography prominently analyzes Hemingway's covert relations with Soviet Russia, which began during the Spanish Civil War. Three of Hemingway's stories set during that war are given very brief mention. Conspicuously absent is any reference to another such story written on the same conflict and at the same time, "Under the Ridge," in which the Russians are depicted in a highly negative light. The Russian officers who perform battlefield executions of a Frenchman and a young Spaniard are avatars of death, violating the prerogatives of the host country and thus betraying hospitality. Hemingway seldom depicted two more sinister characters. They make Max and Al of "The Killers" and the game wardens of "The Last Good Country" look like class acts. The purpose of literary biography is to illuminate the author's life and thus his works; yet in this case, mention of a very highly relevant literary text is omitted entirely. Given the context of the biography, it should have been used to at least illuminate the author's life, if not his works. The world of espionage remained largely unchanged by Hemingway's participation, but he changed the world's literature profoundly and permanently by what he wrote, a fact too often neglected by biographers.

In his 1999 essay, Keneth Kinnamon discusses "the relation of 'The Snows of Kilimanjaro' to its author's life" but takes a more balanced approach (284). He lists and examines seven events in Harry's italicized memories that correspond to events in Hemingway's life, including the parallel between the gangrene Harry suffers and the amoebic dysentery Hemingway suffered during his own safari. He concludes accurately that the submerged politics of "The Snows of Kilimanjaro" constitute "a key transitional point between the disengagement of *Death in the Afternoon* and *Green Hills of Africa* . . . and the social commitment of *To Have and Have Not*" and his Spanish Civil War writings (289). To his credit, Kinnamon keeps his conclusion in perspective, admitting that it "does not negate the validity of other dimensions of meaning . . . nor does it compromise the superb artistry with which this masterful story is executed" (289).

The more recent *Faulkner and Hemingway: Biography of a Literary Rivalry* (2012), by Joseph Fruscione, takes an exemplary approach. Apart from a literary sex scandal, no topic in literary biography offers more opportunity for wallowing in tempting, juicy tabloid-style sensationalism than does literary rivalry. Instead of hack biography sensationalism, Fruscione displays a thoroughgoing understanding of the works of both authors, a detailed analysis of the sequences of events through which the rivalry developed, and—most important of all—how the rivalry and its sequences of events played out *in the various works* of both authors. Nothing in literary biography can be more important than that.

Therefore, while biographical references are necessary from time to time, the text of the story itself must bear the greatest portion of the interpretive weight. Joseph Flora's apt observation should be kept in mind always: "Although [Hemingway's] own life experiences are repeatedly the basis for his stories, the actual experience itself is never the point of a story" (*Ernest Hemingway* xvii). In discussing Hemingway's deletion of some lines of autobiographical material from the story's manuscript, Max Westbrook seems to express the same idea: "The omission . . . lessens the overtly autobiographical nature of 'The Snows' and represents a tangible step in Hemingway's efforts to mold his personal experience into universal meaning" (Lewis and Westbrook, "Texas Manuscript" 92). Carl Jung expressed the same idea decades earlier: "Indeed, the special significance of a true work of art resides in the fact that it has escaped from the limitations of the personal and has soared beyond the personal concerns of its creator" ("On the Relation of Analytical Psychology to Poetry" 309). It is the universal human meaning rather than the biographical motherlode that must be addressed to fully appreciate this particular story's artistry. Ultimately, the most important fact that we must remember about the life of Ernest Miller Hemingway is that he contributed to the world's literature works of the stature of "The Snows of Kilimanjaro." Everything else is a footnote.

Accordingly, the questions of Harry's redemption, the leopard, the hyena, the mountain, and Harry's death flight will be addressed in this study through analysis of the man-on-trail and related hospitality archetypes, especially as they appear in the five sections of Harry's italicized memories. Archetype is defined here in the classic Jungian usage as a primordial image arisen from the collective unconscious of mankind.[9] To use the phrase Henry James employed in his short story of the same name, these archetypes constitute "the figure in the carpet" of "The Snows of Kilimanjaro," which close reading—particularly of Harry's italicized memories—will reveal.

Archetype and Myth

Sigmund Freud's concept of the unconscious mind proved radical enough to change the direction of psychology permanently and opened the door to other radically new ideas. Among the first to storm through this newly opened door was Carl Gustav Jung, Freud's most famous student, who proposed that beneath the personal, individual unconscious mind lay the collective unconscious, in effect the unconscious mind of mankind as a whole. Freud and Jung famously came into conflict over this theory.

In his psychoanalytic practice, Jung found in the dreams of his patients the same images that appeared in ancient myth, religion, folklore, and literature from different cultures in different parts of the world and in different millennia. This universality was crucial for Jung in validating images as originating in the collective unconscious: "An image may be considered archetypal when it can be shown to exist in the records of human history, in identical form with the same meaning" (qtd. in Segal 64). Thus, he posited that certain recurring images—"universal images that have existed since the remotest times"—constituted proof of the collective unconscious teeming below the personal unconscious that Freud had discovered (Jung, *Archetypes* 5). He admitted that some images were consciously transmitted from culture to culture; nevertheless, the indigenous "cases that cannot be accounted for in this way [through human migrations] . . . drive us to the hypothesis of 'autochthonous revival.' These cases are so numerous that we are obliged to assume the existence of a collective psychic substratum. I have called this the *collective unconscious*" (Segal 67). Jung's recognition of these recurring images led to his theory of the collective unconscious and then to his application of the term *archetypes* to those recurring images. Over the decades, he defined *archetype* in slightly varied yet conceptually consistent language, depending on the context. Unlike the images of the individual unconscious, which derive from personal memories—often memories that might well be perfectly meaningless to every other individual in the world—the archetypes are primordial images, vestiges, and memories of the repeated experiences of humankind collectively and are thus applicable to all humanity.

Jung located the archetypes "in the records of human history." And as literature constitutes a significant portion of those records, the effect on literature was immediate and electric. Jack London was among the first to consciously incorporate Jungian ideas into his fiction. His copy of Jung's *Psychology of the Unconscious* (1916) has nearly three hundred notations, indicating how deeply he was impressed with Jung's vision. Sadly, London did not encounter Jung's book until the final year of his life, although he did write a number of stories based on his reading of Jung.[10] This reading actually revitalized his creativity. In the years immediately preceding his discovery of Jung, his work had increasingly drifted toward commercial hackwork whose purpose was simply to raise the money he needed to support his agricultural experiments on his Sonoma Valley ranch. London thus becomes a unique case, intuitively harnessing in his early years the power of archetypes in such compelling works as *The Call of the Wild*, "The White Silence," "To Build a Fire," and, of course, "To the Man on Trail" and then in the final year of his life quite consciously constructing plots from myths Jung had outlined, plots he seemed to have little difficulty developing.

Jung enthusiastically took up the study of myth once he realized that the content of ancient myths coincided with so many of the archetypes he had encountered in his patients' dreams. This coincided with the popular and scholarly interest in myths of all peoples that began before Jung's birth, continued during his lifetime, and continues today. Foremost among the unabashedly popular studies of myth were those of Thomas Bulfinch (1796–1867): *The Age of Fable, or Stories of Gods and Heroes* (1855), *The Age of Chivalry, or Legends of King Arthur* (1858), and *Legends of Charlemagne, or Romance of the Middle Ages* (1863). These were revised and published after his death as *Bulfinch's Mythology*. For many decades, this was the standard popular study—still in print today in multiple editions—until Edith Hamilton's *The Greek Way* (1930), *The Roman Way* (1932), and *Mythology* (1932) came into more common use. Serious, scholarly studies of myth—all still in print—included such works as James Frazer's *The Golden Bough* (1890); Otto Rank's *The Myth of the Birth of the Hero* (1909); Jessie Weston's *From Ritual to Romance* (1920), a study of Arthurian myth, credited by T. S. Eliot as one of the inspirations for his "The Waste Land"; and Robert Graves's *The White Goddess: A Historical Grammar of Poetic Myth* (1948) and *The Greek Myths* (1955).[11] In more recent years the Norse myths have proven to be fruitful sources of material for popular works such A. S. Byatt's *Ragnarök: The End of the Gods* (2011) and Neil Gaiman's *Norse Mythology* (2017) and for more scholarly treatments such as Kevin Crossley-Holland's *The Norse Myths* (1980).

In 1934, Maud Bodkin produced the first great text of archetypal literary criticism, *Archetypal Patterns in Poetry: Psychological Studies of Imagination.* On the very first page of her study, she stated her purpose, which was to "examine" and test Jung's "hypothesis" "of unconscious forces which he terms 'primordial images' or archetypes" in the work of intuitive thinkers, namely poets.

To establish an image as "primordial," the literary critic must move backward in time, through folklore or myth, covering material that establishes the primordial credibility. Thus, it was not long until *archetype* and *myth* became companion terms and companion ideas. With the advent of the mythologist Joseph Campbell's *The Hero with a Thousand Faces* in 1949, the terms became fused permanently. Campbell found by assembling a series of archetypes—drawn from folklore, mythology, religion, and literature from disparate times and locations the world over—that they naturally formed the components of a recurring narrative pattern. This pattern took the form of the hero's journey, one of the most common plots in literature. This pattern he called, using James Joyce's terminology, the Monomyth. From this point forward, it became increasingly difficult to tell whether a writer was naturally intuiting primordial images of the collective unconscious or simply following Campbell's outline. Its influence has continued somewhat abated in literary criticism but completely unabated in cinema, popular culture, and literature. In Hemingway studies, Joseph DeFalco's *The Hero in Hemingway's Short Stories* (1963) applied both Jungian and Campbellian concepts to Hemingway's work.

Three decades after Bodkin's foundational work, archetypal and mythopoeic criticism owned a place in the critical landscape, appearing regularly in anthologies of criticism. Wilbur Scott's *Five Approaches of Literary Criticism* (1962) included a section on, and titled, "The Archetypal Approach: Literature in the Light of Myth," along with other approaches—moral, psychological, sociological, and formalistic. Grebstein's *Perspectives in Contemporary Criticism: A Collection of Recent Essays by American, English, and European Literary Critics* (1968) included a section titled "The Mythopoeic Critic," along with sections on the historical, formalist, sociocultural, and psychological critics. Lionel Trilling's *Literary Criticism: An Introductory Reader* (1970) included myth-based criticism such as Erich Auerbach's "Odysseus' Scar" and Northrup Frye's "Myth, Fiction, and Displacement."

As with all schools of criticism, the initial success waned. Successful schools survive the initial waning; less successful schools go under. Several factors caused the inevitable the ups and downs of archetypal and mythic criticism.

One was a generalized use of the term *archetype*. The classic handbook of literary terms—*A Handbook to Literature,* currently edited by William Harmon—includes a definition of archetype that has stood for decades. It accurately describes the term's Jungian genesis, explains why the archetypes exert an irrationally strong appeal, and discusses the uses to which the literary critic applies the term. Then, inexplicably, it ends with a quotation from Northrup Frye, defining *archetype* loosely and in a non-Jungian context as "a symbol, usually an image, which recurs often enough in literature to be recognizable as an element of one's literary experience as a whole."[12] Elsewhere, Frye makes the same point: "The Symbol in this phase is the communicable unit, to which I give the name archetype: that is, a typical or recurring image. I mean by an archetype a symbol which connects one poem with another and thereby helps to unify and integrate our literary experience" (99). Statements like these, of course, dispense with the need to trace the archetype back to mankind's primordial experiences, reducing the term to application to personal experiences rather than to bona fide, universal, broadly humanistic primordial images. The bar is thus lowered.

Current archetypal studies tend to reverse this unfortunate trend. *Trickster Makes This World: Mischief, Myth, and Art* (1998), Lewis Hyde's extensive study of the trickster archetype, firmly grounds in ancient myths its analysis of such trickster figures as Frederick Douglass, Allen Ginsberg, and Maxine Hong Kingston. One of the following mythic/literary/folklore figures is mentioned on nearly every page: Hermes/Mercury, Greek and Roman; Loki, Medieval Scandinavia; Coyote, Native American; Eshu, the Yoruba people of West Africa; Raven, North Pacific coast of North America; the Monkey King of China; as well as others mentioned less often. Hyde's analysis thus carries significant archetypal credibility. Even more recently (2016) Michael Downing's work on August Wilson emphasizes the playwright's conscious use of archetype. His "The Use of Stereotype and Archetype in *Ma Rainey's Black Bottom*" establishes Wilson's technique of offering white stereotypes of African American characters at the beginnings of his plays and then converting them, by the plays' conclusions, to archetypes of African American experience, thus imploding the stereotypes.

A second reason for the waning of archetypal criticism, ironically, stems from its archetypal/mythic credibility, which remains a thorn in collectivists' sides. Despite the disintegration of the Soviet Union, a primary exemplar of the Marxist experiment, the Marxist school of literary criticism held sway over literary studies for an extended period after and despite the fortunate events of 1989. Literary studies, in the Marxist "base and superstructure" metaphor, constituted part of a superstructure of culture that served to advance the base concept of the continuing revolution by which the proletariat would win its historically inevitable victory in all human affairs over the oppressive aristocracy. Works of literature that did not advance that agenda suffered the label of bourgeois sentimentality, the intention of which is to distract the reader from the real issues, as Terry Eagleton sarcastically asserts in "The Rise of English," the first chapter of *Literary Theory:*

> Since literature, as we know, deals in universal human values rather than in such historical trivia as civil wars, the oppression of women, or the dispossession of the English peasantry, it could serve to place in cosmic perspective the petty demands of working people for decent living conditions or greater control over their own lives, and might even with luck come to render them oblivious to such issues in their high-minded contemplation of eternal truths and beauties. (25)

In fact, all of the topics he lists have made and will continue to make fitting topics for literature. But literature must and does and will go beyond Marxist realism, the worst of which ultimately degenerated into the "Boy Meets Tractor" school of writing. Among the eternal truths and beauties literature addresses is the theme of Death. It's an issue. Try as literary critics may, the death issue resists the Marxist call to "Always historicize." Death predates economics. The Marxists, especially the Russians, do, indeed, read their Hemingway. Fidel Castro admired Hemingway, especially *For Whom the Bell Tolls.* But Marxists have always been a little uneasy about him, as if they knew, dimly, that he had some thoughts about death as a human issue more significant and universal than the war of the classes. In Soviet Russia, *For Whom the Bell Tolls*—which treats the Soviets ambivalently—appeared for many years in abridged editions. Race, class, and gender are issues appropriately treated in literature—as are death, family, friendship, individuation, love, discovery of the self, and all of the topics that confront the hero on his journey through life. It is, of course, inconvenient to some that myth and archetype have deeper roots than the base and superstructure metaphor, and therefore broader human appeal, and that myth and archetype are older than history. This broadly humanistic appeal, however, grants myth and archetype their continuing place in literary studies.

Analysis of the details of plot patterns inevitably involves summaries of plots and multiple references to plot devices and plot elements. To assist the reader in mentally juggling both the similarities and differences of how these elements appear in various stories, comparison tables have been added as conclusions of some of the chapters.

Catalog of Harry's Memories

As Harry's memories would seem a salient feature of the present study, a numbered catalog of the reminiscences is in order, as it will help to facilitate a more disciplined and comprehensive approach. These memories appear in five groups. Most of those in the first group have some connection with snow; even though Mount Kilimanjaro is mentioned only twice, in the opening epigraph and in Harry's death flight, these references have given rise to the reasonable supposition—not well supported by the text—that Harry and his wife, Helen, camp within sight of the mountain and that the snow-covered peak inspires his own first group of memories, which are all related to snow. The five groups of memories, referred to as "italicized memories" here (**IM**), are numbered with Roman numerals; Arabic numbers refer to paragraphs within the Roman numeral groups.[13] Slashes indicate separate incidents or descriptions in the same paragraph; the definition of an incident or description is, of course, my subjective judgment.

IM I

1. Waiting for the Orient Express in Thrace after the Greek retreat / The secretaries sent by Nansen die in the snow.
2. The deserter-in-the-Gauertal incident.
3. Skiing in Schrunz, breathtakingly described.
4. Snowbound at the Madlener-haus. Herr Lent, apparently the proprietor, loses everything gambling / Thoughts on gambling.
5. Barker, the aviator, machine-gunning the leave train of Austrian officers.
6. After the war, skiing, hunting, and discussing the war with Hans, an Austrian soldier.
7. Winters in the Voralberg and the Arlberg / The fox seller / Kirsch / Description of skiing / Arriving at an inn after skiing.

IM II

1. Quarreling with and losing the love of his life, following women who looked like her, writing her a letter asking her to write back / Picking up a woman

to dance with, leaving her to pick up an Armenian woman / Vicious street fight with a British gunner over the Armenian woman / Escaping from the MPs and having sex with the Armenian woman.

2. Leaving for Anatolia the next night / Newly arrived incompetent Constantine Greek officers perpetrate a friendly-fire incident, bringing a British observer to tears.
3. The attack of the Turkish troops on the bizarrely attired Greek Evzone troops and sights of horror / Running in the retreat with the British observer / An American poet in a café talking with the affectatious Tristan Tzara / His current wife sees and asks about the newly arrived letter from his former love, requested in **II.1**.
4. Remembering that he had seen changes in the world and realizing it was his duty to write about them.

IM III

1. The burning of his grandfather's house, including the loss of his grandfather's guns.
2. Postwar trout fishing in the Black Forest and the first way of walking to the trout stream.
3. The second way of walking to the trout stream / Suicide of the proprietor of the Triberg Hotel.
4. Paris: poor neighbors at Place Contrescarpe: Flower sellers / Children in the street / The Café des Amateurs and the Bal Musette / Concierge has affair with an army officer / The tenant whose husband is a bicycle racer / Sharing a glass of wine with the husband of the woman who ran the Bal Musette.
5. The drunkards and the *sportifs*, descendants of the Communards, whose ancestors had been slaughtered / Streets of Paris; apartment where he lived and started his writing career / The hotel where Verlaine died / His writing room.
6. Sights from his Paris apartment: the wood and coal dealer, the butcher shop, drunks.
7. Policeman sleeping with the concierge / Marie's protest of the eight-hour working day as promoting drunkenness of working-class men.

IM IV

1. Introductory paragraph switching the scene from Paris to other memories.
2. Herding cattle at the ranch.
3. Incident of the half-wit chore boy.

IM V

1. Death of Williamson.

This is the order in which these memories are presented in "The Snows"; it is not the chronological order in which these events took place. See the appendix for a speculative chronological listing of the events in Harry's life.

Chapter 1

THE MAN ON TRAIL

> "A health to the man on trail this night; may his grub hold out; may his dogs keep their legs; may his matches never miss fire. God prosper him; good luck go with him."
>
> —Jack London, "To the Man on Trail"

The Deserter-in-the-Gauertal Incident

Keeping all of the various incidents included in "The Snows of Kilimanjaro" straight in one's mind is not unlike trying to keep track of a mercury spill: Little balls roll in every direction. Reading Hemingway first and then Jack London, nobody would be expected to make this connection. However, after first reading London's "To the Man on Trail," a story of substantial length and drama and thus a story easy to remember, and then reading "The Snows of Kilimanjaro," the reader may more easily note a plot shared between the two. The deserter-in-the-Gauertal incident is a mere two sentences; however, with the London story still fresh in mind, the Gauertal incident's similarities to London's story stand out in bold relief upon a reading of "The Snows of Kilimanjaro."

The Gauertal incident:

> It was snow too that fell all Christmas week that year up in the Gauertal, that year they lived in the woodcutter's house with the big square porcelain stove that filled half the room, and they slept on mattresses filled with beech leaves, the time the deserter came with his feet bloody in the snow. He said the police

> were right behind him and they gave him woolen socks and held the gendarmes talking until the tracks drifted over. (7)

Only five pages into the story—a story rich in incident—this episode is indeed easy to forget. It is, however, the plot of the 1899 Jack London Klondike story "To the Man on Trail."[1] The London story is Kiplingesque in its combination of sentimentality and rough masculine camaraderie. Malemute Kid, a miner and recurring London character, shares stories with his mining friends while making a vile Christmas punch—this story, like the Gauertal incident, takes place at Christmas and in the snow. Just as the Kid proposes a toast "to the man on trail this night; may his grub hold out; may his dogs keep their legs; may his matches never miss fire," Jack Westondale, a heavily armed traveler with whom Malemute Kid feels an immediate affinity, arrives: "Though they had never met, each had heard of the other, and the recognition was mutual. A sweeping introduction and a mug of punch were forced upon him before he could explain his errand" (105, 107). And later: "As the young stranger ate of the rude fare, Malemute Kid attentively studied his face. Nor was he long in deciding that it was fair, honest, and open, and that he liked it" (108). After more storytelling, the Kid offers Westondale a bunk, the latter asking to be awakened by four o'clock the next morning. When the Kid wakes Westondale, fifteen minutes early, Westondale finds he has already harnessed his dogs and fully provisioned his sled. The Kid gives him advice on the provisions and on how to locate new dogs when his wear out. The last bit of advice he passes on is this: "Keep a-traveling up to twenty-five, but if it gets below that, build a fire and change your socks" (113). Of course, this statement raises the question of whether Hemingway included the gift of socks in his story to echo a detail he might have remembered from the London story. Multiple elements of hospitality have been offered: spirits (the Christmas punch), food (the rude fare), storytelling, rest, provisions (food for his team), and advice (on changing socks); these constitute rites of incorporation and solidarity.

A few moments after Westondale leaves, a tired Mountie, accompanied by two guides, arrives in pursuit of the man, whom he reveals has robbed $40,000 from McFarland's, a Klondike gambling joint. The Kid gives him a daunting account of how difficult it will be to overtake the rested and provisioned Westondale. He also, threatening violent resistance by making a nod toward his weapons, refuses to give the Mountie aid, despite his attempt to requisition supplies "in the name of the Queen" (116). In this case, the Mounties do not get their man.

So, both "To the Man on Trail" and the Gauertal incident take place at Christmas; both involve a temporary and unofficial sanctuary, aid, and gifts—including a specific reference to socks—all given to a fugitive on the run through the snow; and both involve delaying or impeding the pursuers. In the London story only are other standard archetypal elements of hospitality offered and accepted: food, drink, rest, storytelling, and advice.[2] Two other contrasts with the London story must be mentioned; though they may be implied in the Hemingway story, they are not openly asserted. First is the immediate and unhesitating affinity between the pursued and the host in the London story. Second is that Westondale is depicted as a righteous man and the Kid trusts him without question. After Westondale leaves, Malemute Kid reveals this to his companions:

> A whiter man than Jack Westondale never ate from the same pot nor stretched blanket with you or me. Last fall he gave his whole clean-up, forty thousand, to Joe Castrell, to buy in on Dominion. Today he'd be a millionaire. But while he stayed behind at Circle City, taking care of his partner with the scurvy, what does Castrell do? Goes into McFarland's, jumps the limit, and drops the whole sack. Found him dead in the snow the next day. And poor Jack laying his plans to go out this winter to his wife and boy he's never seen. You'll notice he took exactly what his partner lost—forty thousand. (117–18)

Notice the brotherhood established by the rites of initiation implied by "ate from the same pot" and "stretched blanket." After Westondale leaves and after some debate, the Kid and the assembled miners chant a veritable Greek chorus of their former toast, adding new elements:

> The Kid glanced round the circle of his judges, noted the softening of their faces, then raised his mug aloft. "So a health to the man on trail this night; may his grub hold out; may his dogs keep their legs; may his matches never miss fire. God prosper him; good luck go with him; and—"
>
> "Confusion to the Mounted Police!" cried [fellow miner] Bettles, to the crash of the empty cups. (118)

The Gauertal incident includes several elements that will be established as archetypes of the "man on trail" plot: a fugitive—the man on trail, the gift of clothing, pursuers, and delay of those pursuers by the host. To these, the London story adds rest, food, advice, storytelling, and an affinity and a feeling of brotherhood between guest and host. In addition, other members of the host's household, in this case a celebrating group of miners, at last confront the host as a "circle of judges," another Greek chorus of voices representing the values of the community, which it becomes the Kid's duty to win over.

This plot is not unique to the works of London and Hemingway; the man on trail emerges from far back on the edges of unrecorded history. Although this study attempts to pursue this plot to those far edges, it always comes back to Hemingway and "The Snows of Kilimanjaro," which tale makes the most elaborate use of the widest number of variations of this plot. Did Hemingway read the London story? It matters not, since both stories have characteristics—archetypes—that flow from the same source: from thousands of years of literary traditions, which themselves flow from the collective unconscious of mankind as a whole.

Sorting archetype from analogue from influence is often a tangled and uncertain business, especially for purposes of comparison. Two works of literature may include or derive from the same archetype, since the archetypes are primordial images that arise from the collective unconscious, indeed from time immemorial, through the intuitions of separate authors. In explaining the universality of archetypal possibilities, Frieda Fordham writes that "an archetypal image that might have been drawn in the caves of Auvergne will often appear in the dreams of the most modern of men" (25). The conclusive proof of this was Joseph Campbell's monomyth, which makes the linking of ancient and modern images a simple matter. Analogues are instances in which authors, often without being aware of it, tell stories using similar elements; though they may even be time-honored stories, it may still be possible to determine their genesis. An influence is simply one author having a direct or indirect effect on another. One author may intuitively employ an archetypal plot and influence another to use the same elements. Those plot elements may even become widely accepted cultural icons incorporated into a variety of popular works. To remain honest, the archetypal critic must call an analogue an *analogue* and an influence an *influence.* Joseph DeFalco, in his classic study of the quest myth, *The Hero in Hemingway's Short Stories,* writes about this problem:

> How much of Hemingway's use of the journey artifice and other manifestations of psychological and mythological symbolism is conscious or unconscious is, of course, difficult, if not impossible, to ascertain. Certain assumptions may be made as to the sources of his material, however, no matter what its level of conscious utilization. Principally, as a modern man living in the twentieth century, Hemingway would have available all of the materials from the traditional

> sources of the culture. The cultural inheritance alone can account for his knowledge of the journey pattern. Whether he adapted it consciously or intuitively, he almost certainly observed it in his reading. (18)

Observing it in his reading might well have awakened an intuitive spark. The journey plot is arguably the most common one in literature. The man-on-trail subset of this plot occupies somewhat more obscure corners of the world's literature. Based on the two instances of the man-on-trail plot discussed so far, some questions regarding the authors' conceptions might arise: Did London and Hemingway both intuit the archetypal elements? Did one intuit the plot and the other find it in traditional cultural sources? Did both find it in traditional sources? Did London influence Hemingway—the reference to socks being the key piece of evidence? Were both of them influenced by a previous author or authors? As DeFalco astutely observes, the answers to such questions may be "difficult if not impossible to ascertain." This study, however, will have the advantage of looking at sources that nobody in DeFalco's day could possibly have known were available to Hemingway and will thus have the opportunity to present new evidence to address DeFalco's thoughtful questions.

Lewis Hyde addresses this question in his study of the gift of creativity, *The Gift: Creativity and the Artist in the Modern World:*

> We also rightly speak of intuition or inspiration as a gift. An idea pops into his head. . . . Usually, in fact, the artist does not find himself engaged or exhilarated by the work . . . until this gratuitous element has appeared, so that along with any true creation comes the uncanny sense that "I," the artist, did not make the work. "Not I, not I, but the wind that blows through me," says D. H. Lawrence. Not all artists emphasize the "gift" phase of their creations to the degree that Lawrence does, but all artists feel it. (xvi)

In his *Studies in Classic American Literature,* Lawrence somewhat more famously wrote, "Never trust the artist. Trust the tale. The proper function of a critic is to save the tale from the artist who created it" (2). I certainly do not wish to blow wind into the sails of the death-of-the-author theorists, and Lawrence was susceptible to polemic statements; nevertheless, both Hyde and Lawrence are onto something here regarding the creative spark, and it is certainly applicable to works in which archetypal elements emerge. Archetypes, as they were for London at both the outset and end of his career, are often the "gratuitous element" that gives the artist that "uncanny sense" that the work has created itself.

Other archetypal images, analogues, and sources will emerge from many other diverse authors. It will eventually take them all in order for this volume to come to grips with the two essential conundrums of "The Snows of Kilimanjaro": the leopard in the epigram at the beginning of the story and the majestic death flight Harry makes at the end of the story.

In addition, Hemingway seems to have admitted the possibility of primal connections, whether they be termed genetic, intuitive (as DeFalco describes them), or racial. On 15 December 1929, complaining of the difficulty of writing and taking care of the business end of writing, Hemingway wrote to his editor Max Perkins, "It's hard enough to write—and writing prose is a full time job and all the best of it is done in your subconscious and when that is full of business, reviews, opinions etc. you don't get a damned thing—" (*Letters* 4:20). In his 1958 interview with George Plimpton, in passing and addressing another topic, Hemingway obliquely introduces the topic to the conversation: "Financial security then is a great help as it keeps you from worrying. Worry destroys the ability to write. Ill health is bad in the ratio that it produces worry which attacks your subconscious and destroys your reserves" (114). Plimpton shortly pursues the topic, referencing a previous conversation in Madrid, in which, he recalls, Hemingway "thought the artist's equipment was not an acquired characteristic, but inherited, in the Mendelian sense."[3] Downplaying his response both before and after—ducking behind "two concussions and a skull fracture that year [which] had made me irresponsible in my statements"—Hemingway offers one sentence: "I do remember telling you that I believed imagination could be the result of inherited racial experience" (115). Thus, he may have actually disavowed his previous statement. Or, more likely, he may well have decided that such an admission might prove troublesome if used by the wrong critic. Indeed, Philip Young, whose wound theory Hemingway found highly objectionable, is mentioned in the very questions and responses quoted above. But it is important to note that by his reference to the unconscious it is he, not Plimpton, who has brought the topic into the conversation. DeFalco, whose *The Hero in Hemingway's Short Stories* was published in 1963, does not mention the Plimpton interview.

Finally, Hemingway does not seem to have had much of a hobo period, despite the famous photo of him wearing a backpack and hanging on to the rear ladder of a boxcar (Federspiel 167). His character Nick Adams, however, seems to have had one, as stories such as "The Battler" and "The Light of the World" strongly suggest. London, though, clearly did have a hobo period. Most London biographers devote an entire chapter to it, and London wrote of it in his memoir *The Road,* in shorter essays and chapters of other books, and even in "The Tramp Diary," published posthumously.

In the first chapter of *The Road,* he introduces the reader to the hobo terminology of *throwing,* that is, knocking on a likely looking kitchen door, throwing one's feet under a woman's table, and telling a story calculated to inspire her culinary efforts on the storyteller's behalf: "I have often thought that to this training of my tramp days is due much of my success as a story-writer. In order to get the food whereby I lived, I was compelled to tell tales that rang true" (10). The "throw" that he narrates in that chapter resulted in his hostess providing him with a large dinner, a large lunch to go, and "three pairs of thick red woolen socks," of all things (19). Socks protect the feet, making them an appropriate gift for a man on trail, and London was a man on trail in this episode, not just a traveler, as he was in fear of being arrested at the time. Later in the journey, he actually was arrested for vagrancy and spent some disturbing time in the Erie County Jail. The gift of socks suggests that Hemingway might have read "The Road." Another detail from the same chapter could have inspired the brakeman kicking Nick Adams off the train at the beginning of "The Battler." After panhandling a train passenger for a quarter to buy a meal, "I [London] swung off the platform of that private car with the porter manœuvering to kick me in the face" (2).

In his later years, at his ranch in Glen Ellen, California, London was generous to a fault to strangers who appeared at his door asking for handouts, especially those who claimed to have known him while he was on the road (Haley 307). Hemingway too could be generous to those who knocked on his door (after writing hours), though not to the ruinous financial fault that London was. Both men enjoyed playing host, and the homes where they did so are tourist destinations today: London's ranch is now Jack London State Park; Hemingway's Key West home offers guided tours, and the Finca Vigía, Hemingway's home near Havana, became The Museo de Ernesto Hemingway. Hospitality as regards both host and guest meant much to both men, and it would show in their writing, so much so on Hemingway's part that it would seem to have an unconscious—or intuitive, to use De Falco's term—component.

Joseph Conrad's "The Secret Sharer"

Other authors Hemingway would likely have read include similar elements in their stories. A story Hemingway would perhaps more likely have read than London's is Joseph Conrad's "The Secret Sharer" (1910). It does not take place at Christmas, nor in the snow, nor does it mention socks. It is, however, a tale of aid to a fugitive—a man on trail, one who is literally "legging it" and is appropriately named Leggatt, first mate of a ship who in a moment of crisis has killed an incompetent malcontent of a crewman whose funk during a storm endangered the ship and crew. The story is told by a ship's captain, unnamed, who, unbeknownst to his officers and crew, offers the pursued Leggatt hospitality in the form of rest, clothing, and food; misleads the captain of Leggatt's ship when he comes aboard; gives Leggatt parting gifts (a hat and coins) and advice; and, finally, risks the safety of his own ship and crew to place Leggatt ashore at a favorable location. Not naming the captain/narrator makes it easier for the reader to identify with him.

"The Secret Sharer" is set in the Gulf of Siam. Conrad's narrator, a ship captain on his last night before launching his first voyage as commander of a ship, walks the deck, to the dismay and confusion of his officers: "My action might have made me appear eccentric. Goodness only knew how that absurdly whiskered mate would 'account' for my conduct, and what the whole ship thought of that informality of their new captain" (97). Attempting to pull up a ladder, he finds it is held, quite improbably, by a swimmer, a man about to emerge from the water. Carl Jung reminds us that "[t]he sea is the favourite symbol for the unconscious" (*The Archetypes* 177–78). An absurdly commonplace conversation ensues, ending with the swimmer's decision to come aboard. Once again improbably, the captain neither calls nor notifies any of his crew, stating that "at the time it was pure intuition on my part. A mysterious communication was already established between us two—in the face of that silent darkened tropical sea.[4] . . . The man in the water began suddenly to climb the ladder, and I hastened away from the rail to fetch some clothes" (99). Why, at this point does he not summon someone from his crew to take care of Leggatt? Instead, he brings one of his own sleeping suits: "In a moment he had concealed his damp body in a sleeping-suit of the same grey-stripe pattern as the one I was wearing and followed me like my double" (100). Then, when they reach the captain's cabin, Leggatt reveals he is in the water as a result of "[a]n ugly business," that business being "I've killed a man" (100, 101). The captain's identification with Leggatt becomes irrationally strong with startling immediacy: "The shadowy, dark head, like mine, seemed to nod imperceptibly above the ghostly grey of my sleeping suit. It was, in the night, as though I had been faced by my own reflection in the depths of a somber and intense mirror" (101). What strikes him at this point is that he learns they are both "Conway boys"—this instead of the enormity of the accusation of murder. In fact, the captain even offers a tentative excuse for

Leggatt: "'Fit of temper,' I suggested, confidently" (101). The intuitive feeling of brotherhood sweeps all before it:

> He appealed to me as if our experiences had been as identical as our clothes. And I knew well enough the pestiferous danger of such a character [the crewman whose life Leggatt ended during a crisis in a storm] where there are no means of legal repression. And I knew well enough also that my double there was no homicidal ruffian. I did not think of asking him for details, and he told me the story roughly in brusque, disconnected sentences. I needed no more. I saw it all going on as though I were myself inside that other sleeping suit. (102)

Psychopathic murderers can be the most charming of people. Conrad's captain, nevertheless, making quite a rapid moral judgment, accepts Leggatt on an irrational and purely intuitive level: "I knew well enough"! The speed with which the narrator makes this decision stands in stark contrast to another moral decision—also made on the side of a ship's deck, also involving travelers, pilgrims in fact—made in another Conrad story. In chapter 9 of *Lord Jim,* Jim, the last crew member on board the *Patna,* a rusted, foundering ship full of pilgrims—people on trail, must decide whether to remain on the seemingly doomed ship or jump to the relative safety of a lifeboat in which the rest of the crew has taken refuge. The decision and the chaos during which it must be made are prolonged and agonizing for all involved, including the reader. Jim chooses safety, regrets it bitterly, and spends the rest of the novel attempting to atone.

Conrad, however, makes much of the relationship between Leggett and the captain, describing it as one of deep psychological affinity rather than London's somewhat simpler masculine camaraderie. The two men look the same, are the same size, and wear identical sleeping suits. The captain was recently, like Leggatt, a first mate—this being his first command. Further he refers to Leggatt as his "double" (seventeen times!), as his "other self" (five times), and as his "second self" (five times). Leggatt mentions the ladder:

> "Your ladder—" he murmured, after a silence. "Who'd have thought of finding a ladder hanging over at night in a ship anchored out here! . . . After I gripped it [the ladder] I said to myself, "What's the good?" When I saw a man's head looking over I thought I would swim away presently. . . . I didn't mind being looked at. I—I liked it. And then you speaking to me so quietly—as if you had expected me—made me hold on a little longer. (110)

Several noteworthy points emerge. Leggatt feels the same affinity for the captain. The ladder's uncanny presence is emblematic of the captain's openness to helping Leggatt, which both react to intuitively; it is similar to the synchronicity of Westondale's entry just as Malemute Kid makes a toast "to the man on trail this night"; and it carries the psychological weight of being a conduit to the unconscious or even to the collective unconscious. As Leggatt comes forth from the water, the deserter in the Gauertal and Jack Westondale emerge from storms, which bear similar symbolism.

As the gendarmes pursue Hemingway's deserter and a Mountie pursues London's Jack Westondale, so the captain of the *Sephora* pursues Leggatt into the narrator's very cabin. The interview takes place within earshot of Leggatt's hiding place. The fastidiousness of the narrator's responses to the questions of his new guest result in a tense and prolonged version of Hemingway's "and held the gendarmes talking." The narrator's reluctance to tell a lie makes him seem very much like Conrad's recurring narrator, Charlie Marlow.[5]

Food and storytelling, two key elements of hospitality, are shared. The captain procures hard bread, offers Leggatt his own morning coffee, and from the captain's stateroom locker feeds Leggatt "all sorts of abominable sham delicacies out of tins" (127). Leggatt, as a traveler, does what a traveler is traditionally expected to do: He tells stories—about his voyage: the crisis in a storm in which he kills a crew member, his shipboard imprisonment, and his escape.

All of these elements are explainable as Conrad's understanding and use of age-old cultural traditions regarding hospitality—except for one element: the immediate and complete identification with and acceptance of the man on trail. That is an entirely nonrational and intuitive act, indeed an act that might well be characterized as flouting cultural traditions.

Victor Hugo's Les Misérables

This brotherhood theme is similarly developed in the famous candlesticks episode of Victor Hugo's *Les Misérables*, perhaps the widest known, most culturally accessible iteration of the man-on-trail plot. Indeed, Jean Valjean has become a veritable worldwide byword for what has been called here the man on trail.

Jean Valjean, released from prison but unable to find lodgings because of his status as a convict, finally finds refuge at the residence of the Bishop of Digne. At this point, Valjean is not the pursued man he will become once Inspector Javert picks up his trail. He has, however, been rejected by an inn, the local prison, a dog into whose kennel he tries to crawl, and, finally, the fields under the stars (which were not out, as rain was approaching).

Hugo depicts the scene of each rejection, establishing a mythic tone. The rejections of Valjean echo Ovid's description of the hospitality denied the gods, told in his version of the story of Baucis and Philemon:

> Jupiter came here, once upon a time,
> Disguised as a mortal man, and Mercury,
> His son, came with him, having laid aside
> Both wand and wings. They tried a thousand houses,
> Looking for rest; they found a thousand houses
> Shut in their face. But one at last received them,
> A humble cottage, thatched with straw and reeds. (200–01)

Even before Valjean knocks, the members of the bishop's household, who had heard rumors of his presence in the town, counsel the bishop to have a locksmith install bolts to the door, essentially counseling him against offering hospitality. The bishop's housekeepers, his sister the ladylike Mademoiselle Baptistine, and the peasant Madame Magliore, exhibit less hospitable impulses in contrast to the bishop's generosity. Relevant to these reactions, Jung asserts that "[i]ndividuation always finds itself more or less in opposition to the collective norm" (*Basic* 326). When Valjean knocks—as the housekeepers are discussing the necessity of upgrading the front door to better keep out intruders—the scene has the same sort of synchronicity as Jack Westondale arriving just as Malemute Kid makes his toast "to the man on trail this night."

Each of the bishop's emphatically brief replies focuses on a standard element of hospitality—significantly beginning even before he has met Valjean:

> At this moment there was a violent knock on the door.
> "Come in!" said the bishop. (64)

Shelter has been offered. Here Hugo adds more emphasis by ending a chapter. Valjean then walks in, described by Hugo as looking "fierce" and "hideous" (64), his presence in the doorway is imposing to all but the fully individuated bishop:

> Madame Magliore had not even the strength to scream. She stood trembling with her mouth open.

> Mademoiselle Baptistine turned, saw the man enter, and started up half alarmed; then, slowly turning back again towards the fire, she looked at her brother, and her face resumed its usual calmness and serenity.
>
> The bishop looked upon the man with a tranquil eye. (64)

After a long rant introducing himself and detailing his rejections throughout the town, Valjean asks his questions:

> "What do I care? I have money. I am very tired—twelve leagues on foot, and I am so hungry. Can I stay?"
>
> "Madame Magliore," said the bishop, "put on another plate." (65)

Food has been offered. Valjean rants again about his yellow passport, his history as a convict, and asks again for hospitality:

> "Everybody has thrust me out; will you receive me? Is this an inn? Can you give me something to eat and a place to sleep? Have you a stable?"
>
> "Madame Magliore," said the bishop, "put some sheets on the bed in the alcove." (65)

A place of rest has been offered. The reference to staying in a stable—which had been refused him earlier in the evening—of course evokes the image of holy family. The bishop then invites Valjean: "Monsieur, sit down and warm yourself: we are going to take supper presently, and your bed will be made ready while you sup" (65). In four brief sentences, the bishop has offered shelter, food, a place of rest, and the warmth of his hearth. In the conversation that follows, he refuses payment. At dinner the bishop sees to it that Valjean sits closest to the hearth, which prior to the television was the seat of family communion. When he notices that the light is dim, Madame Magliore, who has by this point become almost an extension of the bishop's will, brings in the famous candlesticks. When he notices something missing from the table, she brings out all six of his silver plates (even though there are only three at table), his usual practice when he has guests for dinner. Drinks, in the form of "good Mauves wine" are served, further establishing brotherhood based on their communal consumption of the wine (70).

A brief chapter is devoted to preparations for bed. Only then, after the house is abed, does Hugo tell the story of Valjean's crime, conviction, imprisonment, and release. The reader now knows what the bishop does not: Like Westondale and Leggatt, Valjean is a good man, his "crime" consisting only of stealing a loaf of bread to feed his sister's hungry children. And, indeed, Hugo challenges the reader regarding both Valjean and the bishop: Has the reader instinctively sided with the bishop or with those who would lock up their doors and deny hospitality? At this point in Hugo's narrative, the reader knows much more about and has more emotional investment in the bishop than he does in Jean Valjean, whom the bishop still knows only as a fierce released convict. Appropriately, when Valjean retires to bed, he does not undress or sleep between the sheets, an indication that he has not yet thrown off his bitterness and ferocity and that he has not fully accepted the hospitality he has been given.

John Valjean's response to the bishop's hospitality is to wake up in the middle of the night, steal the bishop's silver plates, and attempt to make good his escape. The gendarmes capture Valjean shortly after his departure and haul him back to the bishop's residence; like the gendarmes of the Gauertal incident, the Mountie of "To the Man on Trail," and the captain of the *Sephora* of "The Secret Sharer," they are uniformed authority. The bishop, once again without hesitation, protests Valjean's innocence; indeed, he also gives him a gift, the silver candlesticks, and the advice to live a good life. As has been shown, Malemute Kid regards Jack Westondale highly, and Conrad's ship captain regards Leggett as his double. Earlier, the bishop gave Jean Valjean his similar complete acceptance:

> "I tell you, who are a traveler, that you are more at home here than I. Whatever is here is yours. What need have I to know your name? Besides, before you told me, I knew it."
>
> The man opened his eyes in astonishment:
>
> "Really? You knew my name?"
>
> "Yes," answered the bishop, "your name is my brother." (67)

The brotherhood expressed here parallels that shown in "To the Man on Trail" and "The Secret Sharer," though the rites of incorporation embodied in the offer of shelter, fire, food, wine, and a place of rest have been lost on Valjean. The bishop must explain it to him in so many words. Hugo's manipulation of the order in which he feeds his readers information makes the readers confront Valjean on the same terms as the bishop does, making the readers measure their own responses against the bishop's, and making them judge themselves. Are we bishops in touch with the deepest dictates of the collective unconscious, or are we Inspector Javerts in touch with the twisted codes that send to the galleys men who have stolen loaves of bread to feed starving children?

Harriet Beecher Stowe's Uncle Tom's Cabin

It is another twisted code, the runaway slave laws that Harriet Beecher Stowe addresses in *Uncle Tom's Cabin,* the famous abolitionist novel. Like *Les Misérables,* another nineteenth-century blockbuster, Stowe's novel utilizes a pivotal incidence of the man/woman-on-trail plot early in its narrative. One of its main plotlines concerns Eliza, a slave. She learns that her infant son has been sold to a slave dealer named Haley, who will take possession of him the next day. True to her didactic purpose of advancing the abolitionist movement, Stowe leaves no emotional button unpressed; when Eliza makes her escape with her little Harry, she becomes the woman on trail:

> If it were *your* Harry, mother, or your Willie, that were going to be torn from you by a brutal trader, to-morrow morning,—if you had seen the man, and heard that the papers were signed and delivered, and you had only from twelve o'clock till morning to make good your escape,—how fast could *you* walk? How many miles could you make in those few brief hours, with the darling at your bosom,—the sleepy little head on your shoulder,—the small, soft arms trustingly holding on to your neck? (67–68)

From her home in Kentucky she must cross the ice floe–covered Ohio River in order to reach the relative safety of the free state of Ohio. When Haley nearly catches up with her at a village tavern where she must wait for transport across the river, she is forced, in a startlingly cinematic scene, with Harry in her arms, to ford the river by leaping from one ice floe to another. Although the high Victorian sentimentalism of Stowe's style represented everything Hemingway detested in literary expression, we see some of the same details in both Stowe and Hemingway; like the deserter in the Gauertal, she leaves a trail of blood:

> The huge green fragment of ice on which she alighted pitched and cracked as her weight came on it, but she staid there not a moment. With wild cries and desperate energy she leaped to another and still another cake,—stumbling—leaping—slipping—springing upwards again! Her shoes are gone—her stockings cut from her feet while blood marked every step; but she saw nothing, felt nothing, till dimly, as in a dream, she saw the Ohio side, and a man helping her up the bank. (78–79)

The man on the shore turns out to be someone she knows and who is sympathetic. He also turns out to be someone discussed here, the threshold guardian who appears in so many mythic journey narratives. He points the way to a house where she may seek shelter.

At that house, the woman on trail finds the hostess she has been looking for in Mrs. Mary Byrd, wife of Ohio state senator John Byrd who that very day has voted in favor of a new state law similar to the Fugitive Slave Law of 1850. Both laws made it a crime to aid runaway slaves, even in free states. Passage of the federal law galvanized the abolitionist movement. As in London's "To the Man on Trail" and Hugo's *Les Misérables,* there is synchronicity in conversation at the place of hospitality prior to the entrance of the man/woman on trail:

> "Well," said his wife, . . ." and what have they been doing in the Senate?"
>
> . . . .
>
> "Not very much of importance."
>
> "Well; but is it true that they have been passing a law forbidding people to give meat and drink to those poor colored folks that come along?"
>
> . . . .
>
> "There has been a law passed forbidding people to help off the slaves that come over from Kentucky, my dear; so much of that thing has been done by those reckless Abolitionists, that our brethren in Kentucky are very strongly excited, and it seems necessary, and no more than Christian and kind, that something should be done by our state to quiet the excitement."
>
> "And what is the law? It don't forbid us to shelter those poor creatures a night, does it, and to give 'em something comfortable to eat, and a few old clothes, and send them quietly about their business?"
>
> "Why, yes, my dear; that would be aiding and abetting, you know." (98–99)

While it initially appears that Stowe's argument stems entirely from a sentimentalist conception of perceived cultural norms, a closer look reveals an intuitive connection with a deeper consciousness. As their debate continues, Senator and Mrs. Byrd bring "feelings" and "reason" into the conversation:

> "But, Mary, just listen to me. Your feelings are all quite right, dear, and interesting, and I love you for them; but, then, we mustn't suffer our feelings to run away with our judgment; you must consider it's not a matter of private feeling,— there are great public interests involved,—there is such a state of public agitation rising, that we must put aside our private feelings."
>
> "Now, John, I don't know anything about politics, but I can read my Bible;

and there I see that I must feed the hungry, clothe the naked, and comfort the desolate; and that Bible I mean to follow." (100–01)

Of John Byrd's personality, Stowe has already told us with heavy irony, "[O]ur senator has the misfortune to be a man who had a particularly humane and accessible nature, and turning away anybody that was in trouble had never been his forte" (101). He has not acted within the dictates of his own personality but within the dictates of his opposite—his shadow personality, in this case, his political personality. In Jungian terms, he is the "man possessed by his own shadow . . . always standing in his own light and falling into his own traps" ("Concerning Rebirth" 57). Elsewhere, Jung refers to the shadow as "that dark half of the psyche which we invariably get rid of by projection: either by burdening our neighbors—in a wider or narrower sense—with all the faults which we obviously have ourselves, or by casting our sins upon a divine mediator" ("Introduction" 571). Mary, who does not act in accordance with her shadow, of course wins the argument, despite John's projections. She bases her objection not on social norms but on the ancient traditions of hospitality, expressed in biblical texts that predate the political and civil codes John attempts to operate by:

> "Mary! Mary! My dear, let me reason with you."
>
> "I hate reasoning, John,—especially reasoning on such subjects. There's a way you political folks have of coming round and round a plain right thing; and you don't believe it yourselves, when it comes to practice. I know you well enough, John. You don't believe it's right any more than I do; and you wouldn't do it ["Turning a woman out of doors in a snow-storm"] any sooner than I." (101–02)

She does, indeed, know him "well enough," for she knows him by his real character and not by his shadow personality. She knows him better than he knows himself. And it is at this moment in their debate that they are asked into their kitchen to confront the swooning Eliza in all of her distress. As in "To the Man on Trail" and *Les Misérables*, the appearance of the man/woman on trail is synchronous with the discussion occurring at the host home.[6] Mrs. Byrd offers protection; after Eliza goes to sleep, Mr. Byrd suggests two gifts of clothing.

When Eliza tells her story, she appeals to Mrs. Byrd (and by extension all of Stowe's female readers) on a mother-to-mother basis: both have lost children to death (Mrs. Byrd recently), and Eliza now stands to lose her only remaining child to Haley the slave trader, so the pursuer is thus associated with death, an association entirely typical of the man/woman-on-trail plot. Eliza is then offered a bed, a standard element of hospitality, and the senator and wife retire to their parlor, where their debate does not continue. Then the senator formulates a plan to convey Eliza to a safer location, with himself as both key player and cover story. Mary's response: "'Your heart is better than your head, in this case, John,' said the wife, . . . 'Could I ever have loved you, had I not known you better than you know yourself?'" (108).

The climactic emotional moment of the guest/host relationship is Mary's decision to give the gift of clothing: in particular, she gives little Harry some clothes of her recently deceased son. Stowe shows her readers no mercy:

> "Mary, I don't know how you'd feel about it, but there's that drawer full of things—of—of—poor little Henry's." So saying, he turned quickly on his heel, and shut the door after him.
>
> His wife opened the little bed-room door adjoining her room, and, taking the candle, set it down on top of the bureau there; then from a small recess she took a key, and put it thoughtfully in the lock of a drawer, and made a sudden pause, while two boys, who, boy like, had followed close at her heels, stood looking, with silent significant glances, at their mother. And oh! Mother that reads this, has there never been in your house a drawer, or a closet, the opening of which has been to you like the opening of a little grave? Ah! Happy mother that you are, if it has not been so. (108–09)

When Eliza departs, she walks to the senator's carriage "arrayed in a cloak, bonnet, and shawl, that had belonged to her benefactress"; the sharing of clothing here parallels the sharing of clothing—notably the sleeping suits—in Conrad's "The Secret Sharer" and also the socks in the Gauertal incident (110).

For the Byrds's final act of hospitality, the senator, ostensibly on his way to work at the capital, transports Eliza to the remote farmhouse of an abolitionist and former slave owner John Van Trompe, who offers defiance to potential pursuers, much in the manner of Malemute Kid:

> "If there's anybody comes," said the good man, stretching his tall muscular form upward, "why here I'm ready for him: I've got seven sons, each six foot high, and they'll be ready for 'em." . . .
>
> "Now, I say, gal, you needn't be a bit afeard, let who will come here. I'm up to all that sort o' thing," said he, pointing to two or three goodly rifles over the mantelpiece. (113–14)

When the senator leaves, Van Trompe goes with him to show him a better road to take to catch the stagecoach to Columbus. He passes Van Trompe ten dollars for Eliza, the final gift of hospitality, just as Conrad's ship captain narrator gives Leggatt money as a parting gift before he swims ashore, just as Jean Valjean is given the silver candlesticks, just as the deserter in the Gauertal is given socks.

Comparison table 1: The man or woman on trail

Author	Ernest Hemingway	Jack London	Joseph Conrad	Victor Hugo	Harriet Beecher Stowe
Title or incident	Deserter in the Gauertal ("Snows")	"To the Man on Trail"	"The Secret Sharer"	Candlesticks episode of *Les Misérables*	*Uncle Tom's Cabin*, chapters 8 and 9
Host	Harry, likely a journalist at this point	Malemute Kid, Klondike gold miner	Ship captain narrator	Bishop of Digne	Mary Byrd, mother, wife of Ohio state senator
Other members of host's household	"We"	Other miners: "circle of judges"	Ship's crew and disapproving officers	Bishop's sister and a housekeeper	Notably her husband, Ohio state senator John Byrd, recent supporter of a state runaway slave law
Man-on-trail, reason for being on trail	Deserter	Miner/armed robbery suspect	Leggatt, manslaughter (guilty)	Jean Valjean, released convict	Eliza, runaway slave, and her infant, Harry
Acceptance by host	Without hesitation	By host at first, by miners after departure	Total, both before and after confession of crime	Absolute, methodical, and immediate acceptance	Total acceptance at considerable risk to hostess
Relationship of guest and host	Approval implied	Immediate admiration	Double, doppelganger	Bishop expresses brotherhood	Mother to mother
Elements of hospitality extended	Clothing	Shared food and spirits (Christmas punch), rest	Clothing, food, shelter	Food, spirits (wine), rest	Shelter, security, rest, food, clothing, transfer, and continuation of her journey
Parting gifts	Socks	Food for sled team, critical advice	Hat, money	Candlesticks (as well as silver items Valjean had stolen)	Clothing for both Eliza and Harry
Emphasized gift or element of hospitality	Socks	Clothing, rest, supplies	Elaborate risk to set Leggatt ashore	Candlesticks	Clothing for both mother and child

Pursuers	Gendarmes	Royal Canadian Mountie	Captain of ship on which murder was committed	Gendarmes	Slave catchers
Delay of pursuers	Delay by conversation	Threat of violence	Misdirection	Invention of cover story	Illegal transfer of Eliza to a safe house and threat of violence

Chapter 2

THE BOOKS AT WINDEMERE

"Walk in!" said the shepherd promptly.

The latch clicked upward, and out of the night our pedestrian appeared on the door-mat.

—Thomas Hardy, "The Three Strangers"

"You are cold," repeated the old man, "and hungry? Well, step in."

—Robert Louis Stevenson, "A Lodging for the Night"

He lifted his head now and surveyed the stranger in turn. Finally, stretching out his fat hand, he said:

"You are welcome, Brother Edouard."

—Harold Frederic, "Brother Sebastian's Friendship"

"You bear your position well. You are not alarmed at these wild fellows?"

"No—not now. I don't think they would hurt me. Besides—"

"Besides—what?" he asked, as she paused.

"I have your word for them."

"Yes," he answered; "but it is only a highwayman's word."

"I can trust it."

—F. W. Robinson, "Minions of the Moon"

South of the Mackinac Straits, near the northeast corner of Lake Michigan, is Little Traverse Bay. There, on the northwest corner of Michigan's Lower Peninsula, sits the bustling resort town of Petoskey. In 1899, the year of Ernest's birth, Clarence and Grace Hemingway, Ernest's parents, purchased shorefront property and built a summer cottage on Walloon Lake, just a few miles south of Petoskey. In the summer of 1900, they completed the cottage for use and named it Windemere.

The Hemingways lived in Oak Park, Illinois, a fashionable suburb of Chicago, where Dr. Clarence Hemingway had a medical practice. Every year from Ernest's birth through his young adulthood, the family would travel, usually by steamship, from Oak Park to the cottage to spend the summer. The surrounding area, as well as the cottage, provided settings and characters for some of Hemingway's juvenilia as well as some of his most important stories. He spent time there recuperating from the wounds he received in World War I and married his first wife, Hadley Richardson, there.

Upon the death of his father, ownership of Windemere passed to Ernest. He returned only once, many years later, and the cottage remained largely unused during that time. Upon Ernest's death, ownership passed, according to his wishes, to his sister Madelaine, known in the family as Sunny. In 1968, Windemere was designated a Registered National Historic Landmark, though it is not open to the public, as, under the care of her son, Ernest Hemingway Mainland, owner and resident, it is happily still used by the family. In 1975, Madelaine published her memoir of her brother, entitled *Ernie: Hemingway's Sister "Sunny" Remembers*. She passed away in 1995.

In 2012, The International Hemingway Society met for a conference in Petoskey and Bay View, Michigan. As a member of the Hemingway Society and an attendee and presenter at the conference, I availed myself of the rare opportunity to take a guided tour of the cottage and its grounds. During my tour group's time in the cottage, our tour guide directed our attention to a wall of books in the living room. One shelf held cookbooks, another held books by and about Ernest, and a third held books that were at the cottage when Ernest was growing up. We were then told that we could examine any of the books but would need to have one of the family members present take it off the shelf for us. This was a once-in-a-lifetime opportunity, and I found myself in front of the shelf in mere seconds, my eyes intently fixed on the spines of the books in front of me, books that had been long available to Ernest. Knowing my time was limited, I scanned the titles and authors' names as quickly as I could. A red ten-volume set of *Stories by American Authors* sparked some interest, though they were unsuggestively numbered 1–10. Next came a companion set of *Stories by English Authors*, each spine not numbered but labeled—both surprisingly and suggestively—with the name of the country in which the stories in that volume were set. I was scheduled to make my presentation the next day, the final day of the conference. Part of my discussion of "The Snows of Kilimanjaro" was the suggestion that Hemingway had read a story by Robert Louis Stevenson entitled "A Lodging for the Night," a treatment of a fictional, though not improbable, episode in the life of the great medieval French poet François Villon. So I asked to see the volume labeled *France*—in which, as I was delighted to discover, Stevenson's "A Lodging for the Night" was the first selection. He might well have read it from the volume I held in my hand. Never mind that his sister Marcelline had written that she and Ernest both read Stevenson back at Oak Park, because at that moment I felt like Richard D. Altick or Grenfell and Hunt, with a little Indiana Jones thrown in as well.

Well, alas, and sic transit gloria mundi. Leaving at the end of the tour, we walked past the garage where souvenirs were on sale, posters, cups, et cetera. I did not have a copy of Sunny's *Ernie* and could not think of a more appropriate spot to obtain one. It was not a new edition but a reissue. Her son, Ernest, took advantage of the occasion of the 1999 reissue, as he states in his preface, to contribute new photographs and "a list of books in the libraries at Windemere and in Oak Park that might give clues to the early reading habits of Uncle Ernie," which I saw and read on the bus back to Petoskey (vii, 162). So much for Indiana Jones!

The next day, my presentation—with a hastily added paragraph about what I had found at the cottage—met with success, a revised version ultimately finding its way into *The Hemingway Review.* In email correspondence, editor Susan Beegel queried me about two somewhat cryptic bibliography entries for the sets of stories by English and American authors. This led to more research and another article in *The Hemingway Review.* Seeing the listing at the back of *Ernie* had made me assume, falsely, it turns out, that one of the giants of Hemingway scholarship must have noticed the listing and written about it. Surely, in the twelve years since *Ernie*'s reissue, somebody must have picked up on the significance of those twenty volumes. Nevertheless, I obtained and read in their entirety all twenty; meanwhile, my attempts to find out what anyone else might have said about those volumes came up empty. It was not possible to tell whether anybody had investigated them, but it was possible to ascertain that nobody had commented on them.

A number of the stories in the Windemere volumes embody the hospitality themes Hemingway so deftly developed in "The Snows of Kilimanjaro" many years later. Thus, they may have been instrumental in alerting him to the possibilities of the hospitality and man-on-trail plots. (The differences between these two plots are minor and discussed at the end of chapter 3. Suffice it to say at this point that the main difference is that the hospitality plot involves a guest who does not suffer pursuit.) Unlike the case of London's "To the Man on Trail," we can feel confident that Hemingway actually had access to these stories. Hemingway's older sister Marcelline, in her memoir *At the Hemingways,* for example, notes that Clarence and Grace Hemingway, their parents, did not approve of Jack London's "violence and coarseness" (107). How we should interpret this revelation remains unclear. Should we assume that in accordance to his parents' wishes, Hemingway avoided seeking out and reading one of America's, and the world's, best-selling writers? Could he simply have skipped over London? The Reynolds inventory indicates that he may have encountered *The Call of the Wild* during his school days. The Brasch and Sigman inventory of London's books lists only one London volume, published in 1956, two decades too late to have had an effect on "The Snows of Kilimanjaro." Neither the *Selected Letters* nor the first three volumes of Hemingway's letters (1907–22, 1923–25, and 1926–29) index London. However, volume 4 of the letters (1929–31) includes a reference suggesting that Hemingway did indeed read London. In his 12 October 1930 letter to Maurice-Edgar Coindreau, whom he chose as French translator for two of his novels, Hemingway complained bitterly and scatologically about the deeply flawed French translations of London.

So, in startling contrast to their prohibition of London's works, Hemingway's parents made the Windemere volumes available to Hemingway during in his formative years. The small volumes measure a mere 5 by 7 inches and could easily have gone with him on his rambles through the trails and waterways around Petoskey, Michigan.[1] In later years, Hemingway obtained books by some of the authors included in these collections. A number of stories from these volumes contain major elements of the man/woman-on-trail plot. These include, among canonical authors, Thomas Hardy's "The Three Strangers," Robert Louis Stevenson's "A Lodging for the Night," and Harold Frederic's "Brother Sebastian's Friendship," all three of which are discussed below. Among noncanonical authors, they include F. N. Robinson's "The Minions of the Moon," discussed below. While it may be useful to speculate about whether any of the elements of the hospitality plot may have lodged in Hemingway's mind as a result of reading these stories, it is important to remember that they are valuable in their own rights, for they include the variations on the man-on-trail and hospitality plots used by both canonical and popular authors and thus help to gauge the extent to which these archetypal plots permeate both canonical and noncanonical literature. The works by London, Conrad, Hugo, and Stowe discussed so far remain widely available in print in a variety of editions, as do those stories by Hardy and Stevenson included in this chapter, whose authors' reputations precede them. The noncanonical works discussed in this chapter and in chapter 6 (not among the Windemere stories), while less easy to access, are worthy of the reader's time not just for their relevance to this study but for their own inherent readability and literary excellence.

Thomas Hardy's "The Three Strangers"

Thomas Hardy's "The Three Strangers," canonical and widely available, remains his best known and most often anthologized short story, albeit one written in a comic mode not usual for Hardy. He first published the story in 1883, when he was in his early forties, and later included it in *Wessex Tales* (1888), his first collection of stories. He had already published over a half dozen of the novels that would eventually make him famous, so "The Three Strangers" does not qualify as a novice effort. A condemned prisoner escapes from Casterbridge jail, makes his way through a storm—as in, for example, the Gauertal incident or *Uncle Tom's Cabin*—to a wayside farmhouse where the host, hostess, and guests are celebrating a birth and christening. The owner of the house—a shepherd, no less—and his wife welcome the stranger without hesitation. He is afforded three elements suggestive of the rites of incorporation: rest, in the form of a seat by the chimney corner where he could dry out after walking through the storm; the comradeship of smoking together, in the form of some tobacco, as well a pipe in which to smoke it—as he claims to have lost his in the storm; and finally a gift to take with him in the form of a tobacco box, as he claims, once again, that his was lost in the storm. Thus, moments later, when the second stranger arrives—the hangman on his way to Casterbridge to execute the first stranger, the man on trail has already integrated himself into the social construct of the farmer's house and celebration.

The hearth being the center of family life, the first stranger further integrates himself by taking up a poker and tending the fire. The second stranger, the hangman on his way to Casterbridge to perform the execution, then arrives, and he also is offered a seat in the chimney-corner, where they share mead from "the family mug—a huge vessel of brown ware, having its edge worn away like a threshold by the rub of whole generations of thirsty lips that had gone the way of all flesh" (136).

The hangman drinks heartily, dismaying the shepherd's wife, who takes on the role of the counselor against hospitality:

> He [the shepherd] went away to the dark place under the stairs where the barrel stood. The shepherdess followed him,
>
> "Why should you do this?" she said reproachfully, as soon as they were alone. "He's emptied it at once, though it held enough for ten people; and now he's not contented wi' the small, but must needs more o' the strong! And a stranger unknown to any of us. For my part I don't like the look o' the man at all."
>
> "But he's in the house, my honey; and 'tis a wet night, and a christening. Daze it, what's a cup of mead more or less?" (139–40)

The social bond thus grows tighter. Some riddling questions follow regarding the second stranger's occupation, which none are able to solve. Now the hangman draws the social group closer together with music and song, in this case a song the form of a riddle about his occupation:

> O my trade is the rarest one,
> Simple shepherds all—
> My trade is a sight to see;
> For my customers I tie, and take them up on high,
> And waft 'em to a far countree! (141)

Only the first stranger realizes that the last line refers to the undiscovered country, from whose bourn no traveler returns; nevertheless, when the singer shouts "Chorus!" the first stranger "joined him in a deep bass voice of musical relish" (141). The two thus bind themselves even closer, first by drink and then by song. As with London's Jack Westondale, we discover the crime only belatedly, when after a second verse the celebrants realize the identity of the second guest:

> "O, he's the—!" whispered the people in the background, mentioning the name of an ominous public officer. "He's come to do it! 'T is to be at Casterbridge jail tomorrow—the man for sheep-stealing—the poor clockmaker we heard of, who used to live away at Shottsford and had no work to do—Timothy Summers, whose family were a-starving, and so he went out of Shottsford by the high-road, and took a sheep in open daylight, defying the farmer and the farmer's wife and the farmer's lad, and every man jack among 'em." (142–43)

Another veritable Jean Valjean! But we must remember that—exactly as in "To the Man on Trail," "The Secret Sharer," and *Les Misérables*—this comes only *after* the reader has sided emotionally with Timothy Summers. As a guest, he elicits sympathy even before the reader learns of his crimes, similar again to Jean Valjean. As with Jack Westondale, the reader wants him to escape. This response results not from cultural conditioning but rather from a response to an archetype—immediate, a-rational, and visceral—a response once again hard-wired to an image from the collective unconscious of humankind.

The third stranger then appears, brother of the condemned man, whom he sees hobnobbing with his own hangman. Appalled and trembling, he backs away. A shot signals the escape of a prisoner, and the brother beats a hasty retreat. Mistaking the brother for the condemned man, all rush out to apprehend him, and Timothy Summers escapes in the confusion. The local farmers, impressed by Summers's nerve, pretend to search the countryside for him, though in reality they thwart the pursuers in classic fashion and aid in his escape.

Hardy regularly refers to the second stranger as "the man in cinder-grey," invoking "ashes to ashes," for in his occupation of hangman, he brings death. The appropriateness of the color of his clothing also goes a little way in categorizing him as uniformed authority. As has Hemingway, Hugo, and Conrad have already suggested, uniformed authority in pursuit comes to represent death. By thwarting the hunt for Summers, the townspeople rebel against the death that deep inside they know pursues them, that pursues us all.

Robert Louis Stevenson's "A Lodging for the Night"

A second story had already occurred to me before I discovered it in the Windemere books. Robert Louis Stevenson's "A Lodging for the Night" has a pursued man, François Villon, the now famous medieval French poet; a host, an old knight who takes him in for the night; pursuers, the night watch; and tracks in the snow. "A Lodging for the Night" (1877) was Stevenson's first published work of fiction, just as London's "To the Man on Trail," was his first.

Some epistolary and other evidence suggests that Hemingway had read the Stevenson story. First, the first volume of Hemingway's letters includes Hemingway's letter to Sherwood and Tennessee Anderson of 23 December 1921 (almost Christmas!): "And when it's a cold night in the streets of Paris and we're walking home down the Rue Bonaparte we think of the way the wolves used to slink into the city and François Villon and the gallows at Montfaucon." The editors include this note: "In Robert Louis Stevenson's short story, 'A Lodging for the Night' (1877), the medieval French poet Villon muses that it was the kind of weather 'when wolves might take it into their heads to enter Paris again,' [Stevenson,

"Lodging" 26] and he is haunted by the aspect of the gallows at Montfaucon, the 'great grisly Paris gibbet' [15]" (*Letters* 1:313, 315). In another letter, to his father on 28 October 1919, Hemingway mentions having read Villon's "Larger Testament" (209). Second, also during his early Paris years, Hemingway would almost certainly have read "Villonaud for This Yule," Ezra Pound's parody of Villon's ballade style. It too embodies a Christmas reference. Third, D. B. Wyndham Lewis, an acquaintance of Hemingway's from the Paris years and subject of one of the sketches of *A Moveable Feast,* published a biography of Villon in 1928.

In the story, one of Villon's lowlife pals kills another. He then steals Villon's purse and sets fire to the house they are in. Villon flees through the snow-covered streets of Paris, worrying about the tracks he leaves, attempting to avoid the night watch, and finally ending the night comfortably in the randomly selected home of an old knight. The host answers Villon's knock:

> Seen as it [the old knight's face] was by the light of a flickering head-lamp, it looked perhaps nobler than it had a right to do; but it was a fine face, honourable rather than intelligent, strong, simple and righteous.
>
> "You knock late, sir," said the old man in resonant, courteous tones.
>
> Villon cringed and brought up many servile words of apology; at a crisis of this sort, the beggar was uppermost in him, and the man of genius hid his head with confusion.
>
> "You are cold," repeated the old man, "and hungry? Well, step in." And he ordered him into the house with a noble enough gesture. (29–30)

We must note once again here that the host does not vacillate, weigh the pros and cons, or consider his own safety but responds immediately to the human needs of the man at his door. While the old man gathers some food and wine, Villon appraises his belongings and warms himself at the fire. As they converse over their food, Villon slowly but surely reveals his character to the old knight, who eventually calls him out as the rogue Stevenson depicts him as. Despite this, the old knight takes no action against his guest.

Stevenson, ever the moralist, disapproved of Villon and feared romanticizing the shenanigans of someone he considered a disreputable character. Stevenson had earlier revealed his judgement more fully, in his 1872 essay "François Villon, Student, Poet, and Housebreaker," a biting, moralistic screed on the life and work of Villon, "[a] sinister dog, in all likelihood, but with a look in his eye, and the loose flexile mouth that goes with wit and an overweening sensual temperament. Certainly the sorriest figure on the rolls of fame" (179). Accordingly,

Stevenson has Villon stay the night with the old knight; enjoy the hospitality, conversation, food, and wine; and cavalierly go his way the next morning, musing about the value of the old knight's goblets. In effect, Villon exploits the spirit of the time-honored traditions of the guest/host relationship.

Beyond his moralizing, Stevenson depicts in Villon a classic trickster figure. On the trickster archetype, Jung writes: "In his clearest manifestations he is a faithful reflection of the undifferentiated human consciousness, corresponding to a psyche that has hardly left the animal level" ("Trickster" 140). And animal needs—creature comforts—motivate Villon to knock at the old knight's door; primarily he needs a "lodging for the night" to escape the night watch and to get a meal. Only secondarily does he participate in the human bonding rituals of sharing wine and conversation.

In his extended study of the trickster archetype Lewis Hyde sees the trickster involved in three types of plots. In the first, the trickster causes trouble and then moves on without being changed, like a pícaro. In the next, the "trickster is eventually domesticated." In the third, the trickster is defeated (*Trickster* 220–22). Stevenson employs the first of these. Not surprisingly, Hyde places the trickster of the first plot at a door: "From the edge of a group or the threshold of a house there are only a few ways a trickster can move: he can come inside, he can leave entirely, or he can stay where he started, resisting all attempts to civilize or exile" (220). Stevenson's Villon does all three. He does come inside, where, trickster-like, he enjoys what for him are the animal pleasures of food and wine. He stays there through the night until his motives are unmasked by the old knight. He leaves, defeated but unchanged. The old knight is not diminished by his exploited hospitality, and Villon moves on to his next picaresque adventure.

Wine and spirits effect a vulnerability—of judgment, reflexes, basic personal safety. Thus, the ritual of drinking together makes a statement of trust, brotherhood, commitment, and community among the participants. The host runs the risks of this vulnerability when he offers hospitality to the stranger, who may well be a trickster. The host must be fully individuated and secure in his judgment of the stranger. Dithering, he faces the maximum danger by broadcasting his uncertainty. Inviting a stranger into a home involves all of the dangers that tricksters bring along with them, and not everyone measures up to the trickster's challenge.

Finally, it would be a mistake to fail to consider Villon's most famous line of verse, one of the most famous lines in the history of poetry, the haunting refrain from his "Ballade of Dead Ladies": "But where are the snows of yesteryear?" ("*Mais ou sot les neiges d'antan?*") (qtd. in D. Lewis 348–51; see also Oldsey 71 and P. Smith 357.). Hemingway evokes Villon through Stevenson; awaiting his death on the plains of east Africa, Hemingway's Harry contemplates the snows of yesteryear, both literally and figuratively. And Hemingway's Helen plays hostess to Harry, a surly guest as troublesome in his own peculiar way as Stevenson's Villon.

Harold Frederic's "Brother Sebastian's Friendship"

Harold Frederic (1856–1898), a journalist and marginally canonical American novelist, is best known for his 1896 novel *The Damnation of Theron Ware,* still widely available. He wrote "Brother Sebastian's Friendship" early in his career, which began as a journalist at his hometown paper, Utica, New York's *The Observer.* His first fiction, in the form of four short stories, was published in *The Observer* beginning in September 1876 and ending with "Brother Sebastian's Friendship" on June 30, 1876 (see Thomas F. O'Donnell, Stanton Garner, and Robert H. Woodward). Unlike his other *Observer* stories, "Brother Sebastian's Friendship" saw several reprints, including in *Stories by American Authors.* It thus stands above the other *Observer* stories. As with London and Stevenson, his tale of host and guest stands at the outset of his career, though this one was not his very first published fiction. This may be an indication that writers at the beginnings of their careers, less steeped in cultural traditions than their more experienced peers, respond more directly and openly to the call of archetypal plot elements.

Brother Sebastian, a French monk and "a Brother of the Christian Schools," tells the story as first-person narrator some forty years after the events of his tale (143). He opens with his transfer, for health reasons, from Paris to the south of France. The story he tells is the "single exception" to his "reputation as a misanthrope," a man with "no intimates," a man "outside" the usual "social circles" (145). One day, while "killing time in the library," he witnesses a new monk's introduction to the director:

> "You are from Algiers?"
> "I am, Brother."
> "Your name?"
> "Edouard, Brother."

> "Well, tell me more."
>
> "I was under orders to be in Paris in January, Brother. As my health was poor, I received permission to come back here. So I am here. I have these papers from the Mother house, and from Etienne, Director, of Algiers."
>
> Something in the voice sounded peculiar to me. (148)

Several points are noteworthy here. First, the repeated use of the word *Brother* and the associations with Paris and ill health establish an identification between Brother Sebastian and Brother Edouard not unlike that established between Conrad's ship captain and Leggatt. Indeed, Brother Sebastian will play the host to Brother Edouard's man on trail. Further, the description that follows amplifies the uncanniness suggested in the peculiarity of Brother Edouard's voice, a description that bears out both the stress and the charisma of the man on trail:

> a wonderfully handsome face, framed in dazzling black curls. Perhaps it looked the more beautiful because contrasted with the shaven gray poll and surly features of grim Albonus [the Director]. But to me it was a dream of St. John the Evangel. The eyes of the face were lowered upon the Director, so I could only guess their brilliancy. The features were those of an extreme youth—round, soft, and delicate. The expression was one of utter fatigue, almost pain. It bore out the statement of ill-health. (148)

Though the 1879 publication date makes "Brother Sebastian's Friendship" thoroughly pre-Freudian, not to mention pre-Jungian, the reference to "the dream of St. John the Evangel," along with other elements only partially evident at this point of the narrative, establishes Frederic as a writer of intuitive psychological insight.

Beginning the very next day, Edouard and Sebastian become friendly, very uncharacteristically for Sebastian:

> For the hundreds of strangers who came and went in the Paris house . . . I cared absolutely nothing. I did not suffer their entrance nor their exit to excite me. This was so much the case that they called me a machine. But with Edouard this was different. I grew to love the boy from the first evening, when, as he left my room, I caught myself saying, "I shall be sorry when he goes." . . . For that matter most of the brothers petted him. . . . But I was flattered when he chose me as his particular friend. For the first time my heart opened. (150)

Their friendship established, Edouard ventures a question one would ask only of an intimate:

> "You have been good to me, Brother Sebastian. Let me ask you: May I tell you something in confidence—something which shall never pass your lips? I mean it."
>
> He had turned and poured those marvelous eyes into mine with irresistible magnetism. Of course I said, "Speak!" and I said it *without the slightest hesitation.*
>
> "I am not a Christian Brother. I do not belong to your order. I have no claim upon the hospitality of this roof. I am an impostor." (152, emphasis added)

Malemute Kid regards Jack Westondale for the first time: "As the young stranger ate of the rude fare, Malemute Kid attentively studied his face. Nor was he long in deciding it was fair, honest, and open, and that he liked it" (292). After a brief conversation with Leggatt, who is still naked and in the water, Conrad's ship captain reflects on his own behavior: "But at the time it was pure intuition on my part. A mysterious communication was established already between us two—in the face of that silent, darkened tropical sea. I was young, too; young enough to make no comment. The man in the water began suddenly to climb up the ladder, and I hastened away from the rail to fetch some clothes" (99). In "The Three Strangers," when Timothy Summers knocks on the door of Shepherd Fennell he is greeted, "'Walk in!' said the shepherd promptly" (9). There should thus be no surprise that Brother Sebastian speaks "without the slightest hesitation." Moments later, after Edouard first weeps bitterly and then reminds Sebastian that he has promised secrecy, Sebastian reaches a point "when some power of thought returned" (153). Acceptance of the man on trail is not about thinking; it is about acting in accordance with the intuitions that arise from the deepest psychological wells of mankind—for character, for author, and for reader.

Then, without abandoning the basics of the man-on-trail plot, Frederic adds some features that can be described only as Shakespearean. Edouard's health apparently benefits from the relief brought on by his confession, and Sebastian's declines as a result of his anxiety over what he thought must be the approach of Edouard's approaching "hour of trouble" (156).

Elysee, the brother director, returning from a trip, begins a story about a girl named Renée, the niece of a former classmate and an orphan, whom he had placed in a convent. "Last spring she barely escaped compromising the house by an escapade with a young *miserable* of the town named Banin" (157). Brother Albert, a guest at the monastery, picks up the tale: "Banin is in prison." Elysee continues: "The girl was reprimanded. Next week she disappeared. . . . The

Curé [Father Martin Delette, Elysee's former classmate] was nearly heartbroken" (158). A detective eventually appears, revealing he has apprehended Banin, who is serving a twenty-year sentence. Of Renée, he says, "Well, she's off. Good trick, too. She was the decoy. Banin stood in the shadow with club. She brought gentlemen into alley, friend did work." Father Delette, shocked, takes to his bed and dies there. "Brother Albert raised his eyes again, and added, as if he had not paused, 'He was ashamed to hold his head up. He might well be'" (159).

Then, improbably for such a solemn moment, Brother Edouard, "from the other side of the room," speaks up in defense of Father Delette: "Why should he be ashamed? Was he not a good man? Was the blame of his bad niece's acts his? From the story, she was well used and had no excuse. It is he who is to be pitied, not blamed!" (159, 160). Elysee follows Edouard's lead: "Brother Edouard is right. . . . Poor Martin was to be compassioned. None the less, my heart is touched for the girl. In Banin's trial it appeared that he maltreated her, and forced her to do what she did by blows. They were really married. Her neighbors gave Renée a name for gentleness and a good heart. Poor thing!" (160).

It must be revealed here what the Shakespeareans have already suspected—that in a case of disguised gender identity, Brother Edouard is really Renée and that the man on trail is really a woman on trail.[2] Her reputation, like that of the men on trail already discussed, is rehabilitated. She was "maltreated" and "forced." And Jack Westondale robbed McFarland's—a gambling joint and therefore already ethically questionable—of the money his partner blew there. Leggatt's story of the crewman he had to kill to save his ship, while not understandable to "an old judge and a respectable jury," is sufficient for both Conrad's ship captain narrator and the reader (103). Hardy's Timothy Summers was convicted of stealing a sheep to feed his starving family, and as all the literary world knows, Jean Valjean stole a loaf of bread to feed his sister's starving children. These stories are not about mankind's ancient proclivity for theft, hunger, misappropriation of funds, nor are they about the incompetence of sailors at sea. They are about our own proclivity to sympathize and aid the man on trail because he is pursued, at least symbolically if not both symbolically and literally, by the same death that pursues us all.

Brother Sebastian is slow to make the connection between Edouard and Renée. Albonus, the Brother Servitor, understands first:

> "And she was never found?" asked Albonus, eagerly. He spoke very rarely. He looked now at me as he spoke, and there was a strange, ungodly glitter in his eyes which made me shudder involuntarily. . . .

> "It would be remarkable if she should be found now, after all this time," said Albonus, sharply. His wicked, squinting old eyes were still fastened upon me. This time, as by a flash of eternal knowledge, I read their meaning, and felt the ground slipping from under me. (160)

That night, in a one-word written message, Brother Sebastian tells Renée roughly the same thing that Malemute Kid tells Jack Westondale and Conrad's ship captain tells Leggatt: "Fly!" (161). The host follows his duty until the end. But Renée does not fly. During their last meal together, the world of dreams is invoked, not surprisingly, as dreams are the vessels that contain the archetypes: "It is as distinct as a nightmare to me" (162). But of her arrest Brother Sebastian remembers only "a whirling glimpse of uniforms"—of official uniformed authority—before fainting (163). She is eventually pardoned, and Brother Sebastian lives out his life "in the seclusion of a missionary post at the foot of the Andes" (164).

F. W. Robinson's "Minions of the Moon"

Another story in the *England* volume is "Minions of the Moon," by F. W. Robinson (1830–1901). Both the title and author have fallen into obscurity. The tale, best classified as a swashbuckling romance, includes some of the usual man-on-trail elements but in clever and entertaining fashion, making it worthy of discussion.

During the reign of King George III (1760–1820), a group of highwaymen demand hospitality at an isolated but rich estate. Master Reuben Pemberthy being gone, his fiancée, Sophie, realizing she has no choice, admits the Minions of the Moon, as the highwaymen call themselves, and offers hospitality. The group's name comes, appropriately, from a speech Jack Falstaff makes to Prince Hal: "Marry then, sweet wag, when thou art king let not us that are squires of the night's body be called the day's beauty. Let us be 'diana's foresters,' 'gentlemen of the shade,' 'minions of the moon,' and let men say we be men of good government, being governed, as the sea is, by our noble and chaste mistress the moon, under whose countenance we steal" (*1 Henry IV* 1.2.20–26).

Their entrance is, uncharacteristically for the man-on-trail plot, dreaded and delayed; they gain their raucous admission after a threat to burn the house down. Sophie develops an affinity with Guy, their leader, a younger son of the nobility who, without prospects, has taken to the highway. He, in turn, protects Sophie from the rascals and bullies of his crew. The minions are fed at a table already set in anticipation of the return of Master Reuben Pemberthy, and one of them lifts from Sophie the keys to the wine cellar, all of which makes them seem more like Penelope's suitors, from Homer's *Odyssey*, than Timothy Summers, Leggatt, or Jack Westondale. Guy asks her to sing; she impresses all with her voice. The master, having been robbed by the Minions earlier in the evening, returns. He boldly offers hospitality, knowing that a troop of the King's soldiers is on the way, which information he conveys secretly to Sophie so that she may help him delay the minions, by singing again, until the soldiers arrive. She responds with a song that reminds Guy of his mother and the high hopes she had for him, touching him deeply. During a third song, she warns Guy with a look: "She looked at Captain Guy as she sang, and with much entreaty in her gaze, and he looked back at her from under the cock of his hat, which he had pulled over his brows; then he wavered and stole out of the room" (48). This warning constitutes the unhesitating acceptance of the man on trail. It enables Guy and the minions to make good their escape. Guy had indeed protected her from his crew, but all things considered, her warning to him is as a-rational as the aid given to Jack Westondale, Leggatt, Timothy Summers, or Jean Valjean. It stands up to intuition but not to logic.

Fifteen years later, Guy returns and finds Sophie a widow about to be dispossessed, because among the Pemberthys only the males ever inherit. Each of the minions has made his own way to the gallows. Guy's first encounter with Sophie has reformed him, and he is about to inherit his own family estate:

> "Yes, that is it; Richard Guy Isshaw, the younger son, who went wholly to the bad—who turned highwayman—whom you saved. The only one out of eight,—the rest were hanged at Tyburn and Kennington, poor devils. . . .
>
> "You saved me; you set me thinking of my young mother, who died when I was a lad and loved me much too well; and you taught me there were warm and loving hearts in the world; and when I went away from here I went away from the old life." (54)

Sentimental though this conclusion is, it is important to consider why and how Robinson justifies this ending. Guy had protected Sophie, even before she touched his heart with her song, and he had warned her—accurately, it turns out—that Reuben "will not make you a good husband" (47). Sophie, of course, had warned Guy that he must not linger. Apart from the standard cultural traditions of hostess and guest and apart from Guy being moved by Sophie's song—which do not add up to much—there is not much evidence to rationally justify or explain their actions and their attraction to each other. It is a romantic story, of course, so the lovers eventually coming together makes for an ending both entertaining and typical for the genre. If that were the case, would not Robinson have concocted a stronger bond between them during the story? What has really happened is that the storyteller has trusted his own intuition, which assured him, likely without his even being aware of it, that his tale stood solidly on the bedrock of myth and the collective unconscious of mankind, which dictates hospitality for the stranger. It is clear that Guy and Sophie will marry and live happily ever after.

The variety and function of the gifts that have changed the lives of the various men on trail must also be considered. Sophie's song is more of an element of hospitality, of incorporation, than a gift "to go," but it nevertheless changes the direction of Guy's life, just as the gift of silver candlesticks changes the direction of Jean Valjean's. It is notable that Valjean never accesses the practical, financial value of the candlesticks but instead draws his strength from the inspirational value of the bishop's gifts. Hemingway's Gauertal incident includes the practical gift of socks; London's "To the Man on Trail" includes the practical gifts of food, sleep, food to go, and advice; Leggatt receives clothing and money when he is set ashore; Stowe's Eliza gets the gift of clothing for herself and her son; Stevenson depicts Villon as sinister and beyond the redemption of any host's gift.

The selections in *Stories by English Authors* and *Stories by American Authors* give a reasonable picture of the better popular fiction of the century. Hospitality and/or the man-on-trail figures may also be seen in Laurence Oliphant's "The Brigand's Bride" or in C. H. White's "The Village Convict." Hemingway may well have read these stories; he may have been influenced by them, or they may have simply have introduced him to the popular traditions of the short story. Nevertheless, for the purposes of this study they reveal to a certain limited extent the degree to which the archetypes of hospitality and of the man on trail occur in that fiction, some of which eventually achieved canonical status.

Comparison table 2: The Windemere stories

Author	Thomas Hardy	Robert Louis Stevenson	Harold Frederic	F. W. Robinson
Title	"The Three Strangers"	"A Lodging for the Night"	"Brother Sebastian's Friend-ship"	"Minions of the Moon"
Host/hostess	Shepherd Fennel and friends	An old knight	Brother Sebastian, a monk	Sophie Tarne
Other members of host's household	Shepherdess Fennel, frugal, counsels against hospitality	None	Albonus, Brother Servitor, denounces Edouard	Reuben Pemberton, So-phie's fiancé, alerts redcoats
Man on trail	Timothy Summers	Francois Villon, poet and lowlife	"Brother" Edouard	Captain Guy / Sir Richard Isshaw
Degree of acceptance by host/hostess	"sympathy . . . strongly on the side of the fugitive" (156)	Immediate	"I liked Edouard from the first" (150).	Guest gallantly protective of hostess
Relationship of guest and host	Stranger in storm in search of shelter	Strangers	Avuncular	Repressed romantic
Elements of hospitality extended	Spirits (homemade mead), music, fire, shelter	Shelter, food, spirits, candid conversation	Acceptance of Edouard into brotherhood	Shelter, food, spirits, song
Parting gift(s)	Mead and cake	None	None	Song
Emphasized gift or element of hospitality	Mead and a warm hearth	Candid conversation	Retains vow of secrecy to Edouard	Song, inspirational and performed by Sophie
Reason for pursuit	Escaped prisoner scheduled to be executed	Possible association with murder and arson	Mugger's assistant (guilty but coerced)	Highwaymen guilty of road crimes
Pursuers	Hangman, "the stranger in cinder-grey" (144)	Night patrols	"a whirling glimpse of uniforms" (163)	King George's "redcoats"
Delay of pursuers	Unspoken community conspiracy	Shelter until morning only	"Fly" warning (not heeded)	Warns Guy that redcoats approach

Chapter 3

ELEMENTS OF THE MAN-ON-TRAIL PLOT

> But the intended punishment was cruelly disproportioned to the transgression, and the sympathy of a great many country-folk in that district was strongly on the side of the fugitive.
>
> —Thomas Hardy, "The Three Strangers"

The Mythological Context

Writers who describe the world and its workings produce works typically characterized by terms such as *mimetic* or *realistic.* They observe the world and describe it. The great ones do so with insight; with passion for justice, social, civil, and poetic; with an accuracy that astonishes, especially in making the reader see in a new way those things that have been so often taken for granted. While mythic in many of its implications, Steinbeck's *The Grapes of Wrath* takes the Joad family, and the reader, down a clearly recognizable Route 66 to a still somewhat familiar economic exploitation in California; Tennyson's Light Brigade charges into an all too real valley of death; Hemingway's Santiago catches a realistically described marlin and realistically described sharks take it from him. At the same time, Coleridge's "The Rime of the Ancient Mariner," De Quincey's *Confessions of an English Opium Eater,* Browning's "'Childe Roland to the Dark Tower Came'" take us inward through various devices—the opium dream, the sea journey "below the kirk, below the hill, below the lighthouse top" (ll. 23–24), or Childe Roland's final turn into a forbidding landscape: "I turned from him, / That hateful cripple, out of his highway / Into the path he pointed" (ll. 43–45) When the hero, as Joseph Campbell clearly shows, crosses "the threshold of adventure," he enters a strange but uncannily familiar world. It is essentially a world in which things happen that cannot happen—Danny and Peachy become kings in Kipling's "The Man Who Would Be King"; De Quincey sleeps with the obscene crocodile in his opium dreams; and characters appear that cannot appear in reality—the goblins in Christina Rossetti's "Goblin Market," the fairy in Keats's "La Belle Dame sans Merci: A Ballad," or the "cutty sark" at the witches' Sabbath in Robert Burns's "Tam o' Shanter: A Tale."

What can be the purpose of incorporating such unreal elements in a work of literature? The answer is simple: these devices enable the writer to access psychological or spiritual content. The albatross and all of the strange happenings of "The Rime of the Ancient Mariner" may well fall into the category of "things that can't happen," but the mariner's guilt is real, his compulsion to confess is very real and very believable, and the wedding guest's inability to turn away similarly rings true. Keats's fairy child in "La Bell Dame sans Merci" may be symbolic, but the despair of the knight at arms is not only real, it matches the melancholy expressed in so many other of Keats's masterpieces. In the Anglo-Saxon poem "The Dream of the Rood," the Holy Cross tells the story of the crucifixion, using a dream vision to express highly emotional spiritual content regarding the speaker's consciousness of Christ's sacrifice. John Bunyan's *Pilgrim's Progress* similarly uses a dream vision to depict inner personal and spiritual content that would otherwise be difficult to access. Campbell's monomyth provides a structure by which all of these journey plots—both realistic and dreamlike—and a thousand others (Campbell's conservative estimate!) may be analyzed.

Unaccounted for in the monomyth, however, are those plots in which some unreal element from across the "threshold of adventure" invades the world of everyday reality: the mysterious bird arriving from "the night's Plutonian shore" (l. 98) in Poe's "The Raven," a hair of the prophet Mohammad in Salman Rushdie's "The Prophet's Hair," Mr. Hyde in Robert Louis Stevenson's *The Strange Case of Dr. Jekyll and Mr. Hyde,* Dr. Frankenstein's creation, Grendel in the hall of Hrothgar, Keats's Lamia, Faulkner's spotted horses, or the appearance of Tommy Luck at Roaring Camp in Bret Harte's "The Luck of Roaring Camp." These and many other like elements are an inverse of Campbell's monomyth: they are avatars of spiritual or psychological content from the land of "things that can't happen," that is to say from the Freudian unconscious or the Jungian collective unconscious, or from Campbell's psychic "kingdom of the dread" et cetera (246). These elements, while entertaining in their production of horror, suspense, adventure, comedy, and so forth, are in serious works of literature agents of transformation or revelation for underlying issues or conflicts: acceptance of loss in "The Raven," latent Islamic radicalism in "The Prophet's Hair," the evil in us all embodied by Mr. Hyde, the danger of tampering with nature in *Frankenstein,* the con artistry in Faulkner's "Spotted Horses," and the previously latent human yearning for community and civilization amid the raucous anarchy of Roaring Camp.

In the cinema, the necessary contrast between exotic creatures and the everyday people who encounter them—in films such as *ET: The Extra-Terrestrial, Small Soldiers, The Black Stallion, Jaws,* and *Gremlins*—accounts for the hyper-suburbanism of these films. In a painting such as Henry Fuseli's *The Nightmare,* this intrusion creates more horror for the onlooker than the woman under the incubus seems to be suffering. When the nightmare is over, the incubus returns to the land of events that cannot happen. For the viewer, however, the incubus is a sinister presence in a domestic locale—a bed in a bedroom—the incubus's weight palpably on her chest inhibiting her breath—with no indication of relief, as the painting freezes the moment of terror forever in the viewer's present. To the speaker's horror, Poe's raven similarly refuses exit from the narrator's chamber, forever casting its shadow on him.

The man on trail is not a horror, but the man-on-trail plot functions in this mythic context. For the host, the man on trail emerges from the great unknown, from the unexplained. In the plot of the hero's journey, the usual focus is on the hero and the hero's transformation (or lack thereof: Tam o' Shanter, for example, cannot really be seen as having learned any sort of lesson about cutty sarks or witches' gatherings), but the man-on-trail plot has two possible foci: the guest and/or the host. Although it may initially present itself as a moment in a bigger plot—which it actually is in *Les Misérables* or *Uncle Tom's Cabin,* it often is, as has been shown here repeatedly, an entire narrative in itself. This test of the host challenges his individuation, his ability to summon the psychic courage to listen to his own intuition—as opposed to the guidelines and dictates of society and authority—when he confronts the man on trail and all he represents.

The Elements

The mythological host and/or hostess encounters, at or near "his commonday hut or castle" or constructed temporary place of hospitality, a stranger (or strangers) to whom he offers—usually without hesitation or trepidation—the hospitality of his home or home equivalent. The stranger may be a god, a divine or divinely sanctioned agent, a pilgrim, a doppelganger or brother, a runaway slave, a fugitive, or even an enemy combatant, essentially someone from across the "threshold of adventure"—from the world of dreams, from the unconscious mind, from the collective unconscious of humankind, from "the kingdom of the dread," from the night's Plutonian shore, from the horrors of war—who, in distress, has entered the host's world of everyday reality. The stranger, if divine, may have been denied hospitality elsewhere, or, if mortal, may be pursued. Those of the host's household may—like agents of the superego or the social status quo—counsel against offering hospitality, may betray the guest, may aid the host in offering hospitality, or may do all three. The host often feels an uncanny and immediate connection with the guest. The offered hospitality typically consists of food, tobacco, wine or spirits, rest, shelter, money, clothing, intercourse, music, storytelling, and/or advice, all given freely and generously in a ritual of integration or an affirmation or intuition of brotherhood. The encounter may be a test of host's character, humanity, and/or intuitive powers; just as a traditional hero's journey across the threshold of adventure and "to the nadir of the mythological round" leads to "an expansion of consciousness," so can the host's encounter with a traveler from across the threshold of adventure involve a similar challenge and a similar opportunity to expand consciousness. Typically a fully individuated person, the host must intuitively and correctly trust in the essential goodness of the guest, despite his questionable status as fugitive or enemy combatant. The host's unhesitating acceptance of the stranger is all the more remarkable for the sudden and unexpected appearance of the stranger. Hosts who deny or betray hospitality come to unfortunate ends. If the guest is divine, the host may receive "magical aid" or a magical reward. If the guest is pursued, the host may deter, delay, or otherwise frustrate or thwart the pursuer(s). The pursuers, often uniformed, often agents of official authority, sometimes canine or canine in nature, represent death. When the supernatural guest leaves, the host may receive the reward of a supernatural gift or be granted some supernatural aid; those who have denied hospitality (often subordinates of the host) may face supernatural wrath. After the non-supernatural guest leaves, the host may encounter him/her at some crisis in the future and receive from the former guest hospitality or a favor in return. The guest may undergo transformation or expansion of consciousness as well, usually as a result of his or her interaction with the host. The guest's departure, sometimes dramatic, is often the emotional climax of the tale, as his fate is usually in doubt. (All quotations are from Campbell 245–46.)

The Host

The hosts and hostesses already discussed and those yet to be discussed are among the least hesitating and most fully individuated—and therefore the most justly confident—characters in literature. The hosts often reveal a high degree of individuation in the openness and grace with which they receive the stranger, despite the stranger's often unsavory, intimidating, or sinister initial impression. Harry unhesitatingly helps the deserter; Conrad's narrator becomes an instant brother to Leggatt; the bishop offers the bitter paroled convict Valjean his home. The true host seldom hesitates, weighs the possible consequences, considers societal values, or shows anxiety over thwarting official justice, despite that in legal terms, today at least, what the host does often fits the definition of "harboring a fugitive." The law has declared such an act a crime because it happens often enough to impede law enforcement, which impediment occurs because hosts react to an archetypal situation, intuitively offering refuge. And the annals of crime are replete with victims who have offered hospitality to the wrong guests. The host must with complete confidence—engendered by full individuation—distinguish between the man on trail and the murderer.

The host's refusal to hesitate in offering hospitality results not from any shallowness, lack of character, psychopathic disregard of social norms, or kneejerk rebelliousness. Rather, it is due to complete confidence in his or her own intuitive understanding of the archetypal situation and the guest who has appeared, almost always without advance notice or warning.

The Sudden Emergence of the Man on Trail

The man on trail emerges unexpectedly and without buffer, as if hard-wired to the collective unconscious, as does, for example, the threshold guardian, who is a standard element of Campbell's heroic journey plot. This figure serves as the buffer, the warning, that we—along with the hero—are about to cross Campbell's "threshold of adventure." The albatross appears to Coleridge's mariners to show the way through the mist and icebergs, making the ancient mariner's killing of the albatross a crime not just against nature but against myth and against the unconscious itself. Browning's Childe Roland must take his direction from the sinister "hateful cripple" whose purpose seems to him to be "to waylay with his lies, ensnare / All travelers who might find him posted there, / And ask the road" (ll. 2, 7–9). Hemingway was, not surprisingly, aware of this element, aptly demonstrated in "Indian Camp," which clearly follows the heroic journey plot (DeFalco 27–33). Nick Adams's experiences in witnessing birth and suicide within a few moments of each other are certainly transformative, experiences that in his normal everyday world of reality "cannot happen." And multiple threshold guardians are there too: "They came around a bend and a dog came out barking. Ahead were the lights of the shanties where the bark-peelers lived. More dogs rushed out at them. The two Indians sent them back to the shanties. In the shanty nearest the road there was a light in the window. An old woman stood in the doorway holding a lamp" (16). Like the Lotos-eaters or the sirens of Homer's *Odyssey,* the old woman is entirely bereft of plot function. She says nothing and does nothing. She is never mentioned again in the narrative, making her role purely symbolic. The reader intuitively knows, even if Nick does not, that once Nick is past the dogs and the old woman, his experience will be transformative. He will have crossed the threshold of adventure.

The hero on his journey may see a warning in the appearance of these threshold guardians, but these examples all stand in contrast to the host's experience in the man-on-trail plot, for the man on trail appears suddenly and with little or no warning, from the shallows of the unconscious or the depths of the collective unconscious. His appearance bypasses any buffer figures posted by our literary senses or our psychic defenses, as do the images of our dreams. So it is for Roaring Camp when Cherokee Sal delivers her baby: "Deaths were by no means uncommon in Roaring Camp, but a birth was a new thing" (1–2). The appearance of Poe's raven comes without warning: "suddenly there came a tapping" (l. 3). The ogre Grendel appears in Hrothgar's hall when men have fallen asleep as if he emerges straight from their nightmares.

Neither Tommy Luck, nor Poe's raven, nor the ogre Grendel qualifies as a man on trail, nor do the stories in which they appear use what here is referred to as the man-on-trail plot. An important element of the humor and magic realism of "The Prophet's Hair" is the magic realism idea that the hair seems to have a will of its own, appearing suddenly and as a surprise in the lives it transforms. This element is also seen in "The Rime of the Ancient Mariner" in the strong reactions to the mariner's return by those he encounters: the pilot, the pilot's boy, the holy man, the wedding guest, and, finally, "the man that must hear me" (l. 589). However, two parallels must be noted. First, characters from both the realistic and dreamlike groups emerge from the similar places: from the world of dreams, from the unconscious mind, from the collective unconscious of humankind, from "the kingdom of the dread," from the night's

Plutonian shore, from the horrors of war. Second, they appear at the host's door suddenly and without warning. Jack Westondale appears from out of a storm with Jungian synchronicity as Malemute Kid makes a toast "to the man on trail this night" (291). Leggatt's appearance at the bottom of the ladder—as if rising from the deep (a potent symbol of the unconscious)—is similarly sudden. Jean Valjean appears just as the bishop's household begins discussing him, just as Eliza appears when the issue of runaway slave laws arises between the senator and his wife. In all of these cases, the hosts grant hospitality without anxiety, mental or social hand-wringing, or hesitation. The host's companions or members of the host's household serve as foils when they show reluctance. This suddenness is the element of hospitality that cannot be accounted for by cultural tradition or local custom. It is the key that establishes the host's reaction not as culturally conditioned but rather as an intuitive impulse generated in the collective unconscious. The author knows or intuits this, as does the reader. This points backward in time, past current, traditional, or even archaic cultural traditions, back to the time when the values of guest reception were reflexive and intuitive rather than formalized in a code.

Storms, bodies of water, mist, and darkness: each carries out a similar symbolic function. The man/woman on trail emerges from them with regularity: Hemingway's deserter, London's Westondale, Stowe's Eliza, and Stevenson's Villon all appear in snowstorms; Jean Valjean emerges on a rainy night; and Hardy's Tim Summers appears in a rainstorm. In addition, all of the aforementioned except possibly Hemingway's deserter appear at night. And in Harry's death flight at the end of "The Snows of Kilimanjaro", "they were going to the East it seemed, and then it darkened and they were in a storm, the rain so thick it seemed like flying through a waterfall" (27). Mythically, storms and night represent transformation and prefigure rebirth (if the traveler eventually emerges); both the night and storms—as do mist and fog—swallow the traveler whole and leave him or her in another world, as they do, for example, in *Adventures of Huckleberry Finn* (in which the river literally swallows Huck and Jim) or in Homer's *Odyssey.* The traveler's emergence from the storm—as we have often seen with the element of new clothing—can represent rebirth. Odysseus also appears naked when he emerges from the world of the chthonic goddesses (and from a storm) into the land of the Phaeacians. Upon landing, Odysseus snuggles beneath two olive bushes, which share common roots. One is wild, the other domestic, symbolizing the threshold between the dreamlike chthonic world and the civilized world of the Phaeacians.

Sudden Emergence in the Gauertal Incident

The suddenness of the guest's appearance is also evident in Hemingway's Gauertal incident, reflected not so much in the content as in Hemingway's precise yet evocative style. A close reading of the Gauertal incident reveals Hemingway's method:

> It was snow too that fell all Christmas week that year up in the Gauertal, that year they lived in the woodcutter's house with the big square porcelain stove that filled half the room, and they slept on mattresses filled with beech leaves, the time the deserter came with his feet bloody in the snow. He said the police were right behind him and they gave him woolen socks and held the gendarmes talking until the tracks drifted over. (7)

The passage consists of a mere two sentences, totaling seventy-nine words, the first fifty-five long and the second twenty-four. The second sentence focuses entirely on the deserter; the first locates the time of year, the weather, the geographic location, and adds the details of the woodcutter's house, the porcelain stove, and the mattresses filled with beech leaves. At this point the first sentence is already forty-three words long—this by the man who singlehandedly elevated the simple declarative sentence to previously unimagined literary heights. Since the second sentence is shorter, why not add the deserter with his bloody feet to it? That would give one sentence of forty-three words to the host and give a second sentence of perhaps thirty-five to thirty-seven words (depending on how the content might be integrated into the next sentence) to the man on trail, an ostensibly more balanced approach, which many other writers might well have chosen. In, addition, the grammatical connection between the deserter material and the rest of the first sentence is not a strong one; one must process it a moment before realizing that "the time the deserter came with his feet bloody in the snow" refers to "Christmas week," though that phrase is followed by another time reference, "that year up in the Gauertal," which complicates the grammar and time sequence even further. Placing "the time" closer to what it references would produce a version something like this:

> It was snow too that fell all Christmas week, the time the deserter came with his feet bloody in the snow, during that year up in the Gauertal, that year they lived in the woodcutter's house with the big square porcelain stove that filled half the room, and they slept on mattresses filled with beech leaves. He said the police

> were right behind him and they gave him woolen socks and held the gendarmes talking until the tracks drifted over.

Of course, this revision fails wretchedly because the deserter appears too soon. So why not rearrange the sentences as described above—one sentence for the host and one for the man on trail? Although an improvement, this version fails too:

> It was snow too that fell all Christmas week that year up in the Gauertal, that year they lived in the woodcutter's house with the big square porcelain stove that filled half the room, and they slept on mattresses filled with beech leaves. That was the time the deserter came with his feet bloody in the snow and said the police were right behind him and they gave him woolen socks and held the gendarmes talking until the tracks drifted over.

This revision is a little less of a train wreck. Going further, it could also read, slightly improved yet again, as three sentences:

> It was snow too that fell all Christmas week that year up in the Gauertal, that year they lived in the woodcutter's house with the big square porcelain stove that filled half the room, and they slept on mattresses filled with beech leaves. That was the time the deserter came with his feet bloody in the snow. He said the police were right behind him and they gave him woolen socks and held the gendarmes talking until the tracks drifted over.

This, the best of the non-Hemingway versions, still lacks the impact of Hemingway's final version. The reason the Hemingway version is superior to the revised versions is, once again, simple. Hemingway moves from the general to the specific, from Christmas and the Gauertal to the porcelain stove and the mattresses of beech leaves, the latter two of which seem even more cozy, given the snow outside. And suddenly, into this cozy world bursts the man on trail with his bloody feet leaving tracks in the snow without giving the reader a pause to even start a new sentence or fantasize about the warmth of the fire or the inviting mattress. Before readers have fully processed the scene or the breathless first sentence, they are confronted with the man on trail in all of his distress, which thus emphasizes the stress inherent in such an arrival.

Note also that by the second sentence the reader is so precipitously committed to helping the deserter that the potentially momentarily confusing pronoun *they,* which technically might be read as referring to the gendarmes, as the sentence contains no proper antecedent for *they,* does not actually cause any confusion for the reader. The reader knows it refers to Harry (and whoever is with him), because the reader wants it to refer to Harry. Despite the suddenness of the deserter's entry, Harry aids the man on trail without hesitation, and we—except for the Inspector Javerts among us—heartily approve, as we fail to regret missing the mattress and the porcelain stove.

Disregarded are the doubts of others within the household—the circle of miners in "To the Man on Trail," who "were angry . . . at the outraged ethics of the Northland" when they discover that Westondale has committed a robbery (297); the bishop's housekeepers in *Les Misérables,* initially distraught at being under the same roof as a convict; the farmer's wife in "The Three Strangers" upset because too much cider is being consumed; the (would-be) disapproving officers and crew in "The Secret Sharer"; Senator Byrd in *Uncle Tom's Cabin;* and Brother Albonus in "Brother Sebastian's Friendship." Such characters are introduced as foils to the host figures or as representations of the readers' own modern, culturally conditioned resistance to the offer of hospitality. They highlight the host's more fully individuated psyche and the later events that confirm the host's correctness in offering hospitality. The "circle of judges," to use London's phrase, obeys cultural norms: "the ethics of the Northland," or the "law passed forbidding people to help off the slaves that come over from Kentucky" (Frederic 297; Stowe 99). The host, fully individuated and confident, responds intuitively to the archetype, not the cultural norms. This full individuation is the main characteristic of the host, the quality that the reader must grasp. Aware of but unbound by cultural norms, the hero-host fully and confidently confronts the archetypal figure who appears without warning and in distress before him.

The Stranger

The stranger may be a god, a divine or divinely sanctioned agent, a doppelganger or brother, a fugitive, or even an enemy combatant, among other things. Distress is the most common denominator of all of the strangers, even the divine strangers, and it is this distress, along with the role of the host (who must often be regarded as the protagonist) that distinguishes the man-on-trail plot from the many variations of the journey plot outlined in Campbell's monomyth. Assisting any of the men or women on trail is socially unacceptable or even illegal.

The stranger may be a god, but even gods may undergo distress. Jove and Mercury undergo distress in Ovid's tale of Baucis and Philemon, having had a thousand doors shut in their faces. The stranger may be a divine or divinely sanctioned agent, such as the angels who visit Lot or the spies sent by Joshua and taken in by Rahab during the siege of Jericho (Gen. 19.1–16; Josh. 2). In a much later iteration of the divinely sanctioned agent, an angel is sent to earth to learn "what men live by" in Tolstoy's story "What Men Live by." In that story Semyon the shoemaker, coming home late one winter evening, finds Mikhail, the fallen angel, naked and sitting in the snow next to a chapel.

If the stranger is a mortal, he or she may be a pilgrim, such as the Austrian officers going home on Christmas leave (**IM I.5**). The secretaries who die in the snow during the exchange of populations Nansen arranged (**IM I.2**) may be regarded as pilgrims in a more remote way: these exchanges and others in the wake of the Greco-Turkish conflict were based on religion, with Muslims being removed from Greece and non-Muslims being removed from Turkey.

Also among mortals, the fugitive may be a doppelganger or brother/sister. Jean Valjean may be a fugitive of sorts, not yet pursued by the implacable Inspector Javert but clearly marked as an outcast by his yellow passport. Nevertheless, the Bishop of Digne refers to and treats him as a brother. Leggett in Conrad's "The Secret Sharer," is an actual fugitive from justice, but Conrad's ship-captain narrator still regards him as a brother. Hardy's Timothy Summers is under a sentence of death, as are the highwaymen, most of whom are actually hanged, of "Minions of the Moon." As will be discussed in chapter 6, Don José in Mérimée's *Carmen* and Gianetto Sanpiero of his "Mateo Falcone" are criminals, the former having gained a formidable reputation. Eliza, the runaway slave of *Uncle Tom's Cabin* and Jack Westondale, the miner and casino bandit of London's "To the Man or Trail," both flee from very active pursuit because they have absconded with what legally (though not ethically) belongs to someone else.

One of the more extreme acts of hospitality involves aiding in the escape of an enemy combatant; the deserter-in-the-Gauertal incident effectively dramatizes this (though Harry's role in Austria as combatant or journalist remains unspecified). The episode of Priam at the tent of Achilles, the final book of Homer's *Iliad*, elaborately covers similar material. In "The Snows of Kilimanjaro"'s Barker incident the men of the officers' mess openly condemn Barker's killing of enemy combatants in the Austrian officers' leave train, thus validating the same humane value of respecting the humanity of an enemy.

The man on trail almost always embodies redeeming qualities, despite his having done something illegal or socially unacceptable. Jack Westondale lost his money by trusting his partner and wants to return home "to his wife and boy he's never seen" (297). Leggatt committed a homicide to save his ship from disaster in a storm. Timothy Summers and Jean Valjean commit their crimes in order to feed hungry children.

Finally, even Cain is worthy of our understanding. He tills the earth, yet his sacrifice is not accepted; indeed, the angry, uncompromising god of the Old Testament rejects it without explanation. Try as we might to construct philosophical or theological explanations for this rejection, we are, in the final analysis, left with what Genesis tells us. Instructions regarding the nature of the sacrifice are not recorded, nor is a reason for preferring blood over vegetables. Cain's anger is understandable, even though his crime of fratricide is not.

Hospitality Created on the Spot

In *For Whom the Bell Tolls,* as Hilary Kovar Justice has shown, it is the character Pilar who creates hospitality:

> She is the civilizing influence, the guardian of culture (and of Maria), the fixed moral purpose, and the living memory of what things have been, should be, and may be again: her voice dominates the dialogue of the group's values with the world, especially in her narrative of the execution of the Fascists at Ronda. Pilar's instinctive knowledge of food, agriculture, and hospitality as discourses of power and markers of civilization is never far from the surface, and whether or not one has any appetite overtly measures how far an individual and a culture have risen or fallen from that mark.
>
> Pilar's leadership role is expressed overtly through food, governing who may eat, how much, and how. ("Consolation" 29–30)

The tragedy of the Spanish Civil War has pushed civilization back to where it started—to the cave. This is where Pilar becomes "the keeper of the food, the keeper of culture, and the arbiter of what is right and civilized in this home-like den of a cave" (29).

What Helen accomplishes in "The Snows of Kilimanjaro" parallels what Pilar does as the keeper of civilized values. She provides food, shooting a Thompson's gazelle so that broth can be made for Harry's nourishment. She takes care to shoot it away from camp, so as not to disturb the game animals Harry enjoys watching. The broth makes Harry gag, but like a proper guest he does not criticize the hostess's offering. As in "To the Man on Trail," "The Secret Sharer," Priam's meal with Achilles, and "A Lodging for the Night," a meal functions as part of a ritual of integration. Helen's flirtatious "good destruction" reply to Harry's sexual innuendo implies a willingness to rebond sexually, a rite of incorporation. She also rebonds with him socially, through the ritual of drinking spirits, in this case whiskey and soda, another rite of incorporation. Harry accepts her in this role: "The party's over and you are with your hostess now" (24). Harry's acceptance of Helen's created hospitality is partly responsible for the beauty of his death flight in that it enables him to return from cheap bitterness to civil behavior.

Pursuit, Obstruction of Pursuit, and Representations of Death

If the guest is pursued, the host may deter, delay, or otherwise frustrate or thwart the pursuer(s). Obvious examples include the Gauertal incident, in which Harry and whoever accompanies him thwart the gendarmes by talking with them as the snow covers the deserter's bloody tracks; Malemute Kid's gestures toward his weapons when the pursuing Mountie makes his demands; and the bishop lying to the gendarmes who arrest Jean Valjean, telling them that the stolen silver plate was actually a gift. In Robinson's "Minions of the Moon" an implacable force pursues Guy's band of highwaymen in the form of "King George's soldiers." Sophie thwarts the soldiers by warning Guy wordlessly of their approach.

Hemingway develops this delay theme in the posthumously published "The Last Good Country," in which the pursuers are two game wardens: Evans, "the local man"; and "the down-state man." Mr. John, the general store storekeeper, remembers the latter: "'I remember you in Cheyenne the day Tom Horn was hanged,' Mr. John told him. 'You were one of the ones that framed him with promises from the association. Do you remember now? Who owned the saloon in Medicine Bow when you worked for the people that gave it to Tom? Is that why you ended up doing what you're doing? Haven't you got any memory?'" (102). The two are similar to Max and Al; they bring death or would like to. Tom Horn's betrayal by the ranchers who had hired him is, further, associated with the corruption of a place of hospitality, a saloon. Like Penelope's suitors, who force themselves into the home of their hostess and then grossly violate her hospitality, the game wardens bully the locals into providing hospitality in the form of shelter, food, and whiskey. The resistance to the two game wardens becomes communal, much as does the thwarting of authority in Hardy's "The Three Strangers" or the destruction of Penelope's suitors by Odysseus, Telemachus, Eumaeus, and other loyal household members.

In the biblical account of the siege of Jericho, the harlot Rahab hides Joshua's spies, who have been sent to evaluate the city's defenses (an account Hemingway included in the anthology he edited, *Men at War*):

> And Joshua the son of Nun sent out of Shittim two men to spy secretly, saying, Go view the land, even Jericho. And they went, and came into an harlot's house, named Rahab, and lodged there.
>
> And it was told the king of Jericho, saying, Behold, there came men in hither to night of the children of Israel to search out the country. And the King of Jericho sent unto Rahab, saying, Bring forth the men that are come to thee, which are entered into the house: for they be come to search out all the country.
>
> And the woman took the two men, and hid them, and said thus, There came men unto me, but I wist not whence they were: And it came to pass about the time of shutting of the gate, when it was dark, that the men went out: whither the men went I wot not; for ye shall overtake them. But she had brought them up to the roof of the house, and hid them with the stalks of flax, which she had laid in order upon the roof. (Josh. 2.1–6)

Rahab thwarts the pursuers, in this case the defenders of Jericho, by hiding Joshua's spies in the roof of her house.

In Hardy's "The Three Strangers," after the initial chase of the misidentified fugitive (actually the brother of the fugitive Timothy Summers), the locals, in admiration of the nerve of Timothy Summers in sitting and hob-nobbing with his would-be hangman, make a great show of scouring the countryside in search of the fugitive. But it is only a show:

> Next day, accordingly, the quest for the clever sheep-stealer became general and keen, to all appearance at least. But the intended punishment was cruelly disproportioned to the transgression, and the sympathy of a great many country-folk in that district was strongly on the side of the fugitive. Moreover, his marvelous coolness and daring in the hob-and-nobbing with the hangman, under the unprecedented circumstances of the shepherd's party, won their admiration. So that it may be questioned if all those who ostensibly made themselves so busy in exploring woods and fields and lanes were quite so thorough when it came to private examination of their own lofts and out-houses. (156)

The pursuer in this case is the hangman, one who literally brings death, a none-too-well-disguised iteration of the grim reaper. It is no wonder that the locals sympathize with and actively and passively aid Timothy Summers, the condemned man, for Death pursues them just as surely. Similarly, the reader sympathizes with Summers and condones the actions of the locals.

Early in "The Snows of Kilimanjaro," in Harry's first set of reminiscences, Harry and whoever is with him delay the pursuers, "the gendarmes," with conversation while the deserter escapes through the snow. Similarly, Harry's last words depict the police as pursuers—and as death:

> Because, just then, death had come and rested its head on the foot of the cot and he could smell its breath.
>
> "Never believe any of that about a scythe and a skull," he told her. "It can be two bicycle policemen as easily, or be a bird. Or it can have a wide snout like a hyena." (25)

The bicycle policemen (See Hays, "Hemingway, Faulkner") represent death, just as surely as do the vultures and the hyena.[1] And the gendarmes of the Gauertal incident represent death as well.

Harry, too, had been pursued by official authority. In his memory of a vicious fistfight with a British soldier over a "hot Armenian slut" he had picked up, Harry hears, after knocking out the British soldier, "the M. P.'s coming" (16). Hemingway's making the woman an Armenian is significant. In 1915, the Ottoman Turks carried out the infamous genocide of their Armenian population; similar actions during World War II became known as holocaust and more recently have been euphemized as "ethnic cleansing." In fact, the word *genocide* was coined by historians studying the Turks' organized murder campaign on the Armenians. Harry's hot slut has, indeed, been pursued by death. One quite easily imagines that she may have used sex to escape the horrors of her memories.

The guard functions similarly in "A Clean, Well-Lighted Place," another Hemingway story soaked in direct and oblique death references.[2]

> A girl and a soldier went by in the street. The street light shone on the brass number on his collar. The girl wore no head covering and hurried beside him.
>
> "The guard will pick him up," one waiter said.
>
> "What does it matter if he gets what he's after?"
>
> "He had better get off the street now. The guard will get him. They went by five minutes ago." (18)

"The Snows of Kilimanjaro" and "A Clean, Well-Lighted Place" use the same image, that of the man and the woman running from death, which are very much epitomes of *A Farewell to Arms.*[3]

Looking at "A Clean Well-Lighted Place" in the light of man-on-trail plot, some familiar elements emerge: the place of hospitality, the clean well-lighted café; the man on trail, the old man; pursuers, the guard in pursuit of stray soldiers and death in pursuit of the old man who has attempted suicide; the begrudging host, the younger waiter who wants to go home; and the true host, the older waiter, who understands the effect of a clean, well-lighted environment on the old man's dignity. It is appalling when the younger waiter forces the old man out of the café. Further, it is saddening that the older waiter can supply none of the other elements of hospitality—food, clothing, music, advice, or rest—though he too is a kindred spirit who realizes the real pursuer is nothing, the *Nada,* death. Of all the ideas humankind has conceived and applied to life, that have been essential in creating civilization and art, which can possibly be older, more fundamental, more deeply rooted in the collective unconscious than the notion that death pursues all?

Thus emerge two clear, overwhelming, characteristics of the pursuers. First, in the form of Inspector Javert, the game wardens, the bicycle police, the Mounties, the hangman in the cinder-colored clothes, the gendarmes of the Gauertal and the gendarmes of Digne, Agamemnon (discussed in chapter 4), the messengers of the King of Jericho, the Sicilian soldiers of "Mateo Falcone," and King George's soldiers of "Minions of the Moon," the pursuers are represented as official (and often uniformed) authority. And second, they represent death. They are arms of the authority of civilization, happy and willing to stand—to the death—against the call of the unconscious, of the collective unconscious, of the primary instinctive values of the fully individuated person.

And thus a uniformed agent of authority confronts Jake and Brett in the iconic concluding lines of *The Sun Also Rises:* "Ahead was a mounted policeman in khaki directing traffic. He raised his baton. The car slowed suddenly pressing Brett against me" (198). The mounted policeman is death, as are the battle police at the bridge in chapter 30 of *A Farewell to Arms.* In Hemingway's works, the uniformed authority or agents of authority regularly represent death. For, example, the two professional killers in "The Killers," Max and Al, are dressed identically, in gangster fashion, in what amounts to a uniform. They both wear overcoats with guns bulging beneath them and both wear gloves, even while they eat—making them uniform mobsters, agents of death. After fighting alongside highly irregular and certainly ununiformed partisans, who at the conclusion of *For Whom the Bell Tolls* find themselves literally on trail, Robert Jordan's last narrated act is to lie in ambush, protecting their retreat, taking aim at the uniformed troops who pursue them. There is no more heroic death anywhere in Hemingway's works. Uniformed authority of course represents social norms and rationality, both of which are inimical to the intuition of the fully individualized host who, while not rebelling against them, knows when social norms and rationality do not apply and simply bypasses them.

The Hospitality Plot

The hospitality plot, mentioned often in this study, includes the majority of the elements of the man-on-trail plot. The key missing elements are pursuit and, naturally—given the absence of pursuit, the element of delay of pursuit. Plots involving divine agents on earth are the least likely to include pursuit, as neither the gods nor their agents suffer harm from men. This can be seen, for example, in the visit of the angels to Abraham and Sarah and in the visit of Jupiter and Mercury to Baucis and Philemon. Jupiter and Mercury have been refused hospitality and have had a thousand doors shut them out, and while such rejection may take the place of pursuit, it is not the same. Hosts in these plots are humbler. Ovid treats the humility of Baucis and Philemon in a light comic manner, especially in their fumbling and ultimately unsuccessful attempts to catch their only goose to roast for their guests.

Another canonical iteration of the hospitality plot is Hawthorne's "The Ambitious Guest." A stranger appears at the door and is offered hospitality, just as in Hardy's "The Three Strangers," but there is no pursuit. The stranger shares all with the company, including death, making it more of an initiation story. Death does come to the entire household at the end of the story, but it does not come in specific pursuit of the guest.

Transformation stories such as Hemingway's "The Sea Change," which, tellingly, takes place in a bar—an official locus of hospitality and drinking and, thus, initiation and bonding—use many of the same elements as hospitality stories and may even be regarded as forming a subcategory of hospitality stories. However, "The Sea Change" involves no pursuit and, thus, will be regarded here as a hospitality plot rather than a man-on-trail plot.

Initiation stories routinely involve the standard elements of hospitality. In the Child ballad "Robin Hood and Little John" (no. 125), Robin meets a man on a narrow bridge—a point of passage to a new world—and they agree to fight to see who crosses first. After a brutal fight, a ridiculous but time-honored ritual of male bonding, the man is accepted as a member of Robin's band. His name is changed from John Little to Little John; they eat together, feasting on "a brace of fat does" and "humming strong liquor"; he is later clothed in "garments of green"; and the day ends with "musick and dancing" (ll. 30, 31, 37, 38). The name change and shared food, spirits, clothing, music, and dancing constitute the stranger's incorporation into the group. The Sheriff of Nottingham always lurks in the background as a pursuer, but he does not pursue John Little into the forest, nor does the plot involve real pursuit. Incidentally, Hemingway was exposed to this ballad, a selection in one of his ninth grade English class texts, *Old English Ballads*, edited by William Dallam Armes. (See Justice, "Somewhat Rough Withal.")

The elements of hospitality become symbols of bonding and initiation. The same rituals live on ceremonially in weddings and graduations: ritual clothing, name changes, music, food, and dancing. "The Snows of Kilimanjaro" employs elements of both hospitality and initiation and of the man-on-trail plot.

The Stranger's Departure

The guest's departure, often a tale's emotional climax, often involves dramatic events, so the author's language often soars to stress the emotional import of the final scene. Hardy's "The Three Strangers" takes a quiet, yet still inspiring approach:

> In brief, the bass-voiced man of the chimney-corner was never recaptured. Some said that he went across the sea, others that he did not, but buried himself in the depths of a populous city. At any rate, the gentleman in cinder-grey [the hangman] never did his morning's work at Casterbridge, nor met anywhere at all, for business purposes, the genial comrade with whom he had passed an hour of relaxation in the lonely house on the slope of the comb. (156–57)

Note the wry humor of the euphemisms for hanging expressed in "morning's work" and "business purposes," as well as the poetic and ironic lyricism of "bur ied himself." Hardy, too, needs to sanction the man on trail's escape with his own wry approval, as well as with the approval of the good farmers of Wessex.

Conrad's "The Secret Sharer" exploits the epic qualities of his setting to dramatic effect, expressive of the separate destinies the narrator and Leggatt now face:

> Walking to the taffrail, I was in time to make out, on the very edge of darkness thrown by a towering black mass like the very gateway of Erebus—yes, I was in time to catch an evanescent glimpse of my white hat left behind to mark the spot where the secret sharer of my cabin and of my thoughts, as though he were my second self, had lowered himself into the water to take his punishment: a free man, a proud swimmer striking out for a new destiny. (143)

And, finally, the most evocative departure of all, the beautiful death flight of Harry (a guest of Helen at the camp) in Hemingway's "The Snows of Kilimanjaro": "[A]nd there, ahead, all he could see, as wide as all the world, great, high, and unbelievably white in the sun, was the square top of Kilimanjaro. And then he knew that there was where he was going" (27).

The importance of the guest's departure cannot be minimized. It is not a delusion of the host's imagination, because it is so regularly focalized in the third person, as in such examples discussed here as those from London, Hugo, Stowe, Hardy, and Robinson. The dramatic and beautiful flight of the departing stranger validates the host's judgment in offering hospitality in the first place and may also imply a change, Campbell's "expansion of consciousness and therewith of being" in the host, the guest, or both (246).

Chapter 4

THE RACE WAS THE ARTIST

Homeric Men on Trail

> "Is there any other point to which you would wish to draw my attention?"
> "To the curious incident of the dog in the night-time."
> "The dog did nothing in the night-time."
> "That was the curious incident," remarked Sherlock Holmes.
> —Sir Arthur Conan Doyle, "Silver Blaze"

The Curious Incident

Homer's *Iliad* tells of a curious incident—the curious incident of the nap in the night. This episode confirms much of what has been argued thus far and opens up the long view of how far back into time the man-on-trail plot extends.

In book 24, Zeus sends Iris with a message to Priam, ordering him to ransom and retrieve the body of Hector. As is customary in Homer, the mortals act in response to having heard the voice of a god (more on this later, in the discussion of Jaynes). The message is delivered, preparations are made, a prayer is offered to Zeus, and Priam sets off. Hermes, sent by Zeus, guides Priam through the Greek lines to the compound of Achilles. At this point, there are two archetypes associated with rites of passage: the guards are sent to sleep and Hermes draws the massive bolt that holds shut the gates of Achilles's compound: "The gate was barred with a single bolt of pine which it took three men to force into its place, and three to draw back so as to open the gate, but Achilles could draw it by himself" (296). Hermes then retires, saying he "will not enter into the presence of Achilles, for it might anger him that a god should befriend mortal men thus openly" (296).

> Priam slips, unseen, into the tent, where Achilles has just finished dinner with his men, and assumes the traditional posture of the supplicant: "King Priam entered without their seeing him, and going right up to Achilles he clasped his knees and kissed the dread murderous hands that had slain so many of his sons" (297)

Then, remarkably, a most appropriate Homeric metaphor, one referencing a clearly ancient oral-formulaic theme, is employed: "As when some cruel spite has befallen a man that he should have killed some one in his own country and must fly to a great man's protection in a land of strangers, and all marvel who see him, even so did Achilles marvel as he beheld Priam" (297). The metaphor is that of the man on trail, which clearly is what Priam is at this point. That it outlines the man-on-trail plot without naming a specific suppliant and as a generic plot conclusively establishes that the plot is a traditional one, a standard type-scene or theme of the oral-formulaic poets who preceded Homer, and from whom he inherited his formidable repertoire of oral formulas, type-scenes/themes, and plots.

Further, the escaped murderer/suppliant/man-on-trail plot occurs elsewhere in the *Iliad* as well, as Malcolm Willcock points out (187, 270–71). The story of Tlepolemus, son of Heracles and Astyocheia, is told in Homer's account of the contingent of Rhodes in the catalog of ships in book 2:

> When Tlepolemus grew up, he killed his father's uncle Lycymnius, who had been a famous warrior in his time, but was then grown old. On this he built himself a fleet, gathered a great following, and fled beyond the sea, for he was menaced by the other sons and grandsons of Hercules. After a voyage, during which he suffered great hardship, he came to Rhodes, where the people divided into three communities, according to their tribes, and were dearly loved by Jove [Zeus] the lord of gods and men; wherefore the son of Saturn showered down great riches upon them. (25)

It is almost as if Zeus—protector of suppliants—takes on the role of host.

Medon was a Greek who took part in the defense of the Greek ships when the Greek camp was assaulted by Hector and the Trojans: "Of these, Medon was bastard son to Oileus and brother of Ajax, but he lived in Phylace away from his own country, for he had killed the brother of his stepmother Eriopis, the wife of Oileus" (158). Later in the same attack, Hector kills another of the Greeks: "He [Hector] then aimed a spear at Ajax, and missed him, but he hit Lycophron a follower of Ajax, who came from Cythera, but was living with Ajax inasmuch as he had killed a man among the Cythereans" (180).

Epigeus was a Greek whom Hector killed early in the struggle over the body of Sarpedon, one of the sons of Zeus, whom Patroclus had killed: "Epeigeus, son of noble Agacles who had erewhile been king in the good city of Budeum; but presently, having killed a valiant kinsman of his own, he took refuge with Peleus and Thetis, who sent him to Ilius the land of noble steeds to fight the Trojans under Achilles" (198). Medon, Lycophron, and Epigeus are among the countless warriors who make the briefest of appearances in the *Iliad;* they are introduced, characterized enough to reveal something of their humanity, and to give epic sweep to the narrative. Whether they are killed off or not, they are not seen again. Homer's casual, almost perfunctory use of the recurring suppliant-seeking-refuge scenario (the man-on-trail, for our purposes) in depicting these characters lends further proof to the contention that the man-on-trail plot was well developed by generations of singers and audiences long before it came to Homer.

The man-on-trail plot includes a number of differences, notably unqualified and immediate acceptance of the guest, pursuit, and delay of that pursuit. These differences are sufficiently strong that the man-on-trail plot is not strongly associated with the hospitality plot in Homeric studies or in studies of hospitality in general. Steve Reece's detailed study of eighteen hospitality scenes in Homer, *The Stranger's Welcome: Oral Theory and the Aesthetics of the Homeric Hospitality Scene,* lists twenty-five recurring elements (along with seventeen subcategories), which fall into a natural narrative sequence. However, those characters whom Willcock notes—Tlepolemus, Medon, Lycophron, and Epigeus, whose stories constitute "a relatively common theme"—do not fall under the umbrella of Reece's definition of the hospitality scene. The understandable reason, of course, is that Homer's brief sketches of these characters focus on the "exile for manslaughter" theme, rather than the specifics of actual scenes of hospitality (187).

Milman Parry

The findings of Milman Parry (1902–1935) regarding the Homeric poems help explain the sources of these archetypes. Parry earned a reputation as the most notable twentieth-century scholar of the Homeric poems, perhaps the most significant Homeric scholar ever. Through his research of the traditions and techniques of the then still continuing oral poetry of the illiterate oral poets of Bosnia-Herzegovina, Parry established the orality of Homer and his predecessors. He proved the role of the oral formula and the oral-formulaic type-scene as well as those qualities that define excellence and creativity in an oral-formulaic poet, which differ significantly from those of a literate poet. Although Parry published widely in learned journals, his influence outside scholarly classics circles was slow in coming, for he died at the young age of thirty-three, as the result of a firearm accident. His assistant, Albert B. Lord, brought his theories to a wider literary audience in his 1960 volume *The Singer of Tales.* Parry's son, Adam Parry, gathered and edited his papers in 1971, in another landmark volume, *The Making of Homeric Verse.*

Parry defined the oral formula "as *a group of words which is regularly employed under the same metrical conditions to express a given essential idea*" ("Studies in the Epic Technique" 272). Though Parry never completed his work on the oral-formulaic theme, current definitions derive from his studies. Lord writes: "Following Parry, I have called the groups of ideas regularly used in telling a tale in the formulaic style of traditional song the 'themes' [type-scenes] of the poetry" (68). And Adam Parry writes, in his introduction to *The Making of Homeric Verse,* "The *theme* is a sort of basic unit of narration in an oral poem. It may be a unit of action: a single combat, the calling of an assembly, the arrival at a palace; or it may be a description, of arms, or a chariot, or a feast" (xli). As with the theme, the epithet, and the decorative adjective, Parry asserts, that Homeric metaphors are "traditional, and not the work of the original poet" ("Homeric Metaphor" 419). Elsewhere Parry elaborates that "[t]he poetry was not one in which a poet must use his own words and try as best he might to utilize the possibilities of metre. It was a poetry which for centuries had accumulated all such possibilities—all the turns of language, all the words, phrases, and effects of position, which had pleased the race" ("Comparative" 425). The metaphor of the man on trail, with its complement of content and stylistic devices, has its roots in prehistory and emerges in Homer, in this metaphor and in its clearly stated parallel to the story of Priam's supplication, from the depths of an ancient poetic tradition.

Achilles's feeling of marvel in finding Priam at his feet is twofold: first, at the sudden appearance of Priam, and second, at his own admiration and acceptance of Priam. Priam speaks, making his plea to Achilles, whose acceptance of Priam is already established. Both men grieve and weep over the tragedies the war has brought upon them. When Priam refuses his host's offer of a chair, Achilles reacts angrily: "Moreover I know well, O Priam, and you cannot hide it, that some god has brought you to the ships of the Achaeans, for else, no man however strong and in his prime would dare to come to our host; he could neither pass our guard unseen, now draw the bolt of my gates thus easily; therefore, provoke me no further, lest I sin against the word of Jove [Zeus], and suffer you not, suppliant that you are, within my tents" (298–99). Thus, both the audience and Priam are reminded that the situation is governed by the laws of hospitality, which are overseen not by some reluctant local chthonic goddess subsumed into the Olympian system and tucked away on some obscure island in the Aegean Sea but rather are overseen by Zeus, father of the gods. Achilles then personally aids in unloading the ransom and in placing Hector's body on Priam's wagon. Following the laws of hospitality, Achilles ritually prepares a meal that he and Priam partake of together:

> With this Achilles sprang from his seat and killed a sheep of silvery whiteness, which his followers skinned and made ready all in due order. They cut the meat carefully up into smaller pieces, spitted them, and drew them off again when they were well roasted. Automedon brought bread in fair baskets and served it round the table, while Achilles dealt out the meat, and they laid their hands on the good things that were before them. (300)

We must note that the language here, oft repeated in the *Iliad* and *Odyssey,* is dressed in traditional oral formulas, which Milman Parry defined as "a group of words which is regularly employed under the same metrical conditions to express a given essential idea" (qtd. in A. Parry xxxii). The entire scene is what scholars of the Parry/Lord school define as an oral-formulaic "theme": a "basic unit of narration in an oral poem." In this case, the basic unit is a hospitality feast. This leaves the modern reader slightly uneasy, especially knowing that Priam must still make the trip through the Greek camp and back to Troy. Indeed, Achilles has previously stated that he knew that the only way Priam could have made it safely to his compound was with the aid of a god. However, the unease, though mollified by the knowledge that certain ceremonies of hospitality must be observed, is emphasized even further by the fact that Achilles had just finished eating when Priam arrived:

> The old man [Priam] went straight into the house where Achilles, loved of the gods, was sitting. There he found him with his men seated at a distance from him: only two, the hero Automedon, and Alcimus of the race of Mars, were busy in attendance about his person, for he had but just done eating and drinking,

> and the table was still there. King Priam entered without their seeing him, and going right up to Achilles he clasped his knees and kissed the dread murderous hands that had slain so many of his sons." (297)

(Description of the posture of the supplicant is another traditional recurring element of the Homeric poems.) The scene and the accompanying formulaic phrases and acts of hospitality are traditional. Homer follows them. Achilles will eat twice; the modern reader must deal with it.

What happens next, however, strains credulity even further for the modern reader: Priam demands a place to sleep:

> "And now, O king," he said, "take me to my couch that we may lie down and enjoy the blessed boon of sleep. Never once have my eyes been closed from the day your hands took the life of my son; I have groveled without ceasing in the mire of my stable-yard, making moan and brooding over my countless sorrows. Now, moreover, I have eaten bread and drunk wine; hitherto I have tasted nothing"
>
> As he spoke Achilles told his men and the women-servants to get beds in the room that was in the gatehouse, and make them with good red rugs and spread coverlets on top of them with woolen cloaks for Priam and Idaeus to wear. (300)

One wonders what sort of luck modern novelists would have with their publishers, editors, reviewers, and readers in justifying Priam's nap at this point of the narrative. This improbable nap constitutes the curious incident of the nap in the night. Once Priam has received Hector's body, the modern reader wants to see him on his way, not settling down for a pleasant nap in the middle of the enemy camp. Nevertheless, Homer does include the nap, and his reasons invite examination. They are the same reasons that Achilles must eat twice. These reasons go to the heart of the Homeric style and to the ultimate sources of his material. Milman Parry demonstrated conclusively the orality of Homer through his analysis of Homeric style, notably that the Homeric "ornamental adjective" and the Homeric epithet depend "on necessities of meter rather than considerations of meaning" (Adam Parry xxii).[1] Adam Parry asserts this in summarizing his father's theory of such inconsistencies: "When the poet has embarked on a *theme*, he must go through it in the traditional manner whether or not its content makes good sense in relation to other themes in the poem" (lvi). Thus, the poet is "subordinate to the tradition; and it never occurs to him to depart from it, or even to fashion it so as to produce any personal vision of the world" (lii). It seems that the element of Priam's not sleeping since Hector's death—also clearly an improbability—has been added simply to lend occasion and some shred of believability to the apparently nonnegotiable element of offering a place of rest to the man on trail, or, in Greek terms, to the suppliant. It is notable then that Jack Westondale, Leggatt, Eliza, Jean Valjean, and Hemingway's Harry (as well as others) sleep in some of their hospitality scenes.

The Parry theory suggests that elements of oral-formulaic poetic diction have meaning in the aggregate, depicting the qualities of the heroic culture that produced the original narrative lines:

> Such is the need of filling in, and Greek epic poetry took that need not as a necessity but as an opportunity. The words which they chose for the filling were those which generations of poets and audiences had selected as producing the highest artistic effect. . . . The fact that every epic poet used them is nothing to disparage: in their case the race was the artist, and the artist satisfied an artistic need and made of that need an opportunity for extraordinary beauty. (Parry, "Comparative" 428)

All of this argues that the themes of hospitality in the Priam/Achilles episode predate Homer to an extent that scholars cannot even estimate. Even if this theme's entry into the Greek tradition could be located, its true roots would still not have been revealed: "[T]his diction was due to countless poets and to many generations who in time had found the heroic word and phrase for every thought . . . and no one would think of changing it willfully. The Muses it was truly who gave these poets voices" (Parry, "Traditional Metaphor" 374). As Parry asserts, the race was the artist. The voices of the Muses that spoke to the pre-Homeric poets, and that spoke to Homer, were the voices of mankind's collective unconscious. In live oral performance, the poet could see, hear, and feel the reactions of his audience—reactions to the oral formula, to the type-scene, to the poem's overall architecture—and would frame and develop his performance accordingly. So too could and did the performer in intuitive touch with the archetype: the singer of traditional ballads gathered by Child, the blues singer, the *jongleur,* the troubadour, the Anglo-Saxon scop, and the Scandinavian skald. Not just the plots and characters emerge from the depths of the collective unconscious but the very language of the poets themselves.

If we do accept Jung's theory of archetypes, then it is no surprise that the reader accepts the man or trail with no hesitation or compunction and regardless of his status as fugitive or enemy combatant. The critic does not object when Conrad's narrator offers Leggatt refuge, when Malemute Kid aids and supplies

Jack Westondale, or when Harry offers aid to the deserter. The response is ingrained, for humankind has been hardwired for millennia to respond to the man on trail, as Achilles accepts Priam, as Homer and the poets who preceded him accepted the suppliant-seeking-refuge plot, even when the suppliant was a murderer. The artist knows this intuitively and scorns making any a priori defense of the man on trail; he is simply brought on stage, accepted by the host, the poet, and the reader—but not, of course, by the Inspector Javerts of this world.

Julian Jaynes

Discussion of the voices that spoke to Homer leads directly to the theories of Julian Jaynes, which also lend credence to the idea that the content of the *Iliad* has the deepest conceivable social and psychological roots. Jaynes (1920–1997) was, among many other accomplishments, a professor of psychology at Princeton. He is best known for his book *The Origin of Consciousness in the Breakdown of the Bicameral Mind,* which posits a controversial theory. His daring analysis convincingly explains the origins of the voices that spoke to Homer and to his characters. What follows here is an explanation of Jaynes's theory of the decline of bicamerality and the rise of interiority—our belief that we think and make decisions in a space inside our crania, what we call consciousness. It is not a defense or an analysis of Jaynes's controversial theory but an application of it. Jaynes does not need my defense; the depth of his research, the profundity of his thought, and the eloquence of his argument stand on their own.

The crumbling of Mediterranean civilization that marked the end of Greek Mycenaean culture just after the period of the Trojan War (circa 1250 BCE) led to a Dark Age which ended several hundred years later, at about the time of Homer. Homer was followed by the Greek adaptation of the Phoenician alphabet; the emergence of literacy; and the flowering of the Greek classical period of philosophers, poets, politicians, scientists, historians, and military defenses and conquests.[2] Jaynes attributes the advent of the Dark Age to the crumbling of what he calls the bicameral mind and the bicameral civilization that had built up around it. Chaos ensued.

Jaynes posits that modern man (classical Greek man), equipped with consciousness—or interiority, that is, consciousness of his own ability to make his own decisions within himself—emerged during, and indeed because of, the chaos that followed the disintegration of the bicameral world. This theory posits that previous civilization was based on bicameralism—humankind's ability to hear the voices of the gods. Jaynes even suggests the path of the hallucinatory voices from one side of the brain to the other. These voices originated in the brain's right temporal lobe, passed through the anterior commissures, and were heard in Wernicke's area as the voices of the gods. Jaynes thus explains the source of the voices of the gods, which he asserts are similar to the auditory and occasional visual hallucinations often noted in schizophrenia: "[T]he temporal lobes . . . have their own private callosum, so to speak, the much smaller anterior commissures. . . . Here then, I suggest, is the tiny bridge across which came the directions which built our civilizations and founded the world's religions, where gods spoke to men and were obeyed because they were human volition" (104–5).

Like those of the Parry/Lord/Parry school, Jaynes is rightly dismissive of the idea that the gods were the fanciful inventions of poets seeking to account for human motivations. In the brief portion of the *Iliad* discussed here, the visit of Priam to the tent of Achilles, human actions are motivated by what today might be regarded as auditory and visual hallucinations. Thetis, having received a message from Zeus delivered by Iris, visits Achilles, advising him to stop desecrating Hector's body and to give it up for ransom. Achilles agrees without demur (24.120–37). Zeus then has Iris deliver a message to Priam, telling him to ransom the body of Hector (24.142–87). Priam immediately gathers a ransom payment and begins preparations. Next, Zeus sends Hermes to guide Priam through the Greek camp to the compound of Achilles. He appears to Priam as one of the Myrmidons and, convincing Priam of his good intentions, leads him to the door of Achilles' tent (24.349–467). Then follows the tragic, heartrending, and all too human meeting of Priam and Achilles. Afterward, Hermes escorts Priam back through the Greek camp to safety once again. Cursory examination of any other significant event in the *Iliad* reveals the gods acting in similar ways and achieving similar results. The voices and sometimes the actual appearances of the gods determine the human actions that follow. Jaynes asserts that such divine motivations—typical throughout the *Iliad*—are not fanciful poetic inventions but an accurate picture of how bicameral men and women went about their business on a daily basis.

Jung expressed a similar view of the differences between prehistoric and modern man:

> Primitive mentality differs from the civilized chiefly in that the conscious mind is far less developed in scope and intensity. Functions such as thinking, willing, etc. are not yet differentiated; they are pre-conscious. . . . The primitive cannot assert that he thinks; it is rather that "something thinks in him." The spontane-

> ity of the act of thinking does not lie, causally, in his conscious mind, but in his unconscious. (*The Archetypes* 153)

Jaynes develops the idea through further elaboration and by suggesting the actual mechanism by which the bicameral mind operated.

Further we must consider the poet's invocation of the Muses throughout the *Iliad* at key points, such as at the beginning of the catalog of ships in book 2, during the aristeia of Agamemnon in book 11, or before the Greek ships are set afire in book 16. Most important and best known, however, is the invocation in the opening of the first book: "Sing, O Goddess, the anger of Achilles son of Peleus" (1). Willcock sums up the opposing critical views of this line: "The oral poet did not consciously compose his verses. They came into his mind unbidden; and he believed, or affected to believe, that the Muse had told him what to say" (3). If he simply affected to believe—as later poets from Virgil to Milton most certainly did—then the Muse is indeed a poetic fancy, in Willcock's words "the personification of the poet's inspiration" (3). In the poetry of Virgil and Milton, poetic fancy and affectation is, certainly, exactly the function of the Muse. At the same time, if this line is considered from a Jaynesean perspective, then Homer believes he is, in modern parlance, actually "channeling" the Muse. According to Jaynes, then, the poet would have heard the Muse's voice bicamerally as it originated in his own brain. The poet improvises his verses in the right temporal lobe from his stock of oral formulas and themes/type-scenes; the verses then migrate to the left temporal lobe, from whence they emerge as the poet's song. According to Jaynes, the oracles, who spoke in verse, functioned in much the same manner.

In Jaynes's view, "Homer" is the poet of the *Iliad* but not the *Odyssey*. This question is a time-honored element of the famous "Homeric Question," actually a complex of questions regarding the genesis of the *Iliad* and *Odyssey*. Jaynes believes the *Iliad* was composed near the end of the bicameral period and is reflective of bicameral civilization, in which the heroes "were noble automatons who knew not what they did" (75). Eric Havelock asserts a similar theory of character motivation in the Homeric poems: "Achilles may have had a 'self' in our sense of the word, but he was not aware of it, and if he had been, he would not have behaved as a hero of the oralist vocabulary, a speaker of utterances and a doer of deeds" (113–14). Most scholars of a variety of interpretive persuasions agree that the *Iliad* preceded the *Odyssey*, making it a standard and well defended position, though it does not settle the question of whether one poet composed both. Jaynes holds that based on the chaos depicted—suggestive of the chaos of the Dark Age—and the wiles and deceptiveness of Odysseus—suggestive of consciousness—that the *Odyssey* followed the *Iliad,* reflective, as it is, of a later historical period: "In a word Odysseus of the many devices is the hero of the new mentality of how to get along in a ruined and god-weakened world" (273). Their world is god-weakened in that men no longer hear the voices of the gods because bicameral civilization, as a result of its growth, inevitably lost the ability to cue the mass hallucinations necessary for its citizens to hear the voices of the gods telling them how and when to carry out their cultural traditions.

Eric Havelock

In his *The Muse Learns to Write: Reflections on Orality and Literacy,* Eric Havelock focuses on the Greek transition from the oral culture of the Homeric poems to the literate culture of Greek history and philosophy, with the classic Greek tragedies as having characteristics of both. He establishes the function of literacy: "Literacy has supplied us with an artificial memory in the preserved document. We originally had to fashion our memory for ourselves out of the spoken tongue" (71). This memory was contained in and disseminated by the "rhythmic talk" and the "ritualized utterance" of poetry: "Such was the birth of what we call poetry, a performance now relegated under literacy to the status of a pastime, but originally the functional instrument of storage of cultural information for re-use or, in more familiar language, the instrument for the establishment of cultural tradition" (71, 70). So the six iterations of the man-on-trail plot in Homer's *Iliad* are not poetic inventions or fancies. Havelock, invoking the Parry-Lord findings, emphasizes the broad cultural acceptance of the values contained in the recurring themes of heroic verse: "Much of the thematic content, the epic motifs, noted by Lord (1960) . . . continually recall . . . rules of order to be followed in such things as holding an assembly, making a collective decision, conducting a banquet, arming for battle, issuing challenges, organizing funerals, and even carrying out such technical procedures as navigation, ship-building, house-building, and the like" (58). And the proper treatment of guests, even fugitives. Civilization thus passed onward all of the values needed for its continued stability: "Ritualization becomes the means of memorization. The memories are personal, belonging to every man, woman and child in the community, yet their content, the language preserved, is communal, something shared by the community as expressing its tradition and its historical identity" (70).[3] The content and even the language thus enter the collective unconscious.

The story of the man on trail and how he must be treated thus conveys one of the most primordial of all civilized values. The literary evidence, emphasized in the accompanying comparison charts, discussed thus far from writers as far ranging as Conrad, Frederic, Hardy, Hemingway, Hugo, Robinson, Stevenson, and Stowe, as well as others yet to be discussed, indicates by its recurring—yet not completely rigid—parallels that the common source from which the impulse to repeat this plot must emerge is not a conscious literary imitation but a deeper psychological source, one that taps the deepest roots of civilized behavior. In Havelock's words, "[s]uccessful retention in memory is built up by repetition. The children who prefer a retelling of the same story desire to be able to remember it, and so be able to retell it in whole or part and so relish it" (71).

Imagine then the chaos of the Greek Dark Age, when a civilization based on the oral transmission of cultural traditions became too large and unwieldy to support the mass hallucinations necessary for bicameral functioning, when the common man no longer heard the voices of the gods, when fewer poets channeled the voices of the Muses. Nevertheless, the poetry remained, as the stark evidence of the mere existence of the Homeric poems stands as proof. Even well into the period of literacy, the power of orality remained, as evidenced by the Greek tragedies—written by literate dramatists but still proclaimed publicly and communally, as Havelock notes: "Here [exemplified by the *Oresteia* and the *Oedipus Tyrannus*] were the proprieties of civic behavior, its approved attitudes, its rituals implicit in daily life, re-enacted and recommended over and over again" (15). So it is no surprise that Hugo's Bishop of Digne insists (by a glance at his housekeeper) on sticking to his daily ritual of placing all six of his silver plates on his table when even a single guest is present—even though there may not be six at table and even when the guest looks as frightening as Jean Valjean. Mankind's earliest and most primordial values survived oral transmission, the Greek Dark Age, the medieval dark ages, and thousands of years of medieval illiteracy to emerge intact in the writers of the Renaissance and beyond. Indeed, in the chaos of the breakdown of bicameral civilization, which no doubt included hordes of refugees and the invasion of the sea peoples, it is small wonder that the tales of suppliants, refugees, men on trail would resonate with audiences. In modern times the plot emerged often as among the first imaginative works produced by such writers as Mérimée (1829), London (1899), Stevenson (1877), and Frederic (1879) because it arose naturally from the depths of the collective unconscious, part of mankind's psychological inheritance.

Comparison table 3: Suppliants in Homer's *Iliad*

Character	Tlepolemus, son of Heracles and Astyocheia	Medon	Lycophron	Epigeus	Generic murderer	Priam
Book.lines	2.6530–70	13.694–97	15.429–35	16.569–81	24.480–82	24.1–706
Host	Appears to have established his own kingdom	Unspecified	Greater Ajax, (son of Telamon)	Peleus and Thetis, then (at Troy) Achilles	A noble host	Achilles
Place of Hospitality	Rhodes	Phylake	Presumably with Ajax in Salamis	Presumably the court of Peleus and Thetis in Phthia	A foreign land	Compound and tent of Achilles in the base camp besieging of Troy
Reason for fligh-	Killed his father's uncle, Likymnios	Killed a relative	Killed a man in Cythera	Killed a cousin	One who has killed a man in his own country	To retrieve and give proper burial to his son Hector, a ordered by the gods
Pursuer(s)	Sons and grand-sons of Herakles	Unspecified	Unspecified	Unspecified	Unspecified	Ostensibly Agamemnon, if he knew Priam were in the Greek camp

Chapter 5

DIVINITY AND DIVINE AGENTS ON EARTH

> Be not forgetful to entertain strangers; for thereby some have entertained angels unawares.
>
> —Hebrews 13:2

Cain

Ancient treatments of the man-on-trail plot may well be regarded as expressing some of the founding values of civilized behavior. Even the first murderer in the Judeo-Christian tradition is granted man-on-trail status of a sort:

> Cain rose up against Abel his brother and slew him.
>
> And the Lord said unto Cain, Where is Abel thy brother? And he said, I know not: Am I my brother's keeper?
>
> And he said, What hast thou done? The voice of thy brother's blood crieth unto me from the ground.
>
> And now art thou cursed from the earth, which hath opened her mouth to receive thy brother's blood from thy hand; When thou tillist the ground, it shall not henceforth yield unto thee her strength; a fugitive and a vagabond shalt thou be in the earth.
>
> And Cain said unto the Lord, My punishment is greater than I can bear. Behold thou hast driven me out this day from the face of the earth; and from thy face shall I be hid; and I shall be a fugitive and a vagabond in the earth; and it shall come to pass that every one that findeth me shall slay me.

> And the Lord said unto him, therefore whosoever slayeth Cain, vengeance shall be taken on him sevenfold. And the Lord set a mark upon Cain, lest any finding him should kill him.
>
> And Cain went out from the presence of the Lord, and dwelt in the land of Nod, on the east of Eden. (Gen. 4.8–16)[1]

The Cain story in general and this passage in particular leave some difficult questions. Why was Abel's sacrifice accepted and not Cain's? Who might the individuals be who would want to kill Cain? Would they want to kill him because of his reputation as a murderer? Or would they want to kill him simply because he was a vagabond and a fugitive? Was it normal practice to kill vagabonds and fugitives? Why would anyone killing Cain be punished sevenfold? What was the normal punishment for murder if it could be increased sevenfold? What kind of mark upon Cain could possibly prevent anyone from killing him? And if Cain were a fugitive and vagabond, how could he then build a city? "And Cain knew his wife; and she conceived, and bare Enoch: and he builded a city, and called the name of the city, after the name of his son, Enoch" (Gen. 4.17). Ultimately, these questions are relevant theologically perhaps but not archetypally. Jung comments on this loss of meaning: "The fact is that archetypal images are so packed with meaning in themselves that people never think of asking what they really do mean. That the gods die from time to time is due to man's sudden discovery that they do not mean anything, that they are made by human hands, useless idols of wood and stone" (*Archetypes* 13). Note that Cain's concern is that he will be killed. He realizes that he will be the man on trail and that it is death that will stalk him. The Lord's reason for granting the mark remains as unclear in the text as does the nature of the mark. One must, of course, wonder how ancient peoples might have regarded such a text, one that leaves more questions than it answers.

The stranger must not be killed, because civilization could not progress—or even come into being—if every stranger were killed, even if many of the strangers were fugitives or vagabonds. Cain is not killed, and he builds a city. Values must be sanctioned whereby commerce and culture may expand; thus, murder becomes a counterproductive indulgence. So those stories that thrive and are passed on are stories of the best of strangers: the holy family, Orestes and Pylades, angels, divine messengers, heroes under divine protection or favor—Odysseus, Telemachus, Priam, Joshua's spies, or the gods themselves—Jehovah, Zeus/Jove, and/or Mercury. They are stories that nascent civilizations need to canonize. Man creates gods in his own image, then projects the values necessary for the survival of his social group upward onto those gods. Man then creates stories of the gods coming down to earth to determine whether those values have been honored. "Be not forgetful to entertain strangers; for thereby some have entertained angels unawares" (Heb. 13.2). Man must honor the man on trail, indeed all strangers, because according to the many stories, he cannot always tell which strangers are the men and which are the gods or divine agents. Strangers move about freely; civilization flourishes. Respect for the stranger, divinely sanctioned, ultimately becomes an archetype of the collective unconscious.

Abraham and Sarah

In Cain, we see the man on trail. In Abraham we see the mythic host, rewarded for his hospitality. Abraham (patriarch of the Hebrew people) and his wife, Sarah, are childless in their old age when they receive a visit from three strangers:

> And the Lord appeared unto him in the plains of Mamre: and he sat in the tent door in the heat of the day; and he lift up his eyes and looked, and, lo, three men stood by him: and when he saw them, he ran to meet them from the tent door, and bowed himself toward the ground, and said, My lord, if now I have found favor in thy sight, pass not away, I pray thee, from thy servant: Let a little water, I pray you, be fetched, and wash your feet, and rest yourselves under the tree: And I will fetch a morsel of bread, and comfort ye your hearts; after that ye shall pass on: for therefore are ye come to your servant. And they said, So do, as thou hast said.
>
> And Abraham hastened into the tent unto Sarah, and said, Make ready quickly three measures of fine meal, knead it, and make cakes upon the hearth. And Abraham ran unto the herd, and fetched a calf tender and good, and gave it unto a young man; and he hasted to dress it. And he took butter, and milk, and the calf which he had dressed, and set it before them; and he stood by them under the tree, and they did eat.
>
> And they said unto him, Where is Sarah thy wife? And he said, Behold, in the tent
>
> And he said, I will certainly return unto thee according to the time of life; and, lo, Sarah thy wife shall have a son. And Sarah heard in the tent door, which was behind him.
>
> Now Abraham and Sarah were old, and well stricken in age; it had ceased to be with Sarah after the manner of women.

> Therefore Sarah laughed within herself, saying, After I am waxed old shall I have pleasure, my lord being old also?
>
> And the Lord said unto Abraham, Wherefore did Sarah laugh, saying, Shall I of a surety bear a child, who am old? Is anything too hard for Jehovah? At the set time I will return unto thee, when the season cometh round, and Sarah shall have a son.
>
> (Gen. 18:1–14)

The strangers, in this case divine messengers, are treated with courtesy and respect, at least by Abraham if not by Sarah. Because of this, despite her age, Sarah bears children. Notice that upon the appearance of the strangers Abraham immediately prepares food for them. As they partake, they become guests, so they are constrained from punishing or admonishing Sarah for her humor and sarcasm.

Baucis and Philemon

In Greek myth Zeus, the father of the gods, oversaw the sacred laws of hospitality. Aid for the pursued in this myth as well thus takes on a mythic and religious significance. The Greeks actually had a word for it—*philoxenia,* love of the stranger, the antonym of *xenophobia.* Similar to the traditions of Hebrew myth, the stranger is not always a pursued man but often a god.

Ovid's version of the tale of Baucis and Philemon includes a reference to goblets of beech ("*fago pocula,*" *Metamorphoses* 8.669–70), perhaps echoed by Hemingway in the Gauertal incident's "mattresses filled with beech leaves." Hemingway might well have been aware of the story of Baucis and Philemon from his high school reading, but he almost certainly would have been aware of it after reading Ezra Pound's early poem "The Tree," probably in Paris:

> I stood still and was a tree amid the wood,
> Knowing the truth of things unseen before;
> Of Daphne and the laurel bough
> And that god-feasting couple old
> That grew elm-oak amid the wold.

Ovid's treatment, the standard version, has Jupiter and Mercury visit Phrygia in the form of mortal men. A thousand doors are shut in their faces. Finally, they are taken in when they knock on the door of the humble cottage of an old couple, Baucis and Philemon. Baucis seats them and proceeds to boil some cabbage. Her husband reaches up for a side of bacon, "saved up for so long." In "The Snows of Kilimanjaro" **IM V**, which tells of the death of Williamson, Harry gives his hideously and obviously fatally wounded fellow officer "all his morphine tablets he had always saved to use himself" (24), just as Baucis and Philemon offer their bacon "saved up for so long." He treats his fellow officer, who also becomes his guest as well, humanely, giving his best, as do Baucis and Philemon.

The couple also offers a "rustic bench" with a "homespun cover" so that the strangers may rest, and they rekindle their hearth so that the strangers may be warm. They engage in conversation to pass the time. When the bacon and cabbage are ready, they offer wine from a mixing bowl that never seems to empty. After dinner, they offer fruit and nuts. They attempt to kill their goose, which serves in the role of watchdog, but after a comic chase they ultimately fail to catch it, and the gods demur on the offer of a goose dinner. Food, rest, and conversation have thus all been offered freely and cheerfully, leading the gods to repay the couple for their humble hospitality. The unhospitable neighbors are destroyed in a flood, the couple's poor cottage is turned into a marble mansion, and they are granted one wish. Their wish, that neither should outlive the other, is granted. When they finally die, it is simultaneously (though with enough time to say their goodbyes), and they are transformed into two intertwined trees, oak and elm, which the locals honor with garlands. The gods reward hospitality, and the stranger is sacred.

Comparison table 4: Divinity on earth

Source / author	King James Bible	King James Bible	Ovid
Title/subject	Genesis 18 / Jehovah Visits Abraham	Siege of Jericho	*Metamorphoses* / Baucis and Philemon
Deniers of hospitality/conquest	None	Defenders of Jericho	Phrygian villagers of a thousand houses
Gods / divinely sanctioned men on Trail	Jehovah and two others	Spies sent by Joshua to investigate the defenses of Jericho	Jupiter and Mercury
Host/hostess	Abraham and Sarah	Rahab	Impoverished and aged married couple, Baucis and Philemon
Elements of hospitality extended	Bread, butter, milk, freshly dressed calf	Rahab misdirects agents of the King and hides spies on roof	Seats at a clean table, cabbage, fire, bacon, humble delicacies, wine. Goose offered but spared.
Pursuers	Gods are not pursued.	Defenders of Jericho	Gods are not pursued.
Punishment of the unfaithful	Not relevant	Jericho destroyed	Village of a thousand houses swept away in flood
Divine reward	Sarah, despite her advanced age, gives birth	Rahab and extended family spared during the destruction of Jericho	Beautiful new home; their wish to die at the same moment granted; metamorphosis into two trees

Chapter 6

GUESTS BETRAYED AND HOSTS REPAID

He's here in double trust:
First, as I am his kinsman and his subject,
Strong both against the deed; then as his host,
Who should against his murderer shut the door,
Not bear the knife myself.
—*Macbeth* 1.7.12–16

You are no son of Mateo Falcone! Will you let me be taken in front of his house?
—Prosper Mérimée

These hairs which thou dost ravish from my chin
Will quicken and accuse thee. I am your host.
With robbers' hands my hospitable favours
You should not ruffle thus.
—*King Lear* 3.7.37–40

Michael Reynolds's inventory of Hemingway's reading indicates that both *Macbeth* and *King Lear* were included in Hemingway's high school reading (items 1877 and 1878; see also pages 40–41). In his 1958 *Paris Review* interview with George Plimpton, Hemingway said, "I read some Shakespeare every year, *Lear* always" (119). Hemingway seems to have had an interest in various aspects of hospitality. In reading *King Lear,* he would have met with repeated betrayals of hospitality, the most poignant of which would have been the lines in which a generous host, the soon-to-be-blinded Gloucester, is abused by his sinister guests. In *Macbeth,* he would have met a guest murdered by a host, ambitious yet conflicted and aided, indeed harangued, by a sinister household member.

In "The Snows of Kilimanjaro," acts that might be termed betrayals confront the reader, though these are betrayals of groups on trail and not people at the locus of hospitality, for example the secretaries who die in the snow and the Austrian officers. Nansen seems caught up in his own arrogance or self-importance in denying snow and Barker in his own bloodlust in slaughtering the Austrian officers on leave. Hemingway uses "exchange of populations" to describe Nansen's solution of the refugee crisis that came as a result of the Greco-Turkish War (7). The phrase suggests a bureaucratic euphemism not much more palatable than the decades-later "ethnic cleansing." Thus Nansen, unlike Barker, takes some refuge in his denial of the lethality of his decisions. Both, however, prove the undoing of persons on trail. Equally serious are those who betray the place of hospitality. In the stories discussed thus far, hospitality has been exploited (though not betrayed) in Stevenson's "A Lodging for the Night," and Jean Valjean, in his theft of the bishop's silver, betrays his host, though that theft is immediately forgiven. The biblical tale of Rahab and Joshua treats the theme of hospitality repaid.

Betrayed and Repaid: Prosper Mérimée's Carmen

Of all authors, Prosper Mérimée seems most aware of the conflict inherent in harboring a fugitive and develops plots around both the concepts of hospitality betrayed and hospitality repaid. A brief early episode from *Carmen* reveals that Mérimée thoroughly understood the particulars of hospitality customs as they operated in the culture he knew.

Mérimée (1803–1870), who may require a little introduction, was a French nobleman, a noted historian, inspector general of historic monuments, traveler, and courtier, among other things. He perpetrated literary hoaxes and wrote closet dramas, short stories, and novellas. He seldom wrote for financial gain, and some of his fiction was originally written simply to entertain aristocratic ladies. Maxwell Smith's *Prosper Mérimée* adequately chronicles his life and analyzes his literary works.

Although Mérimée did his greatest service to France as inspector general of historic monuments, today he is best known as the author of the 1845 novel *Carmen,* on which Bizet's opera is based. He also retains a reputation as an early master of the short story, based on a handful of short stories, of which "Mateo Falcone" is the most memorable example. His fiction often shows an interest in the primitive, the primal, the paranormal, and the supernatural. "Mateo Falcone" and *Carmen* are among his more realistic productions.

Mérimée was a close friend of both Stendhal and Turgenev, so if Hemingway had done any background reading on either of those authors, he might well have come across references to their relationships with Mérimée. No evidence has surfaced to indicate that Hemingway read *Carmen* or saw the opera. The standard inventories of Hemingway's reading and personal library holdings, by Michael Reynolds and by James Brasch and Joseph Sigman, do not include discrete Mérimée entries. Mérimée is, however, mentioned at least twice in Hemingway's letters.[1] In a 24 April 1926 letter to Maxwell Perkins, his new editor at Scribners, in discussing his reputation in France Hemingway suggests that some have compared him to Mérimée. He also claims that he never read Mérimée because he had assumed Mérimée was not very good. He seems to have subsequently read Mérimée, for he mentions him again, somewhat cryptically, in a 25 July 1929 letter to Owen Wister. At the beginning of a paragraph, he compliments Wister as the better writer of the two, justifying his judgement by his claim to have "read both the gents" (*Selected Letters* 301). It is unclear whether the gents in question are Wister and Mérimée or Mérimée and some other writer perhaps mentioned in the Wister letter to which Hemingway is replying. At any rate, Hemingway's making such a judgement strongly suggests he had read Mérimée.

A few words about the first chapter of Mérimée's novella *Carmen* are necessary to help establish Mérimée's understanding of the elements of hospitality plots. Hospitality is key in both "Mateo Falcone" and "The Snows of Kilimanjaro." This chapter is little known, because it is not used in the opera. Even the *Masterplots* summary of the novel omits this part of the narrative (Magill and Kohler).

Carmen's narrator, a bookish historian, tells of traveling near Córdoba in search of the elusive site of the battle of Munda, one of Julius Caesar's great victories. At a campsite, he meets Don José—Carmen's doomed lover, well into his outlaw period. The narrator's guide regards Don José as a desperado. Despite this, the narrator offers a cigar to Don José, who accepts. The narrator explains, "In Spain, a cigar offered and accepted establishes relations of hospitality, as does the sharing of bread and salt in the East," clearly signaling Mérimée's grasp of cultural traditions (4). Next, he shares food, another element of hospitality.

Through a variety of unspoken hints, the narrator's guide tries to suggest that the narrator end the relationship and leave: "Meanwhile my guide ate little, drank still less, and spoke not at all, though he had been talking nineteen to the dozen ever since the start of our journey together. The presence of our guest seemed to make him uneasy" (4). The guide, without speaking, argues against hospitality, the person who argues against hospitality being another archetype of both hospitality and man-on-trail plots, seen in several narratives already discussed. The narrator ignores him: "I knew the Spanish character well enough to be quite certain that I had nothing to fear from a man who had shared food and tobacco with me" (5). They travel together and arrive at a poor one-room inn, where they bond over food, wine, music, and rest. During the night, the guide slips away to tip off the authorities regarding Don José's whereabouts, but the narrator warns Don José, who escapes. As has been repeatedly shown, aid in a fugitive's flight is another man-on-trail archetype.

After Don José's departure, the narrator considers what he has done:

> I asked myself whether I had been right to save a robber, and perhaps a murderer, from the gallows, merely because I had shared some ham and some Valencian-style rice with him. Had I not betrayed my guide, who was upholding the cause of law and order? Had I not exposed him to the risk of incurring a blackguard's vengeance? Yes, but what about the obligations of hospitality? Primitive notions, I said to myself; I shall be answerable for all the crimes this bandit goes on to commit. Yet can one dismiss as primitive that instinctive call of conscience which is resistant to all reasoning? Perhaps, in the delicate situation in which I found myself, it would not have been possible for me to escape without some self-reproach. (10–11)

The narrator regards "the obligation of hospitality" as a "primitive obligation" but also considers it "the instinctive call of conscience." At any rate, he is fully individuated and makes his decision according to the merits of the case, not in deference to social pressures.

When the narrator next meets Don José, the latter is in jail and sentenced to die. Don José then, trusting in his former host, tells the narrator the entire story of his tumultuous relationship with Carmen. The bulk of the novella consists of this narrative; indeed, the telling of the tale of Don Jose and Carmen might qualify as hospitality repaid. The telling of tales—a standard archetype of hospitality and traditionally a guest's obligation—is one of the most time-honored elements of hospitality. Another tale (not among the Windemere stories) of hospitality repaid worthy of the reader's interest is Alexander Pushkin's "The Captain's Daughter."

Betrayed: "Mateo Falcone," the Chore-Boy Episode, and a 1913 Homicide

The seductive power of Hemingway's personal adventures often obscures other sources he may have used, including literary sources, historical sources, current-event sources, word-of-mouth sources, and his own invented material. Brief as it is, the chore-boy episode of "The Snows of Kilimanjaro" (**IV.2–3**) employs material from multiple sources.

A volume of stories edited by Brander Matthews, *The Short-Story: Specimens Illustrating Its Development* (1907), is listed in the inventories of Hemingway's reading by both Reynolds (item 1435) and Brasch and Sigman (item 4359). It is also listed in the 1940 Key West inventory of Hemingway's books (M. Reynolds 47). The most arresting selection in this volume is Prosper Mérimée's "Mateo Falcone" (1829), an evaluation based not just on its relation to Hemingway but on its stark power as a narrative.[2]

The parallels between Mérimée's story and the chore-boy episode from "The Snows of Kilimanjaro" are notable. More important, however, is the indisputable fact that the homicide depicted in the chore-boy episode is largely based on an actual homicide that took place in Wyoming in 1913. Details of the shooting and trial discussed here come from the contemporary newspaper accounts of the *Northern Wyoming Herald* and the *Park County Enterprise,* both of Cody, Wyoming. The parallels between "Mateo Falcone" and the chore-boy episode reveal that Hemingway used details from accounts of the actual murder, adding particulars from Mérimée's story to shape the episode to his own end; in this regard, the addition of those details constitutes Hemingway's invention added to the raw material of the original accounts. These additions, as well as Hemingway's deviations from the original accounts of the homicide, serve to bring the material closer to the man-on-trail and hospitality motifs.

The chore-boy episode (**IV.3**) from "The Snows of Kilimanjaro" is based on the fatal shooting of rancher James Smith (an alias, though Smith was not a criminal) by ranch hand Tony Rodeschek. Hemingway's biographers have well documented his time at the Nordquist ranch in Wyoming in the late 1920s and 1930s—hunting, fishing, and writing. His stays there resulted in such masterpieces as "Wine of Wyoming" and "The Gambler, the Nun, and the Radio." He knew many of the locals, from whom he may have learned the story. Although local newspapers carried detailed accounts of Smith's murder and Rodeschek's subsequent trial, Hemingway likely learned of the key events and characters by word of mouth rather than by accessing newspaper accounts that were already fifteen years old.

On April 4, 2013, the *Northern Wyoming Herald* reported the shooting of Smith by Tony Rodeschek at the Kitchen ranch, where Rodeschek was a hired hand. Initially and inaccurately described as a dispute over hay, the event took place on Tuesday, April 1, 1913. Smith was described as "an old timer, having been a resident of this section of Wyoming for more than twenty years" ("Quarrel Ended by a Bullet" 5). On April 8, the *Park County Enterprise* reported Rodeschek's age as "about 23." His father's testimony at the trial reported his age as "27 or 28" ("Not Guilty Is the Verdict" 4), hardly the chore boy of Harry's memory. The phrase *chore boy* never occurs in the newspaper accounts; Hemingway likely picked it up through word of mouth or invented it for the story. The *Enterprise* also reported that although he "was by no means a simpleton," he was "not considered as being very sharp of brain" (1). This accords with Harry's referring to him as a half-wit, but Rodeschek did not break out in tears at his arrest, as in the chore-boy incident: "Tony came with the Sheriff but was not arrested until they reached the jail. Apparently, the arrest was a surprise to him," as it was for Harry's chore boy. "He said he killed Smith in self-defense and he could not at first understand why he should be placed in jail" ("Will Soon Face a Jury" 1). He confessed to the killing but pleaded not guilty at his hearing and trial. The newspaper accounts of the preliminary hearing describe Rodeschek as untroubled by his arrest: "The accused man seems to have but little conception of the seriousness of the charge against him. He is impassive, not to say cheerful, at all times, and has no hesitancy in discussing the affair. Without doubt he believes himself thoroughly justified in the shooting" ("Rodoschek [sic] Bound Over" 5).

A witness to the shooting, John Burke, Smith's hired hand, gave a key account in the trial of Rodeschek ("Not Guilty Is the Verdict" 1). Burke and Smith arrived at the ranch in the morning and began feeding their cattle, surprised that Rodeschek, who was indeed in charge of the ranch during rancher Kitchen's absence, did not appear to feed stock along with them. While Smith began walking toward the ranch house to find him, Rodeschek, hidden in the upper section of the barn, opened fire, killing Smith. Burke fled but was easily overtaken by Rodeschek, on skis, who protested that he had no intent to harm Burke in any way. Apparently, there was a history of conflict between Smith and Rodeschek, involving Smith repeatedly bullying Rodeschek, assaulting him, kicking out his teeth, and drawing a gun on him (4). Rodeschek's legal defense would be self-defense and diminished capacity.

Dogs appear in both the chore-boy episode and in the newspaper accounts of Smith's murder. In the former, the body lies in a corral for a week and is partially devoured by dogs, making the chore boy seem unusually callous and the violation of hospitality more egregious. At the trial, the coroner's testimony revealed that Smith's arm was missing. The fatal bullet had passed through the arm, probably breaking bone (thus making detachment of the arm less difficult) and severing a vital artery inside the body, leading to a rapid death. Burke testified that far from acting callously, Rodeschek claimed he had covered the body with canvas and shot one of the dogs that attempted to violate it. Rodeschek also claimed that Smith's own dog made off with the detached arm ("Not Guilty Is the Verdict").

At this point, the particulars of Mérimée's story, especially those that relate to the chore-boy episode, need to be outlined in order to reveal Hemingway's choices in transforming his material and to demonstrate, once again, Mérimée's understanding of the traditions of hospitality.

The chore-boy episode (**IM IV.3**) is set on a remote ranch in the American west, and "Mateo Falcone" is set on a similarly remote farm in rural Corsica. Both begin with evocative descriptions of the essential isolated, rugged high-country locations. Hemingway precedes the chore-boy episode with such a description (**IM IV.2**) of moving cattle through remote, mountainous landscape.

Mérimée begins: "Coming out of Porto-Vecchio, and turning northwest toward the center of the island, the ground is seen to rise very rapidly, and, after three hours' walk by tortuous paths, blocked by large bowlders of rocks, and sometimes cut by ravines, the traveler finds himself on the edge of a very broad *mâquis,* or open plateau." A few lines later, he elaborates: "When the corn is gathered, the straw is left because it is too much trouble to gather. The roots, which remain in the earth without being consumed, sprout in the following spring, into very thick shoots, which, in a few years reach to a height of seven or eight feet. It is this kind of underwood which is called *mâquis*" (137–38). To such a mâquis, Gianetto, the story's fugitive, attempts to escape.

In Hemingway's story, a "half-wit chore boy" is left in charge of the ranch and "told not to let anyone get any hay" (22–23).[3] In Merimee's story, Mateo Falcone leaves his only son, Fortunato, just ten years old, in charge of the farm while he and his wife set out to check on a flock of sheep in the mâquis, said to be a good place to hide when one has committed a murder (Notice the second person point of view so typical of Hemingway):

> If you have killed a man, go into the *mâquis* of Porto-Vecchio, with a good gun and powder and shot, and you will live there in safety. Do not forget to take a brown cloak, furnished with a hood, which will serve as a coverlet and mattress.

> The shepherds will give you milk, cheese, and chestnuts, and you will have nothing to fear from the hand of the law, nor from relatives of the dead, except when you go down into town to renew your stock of ammunition. (138)

While Mérimée thus establishes the themes of communal protection and hospitality for the fugitive, in Harry's reminiscence the supplicant (not a fugitive) is vilified as "that old bastard from the Forks who had beaten the boy when he had worked for him." The old man stopped at the ranch "to get some feed," threatening to beat the boy again when the boy refused to let him take the feed he needed (22). The boy then shoots the old man, thus denying hospitality. He follows orders in telling the old man not to take any feed, but tragically overreacts, resorting to homicide.

In Mérimée's story, Fortunato hears gunshots and is confronted by a bandit, "Corsican for one who is proscribed" (141). Wounded and unable to make it back to the shelter of the mâquis, the bandit—a classic man on trail—demands sanctuary of the reluctant Fortunato: "You are no son of Mateo Falcone! Will you let me be taken in front of his house?" (142). Ironically, the fugitive is named Gianetto Sanpiero—after Saint Peter, the keeper of the keys to the kingdom, the ultimate threshold guardian of the ultimate place of hospitality. He then bribes Fortunato with a five-franc piece, all the money he has, and only then does Fortunato consent and conceal him—in a haystack! Ominously, Fortunato has responded not to the supplicant's demand for traditional hospitality but rather to his bribe. The authorities arrive shortly thereafter, "six men with brown uniform with yellow collars, commanded by an adjutant" (143). As per usual, the pursuers present as uniformed authority. Fortunato refuses to admit he has seen anyone pass by and responds with scorn to the adjutant's threats. A search of the premises, including the haystack, fails to turn up the fugitive. In a final attempt to break Fortunato's resolve, the leader offers "a silver watch worth quite ten crowns" (146). Fortunato is tempted: "His face plainly expressed the conflict going on in his mind between covetousness and the claims of hospitality" (147). The fully individuated hosts discussed so far—the Bishop of Digne, Conrad's sea captain, Malemute Kid, et cetera—do not suffer such conflict. He finally relents and points at the haystack. The fugitive is seized and bound. Like Harry's chore boy, Fortunato has violated the sacred, indeed the primordial, claims of hospitality. Mateo and his wife arrive moments later.

All three narratives include elaboration of the conveyance of the victim. Gianetto's wound has stiffened and has thus limited his mobility. The leader, however, explains how he will be transported: "I would carry you for a league on my back and not feel tired. All the same, my friend, we will make a litter for you out of the branches and your cloak. The farm at Crespoli will provide us with horses" (148). In Hemingway's story, the dead old man was "packed on a sled wrapped in a blanket and roped on and you got the boy to help you haul it, and the two of you took it out over the road on skis, and sixty miles down to town" (22). Several accounts indicate the difficulty and effort required of the local Sheriff to recover Smith's body. This is one of the more outlandish reports: "[I]n places, the grade was so steep the sled could not be held back, so the Sheriff mounted the sled with the body and tobogganed it down the hill, traveling at times at railroad speed and narrowly escaping being dashed to death against trees and rocks" ("Will Soon Face a Jury" 1).

Though their motives clearly differ—the chore boy's being revenge and Fortunato's being greed—each pays a tragic price for denying hospitality. Not so with Tony Rodeschek. The chore boy is turned over to the law: "and when the sheriff put the handcuffs on the boy he couldn't believe it. Then he'd started to cry" (23). Like the chore boy, Fortunato cries:

> "Father," the boy cried out, with tears in his eyes, just ready to fall at his knees.
>
> "Out of my sight!" shouted Mateo.
>
> The child stopped motionless a few steps off from his father, and began to sob. (152)

Mateo, enraged at Fortunato's actions, immediately takes his son out toward the mâquis. Fortunato begs for mercy but, significantly, never defends his actions. After giving Fortunato time to recite every prayer he knows, Mateo executes him with a single shot. Thus, both stories punish the betrayal of hospitality. In Wyoming, the trial took three days, and on its first ballot the jury quickly reached a unanimous verdict of not guilty, with *The Northern Wyoming Herald* reporting "almost universal satisfaction" among those in the "court room . . . thronged with spectators nearly half of whom were women" (1).

To recount the similarities in plot between Mérimée's story and the chore-boy episode: a farm or ranch in isolated high country; a young boy left in charge; the appearance of a fugitive/supplicant; a specific reference to hay; the denial or betrayal of hospitality; elaboration of the conveyance of the dead or betrayed fugitive/supplicant; the boy cries; and, finally, retribution is visited upon the boy.

Several changes in detail must be restated. Accounts of the trial reveal that the motives for Smith's murder were self-defense and revenge. Neither violation of hospitality nor the code of the West were at issue in the killing. If Hemingway did indeed know that Smith had arranged to have his cattle fed at the Kitchen ranch, he suppressed that detail in order to give his chore boy the choice of failing to grant hospitality. By first making the killer a boy instead of a grown man and second having the boy break down in tears, Hemingway brings the episode closer to "Mateo Falcone" and the issue of betrayal of hospitality central to Mérimée's story but not central to the 1913 homicide and trial.

The conclusion to the actual homicide case contrasts with the more pathetic, perhaps even tragic, version Hemingway crafts for the chore-boy episode. Making him a chore boy instead of a grown man not only adds to the pathos but also brings the episode closer to the character of Fortunato Falcone and thus to the theme of hospitality and the proper action of a host. Rodeschek's motives were, arguably, self-defense and perhaps revenge. While Hemingway makes his murder victim a vicious bully whose character seems to accord with Smith's, the violations of hospitality by both Hemingway's victim, who simply takes feed he wants, and Hemingway's killer, who overreacts to a comparatively minor offense, simply have limited genesis in the actual events. Hemingway added borrowings from Mérimée in order to introduce the theme of hospitality.

Mérimée's story is, tellingly, titled not "Fortunato Falcone" but rather "Mateo Falcone." Thus, Mérimée emphasizes that Mateo is the protagonist, for it is his decision, his choice of primal justice over civil justice that is the crux of this compellingly told story. As "Mateo Falcone" was originally published in 1829, the modern reader can too easily dismiss it as the remnant of a more brutal time and place. It is important to note, however, that such codes of conduct still hold sway today. Pashtunwali, for example, the conduct code still practiced by the Pashtun tribes of Afghanistan and Pakistan, still includes the concepts of *Melmastia,* the injunction to respect, serve, and protect one's guests without payment or consideration of any kind, and the concept of *Nanawatai,* asylum. These were depicted in the 2013 film *Lone Survivor,* based on the 2007 book of the same title by Marcus Luttrell, a member of a Navy SEAL team who was taken in and sheltered from the Taliban by Afghan tribesmen, adherents of Pashtunwali, who put themselves at great risk in so doing. Luttrell tells of the village chief who defended him: "He was doing it not for personal gain but out of a sense of honor that reached back down the generations, two thousand years of *Pashtunwalai* tradition: You will defend your guest to the death" (337).

Mateo, significantly, disposes of the watch with which the adjutant bribes Fortunato: "Mateo seized the watch and threw it against a stone with such force that it broke into a thousand pieces" (152). It is not just Fortunato's greed that

Mateo rejects by smashing the watch. Granted, in 1829, such a watch was, indeed, a valuable object, but Mérimée might well have substituted a wide variety of other objects. He chooses a watch not just because of its value but also because it represents time. Mateo lives and acts according not to any code of modern justice but to the dictates of an ancient, primal honor culture, unaffected by the passing of time. Thus, the watch's destruction is entirely appropriate.

A story such as "Mateo Falcone" poses challenges for the modern reader, who naturally feels sympathy for such a young victim as Fortunato. The chore-boy episode seems to err (assuming that we choose to regard it as an error) on the side of the law. As our sympathies tell us, "Mateo Falcone" errs (if, once again, we choose to regard it as an error) on the side of ancient tradition. In our world, where the primitive still comes into contact with societies governed by laws enforced by uniformed authority, this remains an issue. Civilization more often than primitive society holds the power to force its values and concept of justice onto the primitive man—always for his improvement, of course, never for financial gain or political hegemony. In the first chapter of *Heart of Darkness,* Joseph Conrad writes movingly of the "Inferno" of dying displaced native workers brought to the Congo to perform "The work!" of civilizing Africa:

> They were dying slowly—it was very clear. They were not enemies, they were not criminals, they were nothing earthly now—nothing but black shadows of disease and starvation. . . . Brought from all the recesses of the coast in all the legality of time contracts, lost in uncongenial surroundings, fed on unfamiliar food, they sickened, became inefficient, and were then allowed to crawl away and rest. (66)

In a real sense, these workers constituted a sacrifice, one that enabled "civilization" to advance. No doubt the uniformed authority of the US Army and the settlers of the nineteenth-century American West thought that trials and hangings of Native Americans advanced civilization as well. In his *Morning, Noon, and Night: Finding the Meaning of Life's Stages Through Books,* Arnold Weinstein, in writing of the early stages of life, finds abundant examples of the seemingly inevitable sacrifices of the young depicted in the world's literature, providing examples of "familial sacrifice," such as Kafka's Gregor Samsa, Faulkner's Benjy and Quentin Compson, and Ibsen's Little Eyolf, as well as "systemwide sacrifice," such as that in Jonathan Safran Foer's *Extremely Loud and Incredibly Close,* about a son whose childhood is sacrificed in trying to cope with the death of his father in the twin towers attack. Every reader can supply his or her own examples of child victims in literature, from the sons of Medea to *The Diary of Anne Frank,* to the "Moloch" section of Allen Ginsberg's "Howl." Outside of literature, we must consider the deaths of refugee children around the world and whether they propitiate the gods of ethnic cleansing, and in America the accidental gun deaths of children and whether they propitiate the gods of our Militia Amendment. The latter is a choice Americans consciously make. Even when the sacrifice is averted, as in the case of Abraham and Isaac, it is only after a convincing demonstration of a clear willingness and intent to perform the horrid act. The reader's horror of Mateo Falcone's violent act of primitive justice and honor must be seen in context before judgement is passed, and the chore-boy episode of "The Snows of Kilimanjaro" reveals both Hemingway's struggle and Harry's pain in reconciling the conflicting demands of civilized justice and primitive justice. The question of whether justice marches ever forward to higher truth or merely stumbles into exploitative practices sanctioned by what Conrad criticizes as "all the legality of time contracts" foisted upon the uneducated remains unanswered. So does the question of whether primitive justice acts as a link to the oldest and most humane of mankind's prehistoric impulses toward civilization and truth or whether those impulses function merely as atavistic horrors.

Repaid: Rahab and Joshua

Hemingway's familiarity with the tale of Rahab and Joshua at the time he wrote "The Snows of Kilimanjaro" is likely, as he included it in *Men at War* (1942), an anthology of war stories he edited. During the siege of Jericho, Joshua's spies are the guests, and Rahab the harlot, the hostess who, under duress, refuses to betray her guests.[4]

> [A]nd it came to pass, when the people heard the sound of the trumpet, and the people shouted with a great shout, that the wall fell down flat, so that the people went up into the city, every man straight before him, and they took the city. And they utterly destroyed all that was in the city,
>
> But Joshua has said unto the men that had spied out the country, Go into the harlot's house, and bring out thence the woman, and all that she hath, as ye sware unto her.
>
> And the young men that were spies went in, and brought out Rahab, and her father, and her mother, and her brethren, and all that she had; and they brought out all her kindred, and left them without the camp of Israel.

> And Joshua saved Rahab the harlot alive, and her father's household, and all that she had; and she dwelleth in Israel even unto this day; because she hid the messengers, which Joshua sent to spy out Jericho. (Josh. 6.20–26)

And Rahab is not betrayed by her guests or by Joshua, their leader. Once again, the relationship of guest and host is honored as sacred, and its origin drifts back into the mists of time.

How can the modern reader coherently regard the improbable aspects of the myth of the siege of Jericho? Perhaps the walls of the city actually did collapse after the Israelites marched around the city carrying the now lost Ark of the Covenant every day for six days and seven times on the seventh day after which they shouted and blew horns. Perhaps some other cause coincided with the noise they made, causing the walls to collapse. Perhaps the deity intervened at that moment to bring down the walls, thus enforcing the lesson that obeying even the deity's strangest requests at all times ends with miraculous results. More than likely, later chroniclers decided that the actual ruins of Jericho could be used for that very same didactic purpose whether the Israelites or their deity had anything to do at all with the actual demise of Jericho. Looking at the inserted story of Rahab and Joshua's spies, another plausible didactic use of the myth emerges in the suggestions to the Israelites that the deity has chosen them for a special purpose and to everyone else that cooperation with the conquering Israelites is always the safest policy. Thus, the already ancient customs of hospitality find further sanction by being subsumed into tribal myth.

Comparison table 5: Hospitality betrayed and repaid

Author/source	Mérimée	Mérimée	Bible
Title	*Carmen*	"Mateo Falcone"	Joshua and Rahab
Initial host or hostess	*Carmen*'s narrator	Fortunato Falcone	Rahab, the harlot of Jericho
Initial Guest	Don José	Gianetto Sanpiero	Joshua's spies
Element(s) of hospitality extended	Tobacco, food, music, place of rest, warning that uniformed authority has taken up the pursuit	Man on trail hidden from pursuit of uniformed authority	Guests are hidden from pursuit
Betrayer	Narrator's local guide	Fortunato Falcone	–
Method of betrayal	–	Fortunato reveals Gianetto's hiding place	–
Type of repayment	Don José tells the narrator the entire story of his affair with Carmen.	–	Rahab and her family are saved from the destruction of Jericho.

Comparison table 6: The chore-boy incident

Author/source	Ernest Hemingway	Prosper Mérimée	Newspaper accounts
Title	Chore-boy episode	"Mateo Falcone"	*Northern Wyoming Herald* and *Park County Enterprise*
Host and age of host	Chore boy, young but age not given	"Fortunato Falcone," ten years old	Tony Rodeschek, twenty-seven or twenty-eight
Man on trail, fate suffered	"that old bastard from the Forks" (22), death by gunshot	Gianetto Sanpiero, betrayed to official authority, likely to be executed	James Smith, death by gunshot
Need for hospitality	Hay to feed stock	Protection from official authority	Cattle feed
Violation of hospitality	Killing as overreaction to the taking of hay	Fugitive's hiding place revealed	Revenge killing
Instrument of justice	Harry and the sheriff	Mateo Falcone	Arrest by sheriff and trial by jury
Reaction to arrest	Cries upon arrest	Cries when confronted by his father	Surprised but composed and confident of acquittal
Punishment or fate of man on trail	Turned over to Sheriff	Shot to death	Not guilty verdict

Chapter 7

POETIC EXPRESSIONS AND POPULAR MUSIC

> there's a hellhound on my trail
> —Robert Johnson

This chapter includes discussion of several songs by recording artists representing three different genres. None of the musicians or songs can be deemed obscure. All are easily accessible through the usual search engines, including performances and transcriptions of lyrics.

Walt Whitman's Leaves of Grass

While poets may be wired to the collective unconscious differently from prose writers, in the case of Walt Whitman and Harriet Beecher Stowe, the results turn out in a similar fashion. The parallels between Harriet Beecher Stowe's telling of the story of Eliza in *Uncle Tom's Cabin* (1852) may well have influenced section 10 of "Song of Myself" (1855), in which Whitman depicts a runaway slave and the host who aids him, a classic man-on-trail narrative:

> The runaway slave came to my house and stopt outside,
> I heard his motions crackling the twigs of the woodpile,
> Through the swung half-door of the kitchen I saw him limpsey and weak,
> And went where he sat on a log and led him in and assured him.
> And brought water and fill'd a tub for his sweated body and bruis'd feet,
> And gave him a room that entered from my own, and gave him some coarse

clean clothes,
And remember perfectly well his revolving eyes and his awkwardness,
And remember putting plasters on the galls of his neck and ankles;
He staid with me a week before he was recuperated and pass'd north,
I had him sit next me at table, my fire-lock lean'd in the corner. (31)

Stowe's purpose in *Uncle Tom's Cabin* was to advance the abolitionist cause by educating the hearts of her readers about the evils of human slavery. Whitman, however, presents the runaway slave in a larger context as one more character in an epic catalog of Americans. Like Stowe, Whitman wrote at the height of the abolitionist movement, the runaway slave sequence being included in the 1855 edition of *Leaves of Grass*. Though Whitman's purpose in "Song of Myself" was thus markedly different from Stowe's, he still manages in just a few lines to include many of the same elements: sudden appearance, immediate acceptance, reference to a door, medical care, a place to sleep, food, clothing, and protection. Protection is indicated by his reference to "my firelock in the corner," which recalls Malemute Kid's similar intimidation of the Mountie who pursues Jack Westondale: "the kid glanced at his well-stocked arsenal" (296) and Stowe's John Van Trompe who, charged with the protection of Eliza and Harry, points "to two or three goodly looking rifles over the mantelpiece" (114).

The only notable missing element is the pursuer, though in 1855 pursuit by runaway-slave hunters would have been implicit, as outrage over the runaway-slave laws never abated and as part of the culture may have made its way as a matter of course into the narratives of both authors. This does not discount the possibility that both details and the overall contours of the narratives were partially shaped by the psychological inheritance of mankind.

Just as Whitman radically condenses so many of the elements used by Stowe, so does Allen Ginsberg, in the final line of part 3 of "Howl," radically condense his hospitality for Carl Solomon, the poem's dedicatee and the poet's friend and his chosen representative of the anguish post–World War II generation: "I'm with you in Rockland / in my dreams you walk dripping from a sea-journey on the highway across America in tears to the door of my cottage in the Western night" (20).

Bob Dylan's "Shelter from the Storm"

Bob Dylan's usual narrative form, which may be described in literary terms as nonlinear, seems to be what he used in "Shelter from the Storm" (1975). The first line of the second stanza, in which he ponders whether he will "pass this way" in the future has the tone of a summative final stanza. Similarly, stanza four picks up the same theme—what Joseph Campbell would call "the road of trials"—as stanza one, even though stanza three seems to have carried the narrative forward. Nevertheless, elements of hospitality customs as well as the man-on-trail plot surface regularly in the song's ten stanzas. Going beyond the nonlinear and cubist twists, the tale that unfolds embodies a familiar plot. In stanza four, for example, the speaker places himself as "on the trail," and stanza one substitutes a road "full of mud," similar to Townes Van Zandt's "dirty road," discussed below. He is even pursued, "hunted," giving him man-on-trail status. The refrain, repeated ten times in exactly the same way, emphasizes what the hostess offers: shelter from both the literal and metaphorical storms of life, an archetypal element also included in "To the Man on Trail," the Gauertal incident, *Uncle Tom's* Cabin, *Les Misérables,* "The Three Strangers," Pushkin's "The Captain's Daughter," and "Come On in My Kitchen," also discussed below.

The first five stanzas tell a man-on-trail story focalized in the first person from the point-of-view of the guest himself. Unnarrated events then occur, as evidenced by the opening of stanza six, which indicates a breakup with the hostess.

Stanzas seven through nine take on a metaphorical and philosophical quality, with seven and eight purely lyrical and nine picking up the narrative once again. The references are to doom and futility in stanza seven, existential angst in stanza eight, and Christ in stanza nine.

The entire experience is, for the narrator, transformative. In recounting his first entry into the unnamed woman's hospitality, the narrator describes himself, using an artistic term, as lacking "form." When the tale ends, despite his having lost her, he has become an artist in pursuit of "Beauty" which he will eventually "make . . . mine." The entire song thus becomes a tribute to a generous hostess, one in which—despite its narrative gymnastics—the archetypal images of the man on trail and of hospitality break the surface. Successfully experimental though it is in narrative structure and in its combination of narrative and lyrical elements, the song still incorporates—whether consciously or unconsciously—archetypal images and figures.

Townes Van Zandt's "Waitin' Around to Die"

In American country music, Townes Van Zandt's "Waitin' Around to Die" (1968) brings narrative rather than lyric content to the plot. The song, perhaps the signature piece of Van Zandt's career, even bears comparison with "The Snows of Kilimanjaro." Van Zandt (1944–1997), educated and from a prominent founding family of Texas, may have encountered the archetype from literary sources, though it is also entirely possible that he may instead have tapped the archetype directly from the unconscious; the ways of genius are not to be underestimated. Its similarities to "The Snows of Kilimanjaro" convince the reader not that Hemingway served as the source for the song but rather that they both grow from the same primordial images.

The song has five four-line stanzas which tell in brief and linear fashion the narrator's life story. Each ends with some lyrical variation of the "waitin' around to die" refrain.

The first stanza, a general introduction, establishes the speaker's interests as "a-gamblin'," "booze," and "ramblin'" his way down a metaphorical "dirty road." The second introduces a mother who abandons him in order to escape a likely death at the hands of his physically abusive father. The third tells of his first love, who steals his money and abandons him. In the fourth, he helps to commit a robbery, is caught, and does a two-year sentence, "waitin' 'round to die." In the final stanza, upon release from prison, he finds his first true friend, the drug Codeine. The stanza has an extra line, so its refrain can be repeated: "Yeah together we're gonna wait around and die."

The first line of the song establishes the speaker as a man on trail: "Sometimes I don't know where this dirty road is taking me." The refrain establishes the pursuer as death. Part of the song's power is that the pursuer is not symbolic or representative. No image of uniformed authority or canid pursuit is necessary. As Van Zandt bluntly puts it, the pursuer *is* death.

The speaker is haunted by his memories and, like Hemingway's Harry, recounts his life as he waits. The first stanza finds him, like Harry, on a "dirty road" and reveals that, like Harry, he gambles and drinks too much. (Hemingway's *Green Hills of Africa* also begins on a dirty road.) In the second stanza, he witnesses a scene of violence and family tragedy; Harry has seen epic wartime violence and has experienced the burning of his grandfather's house. In the third stanza, he meets a girl who takes his money. Harry loses the love of his life to what is likely her affair with another woman. We can definitely say that both men lose love. He resorts to robbery to gain some "easy money," just as

Harry takes the easy way of marrying Helen for her money.[1] He is pursued by official (perhaps uniformed) authority, in the form of the posse that tracks him down while on the run—on trail. Harry and the Armenian woman are pursued by the MPs, and at the end, Harry can see death in the form of "two bicycle policemen." Finally, Harry is numbed by both alcohol and gangrene, while Van Zandt's narrator is numbed by his newfound narcotic. Fittingly, the train Harry rides on to cover the Greco-Turkish War (**IM II.2**) passes through fields of opium poppies.

And yet we sympathize with them both! The listener does not denounce "Waitin' Around to Die" as a misguided hymn to a criminal junkie. Anyone who has seen enough of his life can understand that the speaker's journey through this world has not brought him into contact with high-quality human beings. The song derives its power from the raw bluntness with which the speaker confronts the inevitable approach of death. And what right does the reader or listener have to condemn either Van Zandt's speaker or Hemingway's Harry without having walked in his shoes? Harry observes "*things that he could never think of and later still he had seen much worse*" (16–17). How long could anyone live with and write of such things, grotesque horrors of war in Harry's case, before seeking out a Helen with enough money to enable him to forget what he had seen?

Robert Johnson's "Come On in My Kitchen" and "Hell Hound on My Trail"

Robert Johnson (1911–1938), an American blues musician and songwriter from Mississippi, has had a disproportionally remarkable influence on world music, considering the relatively small number of songs he was able to record during his short life.[2] A variety of explanations for his enduring popularity have been put forward, none entirely satisfactory. One theory that might partially account for his popularity might be that he had an intuitive access of ancient archetypes.

As the differing lyrics and organization of the two recorded takes of "Come On in My Kitchen" reveal, a blues song is often a variable collection of sometimes related verses. Nevertheless, in a few strokes and with a rolling chorus, Johnson, a man probably free of significant literary influence, hits on some of the key archetypes. The speaker addresses what we can easily deem a woman on trail. The "Come On" of title itself is an offer of shelter, just as the reference to a kitchen is an offer of food, two key elements of the stranger archetype. The approach of winter in the long term and the trembling leaves, both suggestive of storms, mirror the metaphorical and literal so common in man/woman-on-trail narratives already discussed.

In another well-known song, "Hell Hound on My Trail," Johnson develops the man-on-trail theme with an emotional intensity that is shocking, though not uncharacteristic of his recorded performances.[3] The title phrase is repeated three chilling times at the end of the first stanza. It's a difficult stanza for the next three to follow, and they only elaborate on the horror of the first. With the hellhound, Johnson introduces an archetypal nemesis figure in his first stanza. On an obvious level the hellhound was a valid enough symbol for either oppression or just plain old garden-variety death. The third stanza introduces another (nonarchetypal) image—that of "hot foot powder" spread "around my door"—an image of the necessity of moving, ostensibly to stay ahead of death, which could take frightening forms for a young black traveling musician alone and on the move in the 1930s south. The form is lyric and not narrative, but some of the traditional pieces are in place, most notably the pursuit, which here is both mythic and horrific.

By contrast, the second and fourth stanzas work with images of inertness. In the second stanza, the song depicts a Christmas evening and day, idling away the hours with a lover. The fourth stanza depicts a rising wind rustling the leaves, suggesting the approach of something sinister. The portrait drawn in these two stanzas emerges, by contrast with the first and third, as that of persons disturbingly inert in the approach of danger. Having established the horrific pursuit, his stopping to enjoy a Christmas day and to spend idle time with a lover creates a tension, for one cannot imagine the hellhound stopping during its pursuit. The tension and instability, of course, match well with the social and personal conditions a man like Johnson, an itinerant musician, would have had to confront.

Canid Pursuers

As one cannot imagine the hellhound halting its pursuit, so it is hard to imagine the hyena halting its regular passage near Harry's camp on the east African plain, nor can the drunken and addicted William Campbell of Hemingway's "A Pursuit Race" imagine escape from the hallucinated wolf that has pursued him to his shabby hotel room: "Oh, yes. My dear wolf. Every time I take a drink he goes outside the room. He can't stand alcohol. The poor little fellow. . . . He's a lovely wolf. He's just like he always was" (201). Like Harry, William Campbell self-medicates with alcohol to keep at bay the existential dread embodied by the pursuing canid.

Feline predators, enabled by their expansive spines and preponderance of fast-twitch muscles, ambush their prey with dazzling rushes of speed. The rigid-spine canids, however, substitute a determined and prolonged pursuit enabled by their preponderance of slow-twitch muscles for the feline burst of speed. (In birds, slow-twitch muscles are popularly known as white meat and fast-twitch muscles as dark meat.) Usually in a pack, sometimes going on for days, the "dogged" pursuit of the canids finds metaphorical expression in the popular cliché. The relentlessness of canid pursuit makes the canid a fitting symbol for death, in Johnson's song, in Hemingway's story, and beyond

In this regard, an appropriate contrast to the hyena of "The Snows of Kilimanjaro" would naturally be the lion of Hemingway's "The Short Happy Life of Francis Macomber." The hyena "doggedly" passes Harry's camp every night as if waiting for the right moment to feast on the mortally ill Harry, earning his contempt: "That bastard crosses there every night. . . . Every night for two weeks" (14). The lion's final moments waiting in ambush are considerably more noble: "He could hear the men talking and he waited, gathering all of himself into this preparation for a charge as soon as the men would come into the grass. As he heard their voices his tail stiffened to twitch up and down, and, as they came to the edge of the grass, he made a coughing grunt and charged" (137). Actually, the description anticipates Robert Jordan's final moments, described in a similar fashion just a few years later in the final words of *For Whom the Bell Tolls.* Wilson, the safari guide, sums up his own respect, as well as Hemingway's, with his understated "Hell of a fine lion" (138).

Ancient man, living in proximity with predators, would have been aware of this difference and would have responded, marking the canids on the conscious, the unconscious, the cultural, and, finally, the collective unconscious levels. The wolf, the hyena, and the hellhound are all one in their roles as avatars of death; they are the primordial pursuers of humankind, haunting the collective unconscious, a remnant of memory from humankind's sojourn in the primeval savannahs and forests.

In Homer's *Iliad,* the worst threat a fighter can make against an opponent is not just that he will kill him but that he will kill him and feed his carcass to the wild and feral dogs that prowl the battlefield. Achilles makes such a threat to Hector at the end of their climactic single combat in book 22. In classical antiquity, proper burial was deemed necessary before a shade of the dead could enter Hades, the alternative being wandering alone through eternity, which was what being devoured by dogs represented.

In medieval song, the canids continue—in the minds, hearts, and poetry of mankind—the old pursuit begun in the forests of ancient times. The pursuing canid appears in, for example, Fenrir the mythic wolf of both the poetic and prose Eddas of medieval Scandinavia and in the beasts of battle (the raven, the eagle, and the wolf) of the oral-formulaic type scenes of Anglo-Saxon poetry.

In the Norse Eddic writings, Fenrir is a fearsome giant of a wolf, chained at an early age but also prophesied (to Odin in the *Voluspa* or *Prophesy of the Seeress,* the darkest and most profound of the Eddic poems) to be released at the time of *Ragnarök,* the Norse apocalypse. Like Jörmungandr, the Midgard serpent who fatally bites Thor just before Thor kills him, Fenrir engages in direct and immediate combat with Odin in the first clash of *Ragnarök,* eventually killing Odin, when he swallows the Allfather whole.

The regularity with which the beasts-of-battle oral-formulaic theme appears—even in the few remnants of Anglo-Saxon poetry that have survived the centuries—indicates (as in the Homeric poems) both the power and the ancient roots of this theme. Beginning with the most famous of Anglo-Saxon poems, *Beowulf:*

> *ac se wonna hrefn*
> *fus ofer fægum fela reordian,*
> *earne secgan hu him æt æte speow,*
> *þenden he wið wulf wæl reafode.* (3024b–27b)

> but the black raven
> ravenous over the fallen with much to say
> will tell the eagle how to the meal he hastened
> when with the wolf he gulped the [flesh of the] slain.

In another typical passage, the three beasts appear after battle scenes in "The Battle of Brunanburh":

> Many a carcass they left to be carrion,
> Many a livid one, many a sallow-skin—
> Left for the white-tail'd eagle to tear it, and
> Left for the horny-nibb'd raven to rend it, and
> Gave to the garbaging war-hawk to gorge it, and
> That gray beast, the wolf of the weald (translated by Tennyson, section 14.).

The theme appears in "Judith" twice (*Beowulf and Judith*, ll. 205b–212a and ll. 294–96); in "The Battle of Maldon," (mentioning only the raven and the eagle, ll. 106–107), though the Viking foes are described as "slaughterous wolves" (*wælwulfas*) (96); the "Finnsburgh" (64); "Genesis A," referencing only the raven; "Exodus"; and "Elene" referencing the raven, and later the eagle, raven, and wolf (Gordon 64, 98, 115, 212, 213). The theme appears most beautifully in "The Wanderer":

Sume wig fornom,
ferede in forðwege, sumne fugel oþbær
ofer heanne holm, sumne se hara wulf
deaðe gedælde, sumne dreorighleor
in eorðscræfe eorl gehydde. (80b–84)

War took away some,
Sent forth on [their] way, one a bird bore off
High over the sea, one the hoary wolf
Shared with death, one sad-faced
In an earthcave an earl concealed.

The sentiments of these characteristic passages are epic, even heroic in their descriptions of the deaths of both foes and comrades. Indeed, the birds that inevitably gathered on early medieval battlefields may well have been the genesis of the legends of the Valkyries who selected the most courageous from among the fallen to carry to Valhalla.

In "The Snows of Kilimanjaro," the vultures haunting the outskirts of Harry's camp and the hyena that passes by every evening nicely parallel the wolves and birds of medieval poetry. And in death, Harry, like the fallen heroes whom the Valkyries selected, rises through the air to what the Masai call the House of God. This house might well be Odin's great hall in Asgard.

Canids pursue elsewhere in Hemingway's work, as will be discussed later: the hallucinated wolf of "A Pursuit Race" and the sinister Russian battle police who pursue their victims "like hunting dogs" in "Under the Ridge" (146). Its emergence in such a diversified selection of poetry speaks to its origin in the collective unconscious and thus to Hemingway's access to the collective unconscious as well.

Comparison table 7: Novel and poem

Author	Harriet Beecher Stowe	Walt Whitman	Allen Ginsberg
Title	*Uncle Tom's Cabin,* chapters 8 and 9	"Song of Myself" 10 (ll. 189–98)	"Howl"
Host or hostess	Mary Byrd, mother, wife of Ohio state senator	The speaker, Whitman, emotionally if not literally	Ginsberg, in imagination
Other members of host's household	Notably her husband, Ohio state senator John Byrd, supporter of a state runaway-slave law	None	None (though ostensibly "the best minds of my generation" [20])
Man or woman on trail	Eliza, runaway slave, and her infant, Harry	"The runaway slave"	Carl Solomon, proto-beatnik, mental patient
Degree of acceptance by host or hostess	Total acceptance, at considerable risk to hostess	Total acceptance, with eating together signifying solidarity	Former fellow of the same psychiatric institution
Relationship of guest and host or hostess	Mother to mother	Abolitionist to runaway slave	Friend, kindred spirit
Elements of hospitality extended	Shelter, security, rest, food, clothing, transfer, and continuation of her journey	Bath, medical attention, food, clothing, rest, security, recuperation, continuation of his journey north	Emotional support and shelter
Parting gift(s)	Clothing	Clothing	Parting not described
Emphasized gift or element of hospitality	Clothing	"I had him sit next me at table" (31)	"in tears to the door of my cottage in the Western night"
Reason for pursuit	Runaway slave (and child who stands to be sold from mother)	Runaway slave	To enforce society-wide conformity
Pursuers	Slave catchers	Slave catchers	Moloch, representative of forces of oppression and conformity
Delay of pursuers	Illegal transfer of Eliza to a safe house	Reference to "my firelock lean'd in the corner" implies violent resistance (31)	–

Comparison table 8: Popular music

Author or artist	Robert Johnson	Robert Johnson	Townes Van Zandt	Bob Dylan
Title	“Come On in My Kitchen”	“Hell Hound on My Trail”	“Waitin’ Around to Die”	“Shelter from the Storm”
Host or hostess	The singer	A woman on trail and in trouble	Serial betrayers of hospitality	An unnamed “She”
Other members of household	None	None	Parents	None
Man or woman on trail	A woman in trouble	The singer	The singer	The singer
Degree of acceptance by host or hostess	Acceptance is offered but remains unclear	Acceptance freely offered	The guest is abandoned, robbed, incited to crime	Freely offered
Relationship of host to guest	Man to woman	Woman to man	Parents, lover, fellow thief	Woman to man
Elements of hospitality offered	Shelter, friendship, advice	Companionship	The numbness of addiction	shelter
Parting gift(s)	Parting not described	The respite of companionship	Parents, lover, fellow thief all take rather than give	He enters hunted like an animal and leaves in search of “beauty.”
Emphasized gift or element of hospitality	The shelter of the singer’s kitchen	A Christmas Eve celebration	The drug Codeine offers narcotic numbness	Emotional shelter
Reason for pursuit	“trouble”	Death pursues without reason	The posse pursues the singer for the robbery he has committed. Death pursues as a natural inevitability.	–
Pursuers	Societal rejection, An approaching storm:	A hound of Hell	Posse, Death	A hostile world
Delay of pursuers	Not included	Not possible	The numbness of addiction	Not included

Chapter 8

HOSPITALITY IN OTHER HEMINGWAY STORIES

> The religious myth is one of man's greatest and most significant achievements, giving him the security and inner strength not to be crushed by the monstrousness of the universe.
>
> —Carl Jung, *Symbols of Transformation*

Introduction: Places of Hospitality

Taken as a whole, Hemingway's body of work, not just "The Snows of Kilimanjaro," reveals a truly astonishing predilection toward settings in places of hospitality, hosts and hostesses, characters on trail, and often all of the above. Hemingway uses bars, brothels, cafés, campsites, churches, hospitals, hotels, inns, restaurants, and transportation stations and vehicles as settings so often that it ultimately becomes clear that these archetypes constitute the most recurrent lenses through which he viewed reality. In his 3 January 1930 letter to F. Scott Fitzgerald, apparently written in response to Fitzgerald's request for recommendations of places to stay, Hemingway casually mentions eleven different hotels in France and Spain for consideration (*Letters* 4:209). The listings that follow here are broad and exemplary in purpose and make no pretense of comprehensiveness. The goal is to give the reader examples that reveal the wide extent to which Hemingway incorporated these elements in work after work. Individual works in which these archetypes play a crucial role are afforded longer discussions.

In *In Our Time,* "The Battler" takes place at a campsite, at which the hospitality turns sinister, and "Soldier's Home" takes place at a home where the hospitality turns smothering. "Cat in the Rain" takes place entirely at a hotel, and "Out of Season" partially; the first sentence of each mentions the hotel, and the last sentence of each mentions the hotel's padrone. The two stories run consecutively, as well. "A Very Short Story" begins in a hospital. "Cross-Country Snow" ends in a welcoming alpine inn. "Big Two-Hearted River" takes place at the most emotionally healing campsite in the history of literature. Of the "interchapters" chapter 5 takes place outside a hospital; in chapter 6, the wounded Nick waits for aid outside a church, and chapter 7 ends in a brothel.

In *Men without Women,* "In Another Country" takes place in a hospital and rehabilitation center, and the narrator of "Now I Lay Me" mentions hospitalization in the last paragraph of the story. Cafes/bars/restaurants are primary settings for "Hills Like White Elephants," "The Killers," "An Alpine Idyll," and "Today Is Friday." A key scene of "Che Ti Dice La Patria" takes place in a brothel disguised as a restaurant, a fascist perversion of hospitality. "A Pursuit Race" takes place in a hotel.

In *Winner Take Nothing,* two stories, "God Rest You Merry, Gentlemen" and "The Gambler, the Nun, and the Radio," take place in hospitals. "After the Storm" begins in a bar, and "The Sea Change" takes place entirely in one, the Dingo Bar in Paris. "A Clean, Well-Lighted Place" and "Homage to Switzerland" take place in cafés.

Three of the Spanish Civil War stories are set partially or completely at Chicote's Bar. A fourth story, "Nobody Ever Dies," takes place in Cuba but is ostensibly a Spanish Civil War story because it concerns a veteran of the war returning home; its setting is a safe house for returning veterans.

Of the "two fables" (1951) "The Good Lion" ends in Venice at Harry's Bar. Of the "Two Tales of Darkness" (1957), "A Man of the World" takes place in two saloons in the northwestern United States, almost certainly Wyoming.

In *A Moveable Feast,* written during his last years, the title of the first sketch speaks for itself, "A Good Café on the Place St.-Michel." Sketch nine, "Ford Madox Ford and the Devil's Disciple," takes place over drinks at the Closerie des Lilas, as does his conversation with Evan Shipman in sketch fifteen, "Evan Shipman at the Lilas." "With Pascin at the Dôme," the eleventh sketch, takes place at the Café du Dôme. The first of three F. Scott Fitzgerald sketches, "Scott Fitzgerald," narrates Hemingway's first-ever meeting with Fitzgerald, which took place, once again, at the Dingo Bar in Paris. The third, "A Matter of Measurements," occurs at Michaud's restaurant in Paris. Of the sketches included in the restored edition (2009), "The Education of Mr. Bumby" takes place at various cafés at which Hemingway did his work while he took care of Bumby, his oldest son.

In Our Time

"On the Quai at Smyrna" depicts an entire people on trail, the refugees of the Greco-Turkish War, a connection between *In Our Time* and "The Snows of Kilimanjaro." Hemingway also wrote movingly of the same refugees in his journalism, notably "A Silent, Ghastly Procession" and "Refugees from Thrace," during his time with the *Toronto Star;* the latter includes Madame Marie, whose cynical attitude and lice-ridden hotel reveal the corruption of hospitality that the conflict inevitably brought about. "Indian Camp" is the first of several stories that depict Nick Adams on trail. Nick does go to an Ojibway hut in the story, but for him it is not a locus of hospitality and his purpose in going there is not to receive hospitality. He does not enter the story as a pursued man on trail, but by the story's climax he is confronted by the reality that death is the pursuer, though he manages to escape into denial at the story's end.

In "The Battler," Nick, especially after having been unceremoniously booted off a train by a nasty brakeman, is on trail, though he is not pursued and his destination is unclear. Having been cut and scraped in his fall, he needs the hospitality of the campfire of the punchy ex-prizefighter Ad Francis and his companion, Bugs. There he is offered a seat by the fire, conversation, advice, and a ham and egg sandwich. Unfortunately for Nick, the host is demented, his companion has a quietly disturbing quality, and their hospitality goes sour.

The man on trail appears also in "The Revolutionist," included in both *in our time* and *In Our Time.* Like Nick Adams in "The Battler," the revolutionist is wounded on his journey: "Horthy's men had done some bad things to him."[1] As hospitality goes bad for Nick in "The Battler," the trail goes bad for the revolutionist, ending in jail.

Another campsite figures as a major feature of "Big Two-Hearted River." Nick makes his own fire and builds his own place to sleep when he pitches his tent. When he returns wounded from the war, his therapy is to establish his own, albeit temporary, place of hospitality: "He was there, in the good place. He was in his home where he had made it" (186–87). He then cooks his own meal of canned spaghetti, beans, and bread. Eating the meal constitutes a rite of passage, in this case a rite of incorporation with the wilderness and its healing powers.

The hospitality that Nick established for himself makes him a notable contrast with the less fortunate Harold Krebs of "Soldier's Home," who cannot find the hospitality he needs even in the home he has returned to after the war. The food highlights the contrasts. Remarkably, and against all culinary probability, Hemingway contrives to make the canned spaghetti and canned baked beans, appallingly (from a culinary standpoint) mixed together in the same frying pan, sound delicious. Poor Harold, on the other hand, must listen to his mother's inanities as he watches the bacon fat harden on his plate. All Harold can do is to leave his home, where his parents' hospitality has failed him, just as Nick must leave the sinister hospitality offered Ad and Bugs's campsite in "The Battler."

"A Very Short Story" begins in a hospital—most certainly and by definition a place of hospitality. When the unnamed main character leaves the hospital, his romance with Luz ends. As mentioned, "In Another Country" from *Men without Women,* and "God Rest You Merry, Gentlemen" and "The Gambler, the Nun, and the Radio" from *Winner Take Nothing* also take place in hospitals, and, as Hemingway was not a writer to repeat himself, each story approaches the hospitality offered by its hospital in a different way. "Great News from the Mainland," first published in 1987, is structured around telephone calls between a son in a hospital and his doctor to the father at home.

Hotels also appear regularly in the short stories. Both "Cat in the Rain" and "Out of Season" mention—in their opening sentences, no less—the hotels at which the plots take place. The final sentence of each mentions the padrones of the respective hotels, framing and thus emphasizing the hospitality themes. "Cat in the Rain" tells of a wife whose husband neglects her emotional needs. The padrone recognizes her need, expressed only as a longing for a cat. A true and caring host, he has a cat delivered to her room.

"Cross-Country Snow" begins and ends with Nick Adams and his companion, George, skiing in the Swiss Alps, but the bulk of the story takes place at a warm and welcoming Alpine inn: "They stacked the skis against the side of the inn and slapped the snow off each other's trousers. . . . A big porcelain stove shone in the corner of the room. There was a low ceiling. Smooth benches back of dark, wine-stained tables were along each side of the rooms" (142). The reference to the porcelain stove would be echoed years later in the Gauertal incident of "The Snows of Kilimanjaro," and the description of arriving at the inn would be echoed in **IM I.7**: "Knocking your bindings loose, kicking the skis free and leaning them up against the wooden wall of the inn, the lamplight coming from the window, where inside, in the smoky, new-wine smelling warmth, they were playing the accordion" (8). Hospitality is extended immediately, and the waitress brings them wine.

Two Novels

THE SUN ALSO RISES

In *The Sun Also Rises*, Jake Barnes's problem is that his war wound has rendered him incapable of intercourse while leaving him with an unreduced level of sexual desire. This emerges early in the narrative. Though no scenes in the novel take place in a hospital, the backstory reveals Jake's initial meeting with Brett. They meet when he is hospitalized for his war wounds. In Paris, prior to their travel to the festival in Pamplona and before Robert Cohn's brief affair with Brett, Jake reveals to Cohn that Brett "was a V. A. D. in a hospital I was in during the war" (38). "V. A. D." refers to Voluntary Aid Detachment, hospital volunteers not associated with the military. The number of watering holes visited and the amount of alcohol consumed by the characters of *The Sun Also Rises* reaches epic proportions. Montoya, the proprietor of the Hotel Montoya and an aficionado of the corrida, plays the most important role for a provider of hospitality in the novel. In introducing Brett to a young matador, Jake sacrifices his friendship with Montoya, betraying his host by potentially damaging the matador's promising career, involving him in a relationship with a dangerous woman.

Further, the number of scenes in the novel that take place in watering holes reveals a group of characters in search of hospitality at what must be more than a simple social level. A full analysis of the role of hospitality in the novel must wait for another day. What follows is merely a sampling of the locations of hospitality in book 1, which includes only chapters 1 through 7, pages 1 through 53. Scenes take place at the Café de Versailles (5), the café on the ground floor of the building housing Jake's office (9), the Café Napolitain (11), Lavigne's Restaurant where Jake has dinner with Georgette (14), the bal musette where Jake leaves Georgette and meets Brett (16), the bar next door (20), Café Select (23, 45), Vetzel's [Wetzel's] Restaurant (31), Café de la Paix (33), Hotel Crillon (34), the Closerie des Lilas (37–38), and Café Dôme (38). Also mentioned are the Dingo bar (30) and the New York Bar (35). A comprehensive study of these establishments and those that are mentioned or that play key roles in books 2 and 3, as well as the providers of hospitality associated with each—bartenders, padrones, concierges, et cetera—would seem a fruitful topic of inquiry and might reveal aspects of the novel heretofore unnoticed.

A FAREWELL TO ARMS

Somewhat more famously, Frederic Henry and Catherine Barkley of *A Farewell to Arms* meet in the same fashion. Indeed, little of this novel would remain if scenes in barracks, cafés, brothels, hospitals, restaurants, and hotels were deleted.

The novel's opening line describes the house where the ambulance drivers lived. Two of Henry's companions there, especially the priest and Lieutenant Rinaldi, form a loose but sometimes functional family for him. By chapter 4, he meets Catherine Barkley, an English nurse—a professional provider of hospitality—and soon falls in love with her. In chapter 9 he is seriously wounded. In chapter 10 Rinaldi visits him in a field hospital, and in chapter 11, the priest visits, as family members might.

He is transferred to a hospital in Milan at the beginning of book two, (chapters 13–24). Catherine appears in chapter 14, and by the end of the book their love reaches existential profundity, each looking at the two of them as one, similar to the love of Catherine Earnshaw and Heathcliff of Emily Brontë's *Wuthering Heights.* In chapter 23, just before Frederic returns to the front, he and Catherine check into a hotel. Catherine reacts negatively to the hotel's distortion of hospitality, its overwrought décor making her feel like a whore.

In book 3 (chapters 25–32), Frederic returns to the front and gets caught up in the disastrous Italian retreat from Caporetto. A brothel, relocated from one town to another, is one of the few images or places of hospitality developed in this section, but there are rites of passage appropriate to the man on trail. Before leaving for the front, Frederic speaks with Rinaldi and the priest for the last time; when he leaves, he leaves behind the two extremes of living these two men represent: the sensuality of Rinaldi and the asceticism of the priest. His departure thus constitutes a rite of separation, which always involves leaving something behind. The second, the incident of the carabinieri at the bridge, is a rite of transformation. They are battle police, the Inspector Javerts of the army. Witnessing their seemingly righteous, but actually random, unjust, and sanctimonious search for candidates for execution, Frederic experiences a moment of epiphany. The hideous randomness of the executions, as well as other meaningless deaths he has seen, convinces him that the war can no longer provide meaning for him, for, in Jungian terms, the war and the "monstrousness of the universe" have conspired to drain the war's deaths of significance. He escapes the execution squad by diving into the Tagliamento River, his immersion in and emergence from the water represent symbolic rebirth, as we all float in amniotic fluid prior to birth and thus emerge from the water at birth. A fugitive, Frederic becomes a man on trail, pursued by battle police and local police. His full intent is to find Catherine and build a meaning for his life with her.

In book 4 (chapters 33–37), Frederic searches for Catherine. Man-on-trail (actually couple-on-trail) images and traditions predominate. Chapter 33 introduces two helper figures. Aid appears almost magically to the hero on trail; arriving by train in Milan, Frederic immediately enters a wine shop run by a friendly proprietor—with whom he shares drinks, another rite of incorporation, and receives good advice. He also eats there, having bread and coffee. From there he goes to the apartment of an acquaintance named Simmons, who supplies him with civilian clothing, another rite of incorporation. From Simmons he receives detailed advice on making the passage to Switzerland.

In chapter 34 he takes the train to Stresa and arrives at the hotel where he expects to meet Catherine. He wears his newly acquired civilian clothes, symbolic of his incorporation into a civilized setting. He goes to the bar and eats and drinks much more heartily, partaking of snacks, sandwiches, and drinks, again symbolic of incorporation, and he becomes friendly with Emilio the bartender. Emilio, another mythic helper figure, later provides them with the boat they need to make the long row to safety in Switzerland.

Later, after Catherine's arrival, he meets the elderly Count Greffi, bonding through a game of billiards and sharing drinks. From the count he receives both practical and philosophical advice. That night, sharing a bed with Catherine, he recounts, "[W]e were never lonely and never afraid when we were together" (216). Their finding of their own identities and purposes in each other reveals the existential quality of their love. The idea is developed extensively and in their stay at the Stresa hotel, most significantly validated by the wisdom of the count, who speaks with Frederic for the last time at the end of chapter 35:

> "Maybe it is too late. Perhaps I have outlived my religious feeling." [said the Count.]
>
> "Mine comes only at night."
>
> "Then too you are in love. Do not forget that is a religious feeling."
>
> "You believe so?"
>
> "Of course." (227)

Or, in terms Lady Brett Ashley might have used, it's what people have in place of religious feeling.

Finally, the element of pursuit enters the story, as Emilio the bartender knocks on their door at night and informs Frederic that he is to be arrested in the morning. Emilio informs him that he should escape to Switzerland by rowing up Lake Maggiore. He carries their bags to the boat and provides a can for bailing, sandwiches, bottles of brandy and wine, and an umbrella to protect Catherine from the stormy night.

The food, libation, advice, clothing, and means of flight from his pursuers that Frederic and then Frederic and Catherine receive at the hotel and during Frederic's journey to Stresa parallel the hospitality Jack Westondale is given when he arrives at the cabin of Malemute Kid. The parallels, though more elaborated in *A Farewell to Arms,* are truly remarkable, raising once again the question of whether Hemingway was influenced by cultural conditions or Jack London, or whether he intuitively responded to images from the collective unconscious, or somehow responded to two or even all three of those possible sources.

After the grueling nighttime row up the lake—the storm representing a rite of passage, they immediately go to a café for breakfast. After their arrest, they are released as tourists. Then they find a place to stay, with *hotel* being the final word of book 4.

In the second sentence of book 5, Hemingway establishes the house that they find to live in. This parallels the first sentences of book 1, which establishes the house he lived in. (The first paragraph of *Islands in the Stream* similarly establishes a house.) After they settle in, they continue trying to become the same person. Catherine wishes she could have gonorrhea because Frederic had it previously. She asks him to grow his hair long so that their hair styles, if not colors, would be similar and also offers to cut hers short. "Then we'd both be alike. Oh, darling, I want you so much I want to be you too" (257). This is a serious philosophical reaction to the human condition, not merely lovers' prattle. All too often, critical commentary on such passages does not go beyond Hemingway's alleged "hair fetishism." The real purpose here is another very persistent Hemingway theme: becoming one with one's beloved as the only meaningful response to the chaos and the inherent lack of any discernible a priori meaning in life, with only the meaning and identity one creates for one's self having any existential value. The point is driven home repeatedly:

> "Why, darling, I don't live at all when I'm not with you"
>
> "I won't ever go away," I said. "I'm no good when you're not there. I haven't any life at all any more." (258)

Book 5 concludes with one of the most famous references to a place of hospitality in literature. A good portion of the final book takes place in another place of hospitality, the hospital in which Catherine dies in childbirth. Death catches up in peace as well as in war. After an unsatisfying goodbye, Frederic returns to a place of hospitality, ending the novel with two hospitality references in the famous final sentence: the hospital and the hotel.

Men without Women

"HILLS LIKE WHITE ELEPHANTS"

In *Men without Women,* Hemingway's second collection of short stories, "Hills Like White Elephants" depicts a man and woman at a crucial juncture of their life on trail together, though they are not pursued. Fittingly, they are at an isolated train station, and most of the story takes place at a table outside the station's bar.

"THE KILLERS"

"The Killers" takes place first at a restaurant, then at a boardinghouse, with Max and Al, two hired killers, violating the hospitality and friendly atmosphere of Henry's lunchroom. Mrs. Hirsch's rooming house, where Nick warns Ole Andreson that Max and Al plan to kill him, proves to be an ineffective sanctuary. Andreson, knowing that he will not be safe and that his death is almost inevitable, has given up and is simply "waitin' round to die." When Nick sees him, he is in his bed; Hemingway mentions twice that he was looking "at the wall" (92), once that he was "talking toward the wall" (93), and finally that he "rolled over toward the wall" (93). He is both literally and figuratively up against the wall. At the story's end, Nick reveals to George the counterman how he feels about what he has seen: "I can't stand to think about him waiting in the room and knowing he's going to get it. It's too damned awful" (96). Nick cannot deal with the situation because it takes him back to a nightmare situation he has been in before. In "Indian Camp" the action of another suicidal man, also literally and figuratively up against the wall, is described by Hemingway in nearly identical language, emphasized by presenting the sentence as the entire paragraph: "The husband in the upper bunk rolled over against the wall" (17). For the husband at least, the hut should have been a place of comfort and hospitality, but it is not, as he commits suicide during the childbirth taking place in the bunk below him.

Another compelling episode of *In Our Time,* "Chapter 5," includes a place of hospitality and men both literally and figuratively against a wall: "*They shot the cabinet ministers at half-past six in the morning against the wall of a hospital*" (63). Hospitality there is out of joint and perverted. It is also not quite right in "The Killers," where the designated providers of hospitality—equivalent in their professional roles to the padrones of "Cat in the Rain" and "Out of Season"—are not to be found. "Henry's had been made over from a saloon into a lunch-counter" (83), and Henry never appears, just as Mrs. Hirsch, who owns the rooming house never appears; Nick, thinking he is talking to her, discovers that he is actually talking to Mrs. Bell, who runs it for her. Similarly, the shutters of the hospital in "Chapter 5" are "*nailed shut*" (63). Hospitals are intended to be open and welcoming spaces to the sick and injured, not settings for executions.

"A PURSUIT RACE"

"A Pursuit Race," another tale from *Men without Women,* includes the man-on-trail archetype and also bears other similarities to "The Snows of Kilimanjaro." William Campbell, the advance man for a burlesque show, has a job whose main requirement is to stay ahead of the show as it progresses around the country. The narrator uses the bicycle pursuit metaphor to describe Campbell's predicament, and Campbell uses the metaphor himself. Most games have the idea of death built into them; when baseball began, for example, baserunners tagged or forced were said to be *dead,* rather than the current *out.* Double plays are still referred to as *twin killings.* Similarly, in bicycle pursuit races a rider who is passed is thereby eliminated. When the show catches up with Campbell in Kansas City, he loses his job and thus his pay. When Mr. Turner, the show's manager, visits him in his hotel room, Campbell refuses to come out from under the sheet on his bed, mentioning the sheet an ominous thirteen times. A junkie and an alcoholic, Campbell may soon have death catch up with him. The sheet takes on the quality of the burial shroud under which he may soon find his final rest. Turner, who is "very fond" of Campbell, tries to convince him to seek treatment for his addictions, but—like Harry, who similarly dismisses Helen's ministrations and advice—he simply keeps drinking (204). And like Harry, he is haunted by a canine. The wolf—whom he deludes himself into thinking is forced out of the room every time he takes a drink—prefigures Harry's hyena. Like Ole Andreson from earlier in *Men without Women* and Harry yet to come, he has had to stop on trail. In all three cases, it is death who has been the pursuer. It is death who always pursues the man on trail, and in all three of these cases death catches up.

Winner Take Nothing

Winner Take Nothing deals extensively with the hospitality and man-on-trail archetypes. In addition, key selections, most notably "A Clean Well-Lighted Place" and "The Gambler, the Nun, and the Radio," address the issue of the *Nada*, Hemingway's term for cosmic nothingness.

The first words of "After the Storm," the first story in the collection, set an existential tone: "It wasn't about anything" (3). In short, it was about nothing. The nothing that it is about is not plain old *Seinfeld*ian nothing, but a bigger, more sinister nothing. The protagonist narrator of "After the Storm," who sounds much like Harry Morgan of *To Have and Have Not*, gets into a bar fight, knifes his assailant, and is then pursued into the night by the assailant's friends, putting him on trail. He escapes out to sea in his boat, finds a newly sunken liner before any of the other salvagers are able to put out to sea, but manages to salvage from it exactly nothing, a fitting metaphor for life's journeys and endeavors.

"A CLEAN, WELL-LIGHTED PLACE"

"A Clean, Well-Lighted Place" makes one of Hemingway's most profound statements on hospitality at the existential level. It qualifies as a hospitality story in no uncertain terms, as it includes so many of the key elements: the provider of hospitality (the older waiter), the person who argues against hospitality (the younger waiter, who wants the old man to go home so he can close up for the evening), the dedicated place of hospitality (the clean, well-lighted café), and the guest (the old man who has recently failed in a suicide attempt). Elements of the man-on-trail plot, touched on more lightly, also play their parts in the story: the man on trail (the old man); death, the pursuer (in two forms: literally in the old man's suicide attempt, and figuratively in the guard that passes by, reminiscent of the "two bicycle policemen" whom Harry associates with death in his final words in "The Snows of Kilimanjaro" [25]). Of course, the *Nada*, which plays a bigger role in "A Clean, Well-Lighted Place" than in any other Hemingway story, also makes its presence strongly felt in "The Snows of Kilimanjaro," as will be discussed later.

On the topic of religion, Carl Jung wrote one of the most profound underhanded compliments of all time: "The religious myth is one of man's greatest and most significant achievements, giving him the security and inner strength not to be crushed by the monstrousness of the universe," a compliment in that it praises religion, underhanded in that it categorizes it both as "myth" and as an achievement of humankind, as opposed to the construct of an ostensible deity (*Symbols* 231). "A Clean, Well-Lighted Place" tells the story of two men who have lost that security and inner strength in the face of the monstrousness of the universe, represented in the story as *nada*. The waiters' conversation about the old man brings in the idea of existential despair in the first passage of dialogue:

> "Last week he tried to commit suicide," one waiter said.
> "Why?"
> "He was in despair."
> "What about?"
> "Nothing." (17)

The "nothing" in this case is existential despair. The old man has no solution but to drink, though he strives, as anyone must, to retain his dignity. The younger of the two waiters, a married man, says (albeit in reference to the older waiter's joke regarding the faithfulness of the younger man's wife), "I have confidence. I have all confidence" (22). It is the older waiter who, like the old man, wrestles with his despair and lacks confidence in the benignity of the universe. He stops for a drink on the way home and recites to himself the Lord's Prayer and part of the Hail Mary, but substituting *nada* for most of the key words. He does not regard himself as a child of the universe. He cannot sleep without a light, and he wonders at the cause of his despair. Ironically and sadly, he does not realize that in his vocation as a provider of hospitality he has found and actually practices the solution to existential dread. He provides a clean, well-lighted place for those whom he clearly perceives badly need it. His café parallels the Good Place where Nick Adams camps beside the Big Two-Hearted River. The older waiter thus establishes a purpose and therefore a meaning for his life on the existential level.

In fewer than five pages, Hemingway dramatizes life's most significant problem, existential dread—the difficulty of establishing a purpose and identity in defiance of the monstrousness of the universe and in the absence of the a priori purpose and identity that religious myth increasingly fails to supply—and also dramatizes the solution to it, the creation of a personal metaphorical clean, well-lighted place for one's self and for others. In that regard, critical response to this story as gloomy never fails to appall, for it remains one of the most life-affirming and liberating texts ever written.

"The Sea Change," a transformation story, takes place at the Dingo Bar in Paris, according to Charles Oliver ("Dingo Bar") with the bartender playing a key role in validating the transformation that the protagonist feels has taken place within himself. Each of the three sections of "Homage to Switzerland" takes place in a station café along the route of the Simplon–Orient Express—which is where the reader first meets Harry in **IM 1.1** of "The Snows of Kilimanjaro."

As "The Light of the World" begins, when Nick and his friend Tom enter the bar, the bartender covers up the free-lunch bowls, thus denying hospitality. From that locus of denied welcome, the plot moves to a transit point, a train station.

"WINE OF WYOMING"

"Wine of Wyoming," while not a man-on-trail story, clearly merits discussion as a hospitality story. It may be seen as Jamesean, in that it contrasts European traditions with American prohibitions (and Prohibition). The Fontans, a French couple who have immigrated to Wyoming, personify ancient hospitality traditions. During the depths of the prohibition era, they make their own beer and wine and are pestered by various ugly American types who perpetrate various gaucheries upon their hospitality: pestering them for beer and wine, vomiting at their table, and spiking their beer with whiskey. In addition, the government stiffly fines the Fontans for engaging in the ancient tradition of making beer and wine.

Carlos Baker reports that the Fontans were based on a couple Ernest visited in Sheridan, Wyoming, while on a hunting trip in 1928 (*A Life Story* 196). Joseph Flora has argued convincingly that the story's narrator is Nick Adams, and he will be referred to as such (*Hemingway's Nick Adams* 223–24). Nick's sensitivity to and appreciation of the Fontans' hospitality leads to the story's emotional climax. The tale's themes of marriage and politics have been discussed by several critics. These are clearly secondary issues, however; the story's real impact on the reader in its treatment of the guest-host dynamic, especially in the fourth and final section, requires more discussion as it constitutes the emotional heart of the story.

Put simply, forces outside their control conspire to prevent both guest and host from fulfilling their proper roles. In part 1 of four (Hemingway did not number the parts), Nick, the story's guest and narrator, drinks a beer and converses with Madame Fontan on her porch about American restaurant and hotel food and about her daughter in law, who does not prepare dinner for her husband when he comes home from work. A couple of drunks who drive up in search of beer interrupt them. Madame Fontan invites Nick to dinner. Like the café of "A Clean, Well-Lighted Place" Madame Fontan's "house was very clean and neat" (159).

That evening, Nick and his wife have dinner with the Fontans in their dining room. The Fontans' role is similar to that of the older waiter of "A Clean, Well-Lighted Place." Both the older waiter and the Fontans offer cleanliness, order, and heartfelt hospitality. The only time Nick actually drinks the Fontans' wine is during this occasion: "We ate in the dining-room and there was a clean tablecloth. We tried the new wine. It was very light and clear and good, and still tasted of the grapes" (161). The pristine sentences reflect the pristine room.

In part 3, the next afternoon, Nick escapes the heat by sharing beer and conversation on the back porch first with Madame and then with Madame and Monsieur Fontan. Madame is described once again as clean: "She looked like Mrs. Santa Claus, clean and rosy-faced and white-haired" (171). Her wholesomeness is a stark contrast to the guests she tells Nick about. She confesses to locking the door when they showed up a second time. Fontan refers to them, "delicately, hesitatingly" as "cochon," swine (175–76). They invite Nick to dinner, and he promises to return the next night, the last night before he must leave. Fontan promises to have more wine.

The next afternoon, after a long day of hunting, Nick stops at the Fontans' home for a beer and leaves Madame the gift of a couple of game birds he had shot that day. He agrees again to return with his wife that evening for dinner and wine, but as in all tragedies, malignant fate intervenes, in this case, in the form of the many duties that must seen to in preparation for leaving, in the form of a cut tire, of telegrams to be sent, and of Fontan's love of his own wine. The next day, Nick and his wife pack, leave their hotel, and drive to the Fontans' home to say their goodbyes.

When they arrive, Fontan's first reaction is to tell Madame to get some wine. She reminds him that he has drunk it all: "Fontan looked very upset" (181). Fontan insists on going to the house of a neighbor who has bought some of his wine, and Nick offers to drive him. The house is locked, but when he looks in, Nick notices its kitchen is "dirty and sloppy," a contrast to the Fontans' clean, well-lighted place. Fontan, in desperation, attempts to dig under the wall of the house to retrieve the wine, but Nick politely dissuades him. On the way home, "[h]e was incoherent and crushed" (183). Arriving back at their home, "[a]ll the happiness went from Madame Fontan's face" (183). As Nick says goodbye, "Fontan shook his head. He was disgraced. Madame Fontan looked sad" (184). Later, Nick tactfully asks them to drink some for him and his wife: "Fontan shook his head. He did not smile. He knew when he was ruined" (184). Hemingway was, indeed, the master of the simple declarative sentence. All of the story's conversation and action lead up to this emotional climax, driven home by the force of this series of simple sentences. The host feels disgraced; in his visceral reaction to failing to have wine for his guests, as well as in his placing ancient tradition over current laws, Fontan is reminiscent of Mateo Falcone.

What it all adds up to is a condemnation of one of America's most ridiculous and disastrous of its many exercises in sanctimony: prohibition, the root cause of the emotional devastation of both couples. But the story is not about the Eighteenth Amendment. It is about an all-too-human reaction to the crushing of an ancient tradition of hospitality. Hemingway does not even indicate who the speakers are as Nick and his wife drive away, for they both feel the same way:

> "They felt so badly. Fontan felt terribly."
> "We ought to have gone last night."
> "Yes, we ought to have." (185)

The real crime is the sanctimonious repression of tradition. Earlier in the story, when Madame tells Nick about Fontan's arrest, he responds with simple sentences: "'He's a good man,' I said, 'It's a crime." Similarly, regarding the crippling $755 fine, he replies: "It's wicked" (172). The arrest was indeed a crime, and the fine was indeed wicked. As examination of the archetypes of hospitality has shown, the roots of humankind's emotions and intuitions run deeper than loyalty to the law.

"THE GAMBLER, THE NUN, AND THE RADIO"

Mr. Frazier, the writer protagonist of "The Gambler, the Nun, and the Radio," suffers from much the same malady as the older waiter of "A Clean, Well-Lighted Place": existential dread. Unlike the waiter, however, he finds himself trapped in a place of hospitality, in this case a hospital, rather than creating one. He cannot leave the hospital until his badly broken leg heals and is thus trapped by his need for hospitality; so he must cope with his own thoughts in much the same way as Nick Adams of "Now I Lay Me." Speaking with the gambler and the nun and listening all night to the radio enable him to keep his tenuous grip on sanity in the face of the monstrousness of the universe. At the end of "A Clean, Well-Lighted Place," the older waiter generalizes his dread through his thought that "[m]any must have it" (24) Similarly, Mr. Frazier runs through the various "opiums of the people," the ideas and activities humanity would rather drug itself with rather than confront the *Nada:* Religion, of course, has the first claim but is closely followed by music, economics, patriotism, sexual intercourse, drink, the radio, gambling, ambition, belief in any new form of government, and bread (218–20).

Providers of Hospitality

Providers of hospitality, often in an official capacity, figure regularly in Hemingway novels and stories, and a review here is necessary. The hotelkeeper is the thoughtful hero of "Cat in the Rain," sending a cat for the American woman when she most needs it. Montoya, proprietor of the Hotel Montoya, plays an important role in *The Sun Also Rises.* The injuries Pedro Romero, the bullfighter, suffers at the hands of Jake Barnes's companions Brett Ashley and Robert Cohn create a permanent rift between the host (Montoya) and the guest (Jake).

Several innkeepers, wait staffers, and bartenders are featured in *Men without Women.* It is George the counterman in "The Killers" who must deal with the two hit men, who helps Nick Adams in processing the whole episode, and who gives Nick the key advice in the story's closing line: avoid thinking about the whole horrible experience. Ole Andreson's pursuers—dressed almost comically in similar "uniforms"—may be seen as the uniformed authority who have pursued Hemingway's characters as well as those of so many other writers. In "Che Ti Dice La Patria?" the two travelers in Italy find that fascism has perverted the traditions of hospitality so much that women who appear at first glance to be waitresses are really prostitutes. In "Ten Indians," Dr. Adams, after breaking the news to Nick that his girlfriend, Prudie, is enjoying the company of another young man, takes on the unofficial role of hospitality provider, serving Nick the memorable meal of cold chicken, milk, and huckleberry pie. In "An Alpine Idyll" it is the innkeeper, having been invited to share a drink with the narrator and his companion John, who engages his guests in storytelling, a significant element of hospitality, typically a rite of incorporation.

"Today Is Friday," in the form of a one-act play, is set in a drinking place peopled by a squad of Roman soldiers who have participated in the crucifixion and a Hebrew wine-seller who, improbably, shares the name "George" with the counterman of "The Killers." Another George also provides hospitality: as bartender at the Crillon in Paris in *The Sun Also Rises,* he mixes a Jack Rose cocktail for Jake Barnes and several for Bill Gorton (34, 60). Harry and Helen also stayed at the Crillon (8). Philip Greene points out that David and Catherine of *The Garden of Eden* first meet in the bar of the Crillon and that in *A Moveable Feast* Hemingway admitted that he too drank at the Crillon (134–35). Praising Pedro Chicote, the proprietor of Chicote's—the bar at which several of Hemingway's Spanish Civil War stories are set—the narrator compares him to George, a chasseur of the Ritz of Paris, a hotel and bar Hemingway regarded as among the most hospitable ("The Denunciation" 89).

In *A Farewell to Arms,* after escaping the chaos of World War I Italy, Frederic Henry and Catherine Barkley flee to Switzerland. There order and hospitality are summed up in a single truly classic sentence: "They arrested us after breakfast" (240). A meal is not to be interrupted in a civilized, hospitable country; the reader will recall that in Italy during the war Frederic Henry and his companions are hit by a shell while they share a meal of cold spaghetti noodles and cheese (47).

"The Short Happy Life of Francis Macomber" is very much a companion piece to "The Snows of Kilimanjaro."[2] Wilson, the Macombers' safari guide, thinks of the phrase "[s]till drinking their whisky," code language among the guides for indicating that a safari had gone bad (125). Drinking the client/host's whiskey was merely the formality of hospitality that must be observed to save face when the host/client and guide/guest relationship was irretrievably broken, though the safari might not be over.

Stories of the Spanish Civil War

Hemingway's lesser known writings about the Spanish Civil War treat the hospitality and man-on-trail themes thoroughly, perhaps even comprehensively. His Spanish Civil War play, *The Fifth Column,* takes place largely in a hotel, Madrid's Hotel Florida.

In the short stories, the violation of hospitality by guests and hosts and the intrusion of death by uniformed authority mirrors war's breakdown of civilized behavior. Three of the four stories take place all or in large part in an elegant Madrid bar still known today as Chicote's. "Night before Battle" takes place partly there and partly in a notably lesser restaurant across the street. "The Denunciation" and "The Butterfly and the Tank," however, both depict the degradation of civilized behavior—embodied in the corruption of hospitality—brought about by the civil war—and, by extension, war generally. In "Under the Ridge" murderous uniformed authority pursues two men, one clearly a man on trail. All four stories are in the narrative voice of Henry Emmunds / Edwin Henry, an American writer making a film about the war in order to raise money to buy ambulances for the royalist/republican cause in the war.[3] On an obvious level, he is a fairly naked alter ego for Hemingway, as both Martin Light and Allen Josephs clearly establish and analyze. On a less obvious level, Henry is the formal name for Harry, Hemingway's protagonists in both "The Snows of Kilimanjaro" and *To Have and Have Not.*

An overall review of Hemingway's uses of the name Harry reveals even more than his perhaps even more famous use of variants of George/Georges/Georgette/Georgetti—of which Charles Oliver lists thirteen, several associated directly or indirectly with hospitality. The use of Harry/Henry—along with variants such as "Harold," "Harris," "Harrison," or "Enrique"—begins early enough in Hemingway's body of work, with Henry Adams, Nick Adams's father. More of Hemingway himself, returned from World War I, appears in Harold Krebs of "Soldier's Home," the sour hospitality of which has already been noted. Wilson-Harris is an English fly fisherman Jake Barnes and Bill Gorton meet and like very much during their fishing trip in *The Sun Also Rises.* Even more so than Harold Krebs, much of Hemingway himself appears in his portrait of Frederic Henry, the narrator of *A Farewell to Arms.* Some have suggested that Hemingway borrowed the name from Stephen Crane's protagonist from *The Red Badge of Courage,* Henry Fleming. The story of Frederic Henry, as the title *A Farewell to Arms* clearly suggests, takes him away from commitment to war and political causes, which for him have gone murderously bad. At that point in his career, Hemingway seemed to retreat into writing about hunting, bullfighting, fishing, and sports. As world crisis began to come to a disturbing head in the late 1930s, Hemingway started to feel the pressure for social commitment. As Keneth Kinnamon aptly concludes in his biographical study, "Placed in the context of Hemingway's literary career in the 1930s, 'The Snows of Kilimanjaro' is not only his greatest artistic achievement since *A Farewell to Arms* but a key transitional point between the disengagement of *Death in the Afternoon* . . . and *Green Hills of Africa* on the one hand and the commitment of *To Have and Have Not* . . . , *The Spanish Earth, The Fifth Column,* and *For Whom the Bell Tolls* on the other" (289). Not surprisingly, Hemingway choose "Harry" as the name for the protagonist who represented his awareness of the transition that he—Hemingway had to make. Granted, Captain Henry Morgan, pirate of some historical note, made for an appropriate moniker for Hemingway's fictional hero, the fishing-guide-for-hire Harry Morgan. Further, the first two Harry Morgan stories, "One

Trip Across" (*Cosmopolitan,* April 1934) and "The Tradesman's Return" (*Esquire,* February 1936), which make up the first third of *To Have and Have Not,* were published prior to the first publication of "The Snows of Kilimanjaro" (*Esquire,* August 1936), indicating his already shifting commitment to addressing the issues of social classes as well as those of individuals.

"THE DENUNCIATION"

In "The Denunciation" a guest with some characteristics of the man on trail is denounced to uniformed authority and to the death implied thereby. Enjoying the drinks that due to war-related shortages can only be had at Chicote's, Henry Emmunds notices Luis Delgado, an old gambling acquaintance (another connection to Harry of the "The Snows of Kilimanjaro," as indicated in Harry's thoughts on gambling in **IM I.4**) who is now on the side of the Franco's fascists. Henry establishes early in the narrative that "you didn't talk politics at Chicote's" (89). The war has changed all that, and even the waiters have become political. When Henry happens to mention that Delgado is with the fascists, one of the waiters becomes determined to denounce him to the government authorities. Henry tells him how that might be done, though he soon feels guilty for doing so: "But I had given him the shortest cut to having Delgado arrested in one of those excesses of impartiality, righteousness and Pontius Pilatry, and the always-dirty desire to see how people act under an emotional conflict, that makes writers such attractive friends" (97). As Henry leaves, authority, in the form of two plain clothesmen (plain as Max and Al, if those two hitmen are recognizable as plainclothesmen) and "[s]ix with submachineguns," arrives to make the arrest (98). The violation of hospitality feels similar to Barker's slaughter of the Austrian officers' leave train or the betrayal of "Brother Edouard" in Harold Frederic's "Brother Sebastian's Friendship." "All we old clients of Chicote's had a sort of feeling about the place. I knew that was why Luis Delgado had been such a fool to go back there" (100). Delgado, whom Henry refers to as a "fool" five times and "crazy" one time, is betrayed at a place of hospitality where the bond of drinking occurs. He is betrayed by an agent of hospitality, a waiter whose power, because of the intrigues of war, has been unduly inflated. Later, Henry's guilt leads him to call "my friend Pepé at Seguridad" with the request that Delgado be told before his execution that he was denounced not by the waiter but by Henry himself (100). Quixotic though it is, Henry's act emphasizes the high value of hospitality uncorrupted by war. He does not want Delgado to die "disillusioned or bitter about the waiters" (100). Harry of "The Snows of Kilimanjaro" has no such guilt, for he has not committed any such betrayal.

The denunciation of Delgado has some Homeric precedent. Supplication scenes abound in the Homeric poems. In Homer's *Iliad,* the supplications of Chryse to Achilles (1.407), Thetis to Zeus (1.500–502), and Priam to Achilles (24.476–80) are all granted. At the same time, of the supplications that take place on the battlefield—that of Adrestos to Menelaos (6.37–65), of Peisandros and Hippolochos to Agamemnon, of Tros to Achilles (20.463–72), of Lycaon to Achilles (21.34–135), and of Hektor to Achilles—none are granted, and all of the suppliants are slain (see Edwards 311–12). Even the laws of Zeus, protector of suppliants, do not apply in war. War has entered Chicote's, and Henry Edmunds characterizes Delgado as a fool five times. Henry's relation to Delgado does not parallel Harry's relationship with the deserter in the Gauertal. Harry lives in the Gauertal apparently as a civilian, a genuine host not involved in the conflict, thus obligating him to fulfill the proper role of host. As a writer and filmmaker, Henry is committed to the republican cause and as a guest at Chicote's, he is not committed to protecting every enemy combatant. Those who condemn Edwin Henry as Delgado's betrayer should also condemn Achilles for killing the pathetic Lycaon—whom Achilles had captured once before, who had escaped, and who, upon being captured a second time, assumed the suppliant's position and begged Achilles not to kill him. Granted, such a condemnation can be mounted and defended, but war is hard, and Achilles is the hard man who can carry out what the hard realities of war demand. The hard reality is that Edwin Henry's old gambling acquaintance is a fascist; Edwin Henry was committed to ending fascism, the eventual destruction of which was a blessing to all of humanity.

Paul Smith cites a conference paper delivered by William Watson that presents the thesis that "The Denunciation" constitutes Hemingway's self-therapy for guilt over not aiding John Dos Passos in investigating the disappearance of José Robles Pazos. Such a view illustrates the potential distortions of biographical criticism (370–71). Psychobiographical speculation is simply beside the point. Hemingway published the story (in *Esquire,* November 1938). He expected his readers to take something from it. It must stand on its own, and it is on that stance that it must be understood—even if the psychobiographical speculation somehow proves valid. What the story reveals is that like the laws of Zeus, protector of suppliants, the customs of hospitality are painfully distorted by the horrors of war. Henry's act of mercy for a condemned man reveals his own understanding of this truth. The bond of gamblers is less sacred than that between host and guest. "The Butterfly and the Tank" makes much the same point, emphasized by its being set in the very same bar, Chicote's. The killing of the flit-gun man—in the very same locus of hospitality—similarly depicts the erosion of civilized behavior brought about by war.

Tragedies at the Front

In their varied handlings of the man-on-trail archetype, both "Under the Ridge," published in *Cosmopolitan* in 1939, and the later World War II story "Black Ass at the Crossroads," the latter published for the first time in 1987 in the *Finca Vigía* story collection, invite comparison with the Gauertal incident. The man on trail in "Under the Ridge" is the Frenchman who attempts to walk out of the battle. The retreating German soldiers in "Black Ass at the Cross Roads" do not exactly qualify as men on trail—which is the source of the narrator's "black ass," Hemingway's own phrase for wretchedness and despair. Each tale holds up a mirror to our own times, as in them we see the issues of cynical and overreaching Russian intrusion in the affairs of other nations and of the unrepayable emotional debt accumulated by those who carry out the often morally unsatisfying duties required of those we refer to today as boots on the ground.

"UNDER THE RIDGE"

The unnamed narrator of "Under the Ridge" has many of the same characteristics of Henry Emmunds, the narrator of the other three Spanish Civil War stories—the Chicote's stories. He is a writer and part of a film crew covering the conflict. The story takes place during a battle but within the protective shelter of a ridge where reserve forces wait in safety before being called up, which might be stretched to qualify as a locus of hospitality. Besides the narrator, the key characters are a boy, Paco, who has lost a hand in a self-inflicted injury; a Frenchman who decides to simply walk away from the battle; and an Extremaduran who converses with the narrator about why he hates all foreigners. Preceding the appearance of the Frenchman, the narrator speaks with the Extremaduran who, since he hates foreigners, thus rejects hospitality for strangers:

> "What are your politics?"
> "I hate all foreigners," he said.

> "That's a broad political program."
>
> "I hate the Moors, the English, the French, the Italians, the Germans, the North Americans and the Russians."
>
> "You hate them in that order?"
>
> "Yes. But perhaps I hate the Russians the most." (143)

He makes six "hate" statements during the course of the conversation. The guest/host relationship is invoked by another soldier who addresses the Extremaduran: "'Shut up!' said the friendly soldier. 'I command here, and these comrades are our guests'" (144). Nevertheless, the Extremaduran angrily catalogs the atrocities perpetrated by foreigners upon the Spanish from the time of Napoleon to deaths in his own family.

During the course of this exchange the Frenchman appears:

> Down the gap, walking beside two stretcher-bearers and seeming to pay no attention at all to where he was, came a tall man in International Brigade uniform with a blanket rolled over his shoulder and tied at his waist. His head was held high and he looked like a man walking in his sleep. He was middle-aged. He was not carrying a rifle and, from where I lay, he did not look wounded.
>
> I watched him walking alone down out of the war. (143–45)

Hemingway never describes the gendarmes who pursue the deserter in the Gauertal, but they must have looked much like the two Russians who next appear in pursuit of the deserting Frenchman: "Just then two men in leather coats, one short and stocky, the other of medium height, both with civilian caps, flat, high-cheekboned faces, wooden-holstered Mauser pistols strapped to their legs, came out of the gap and headed toward us" (145). "News on the March! Max and Al go to war! Notorious Chicago gangsters and minions of *Nada* find their true calling as battle police in the Spanish Civil War!" They question the narrator and his party, follow the Frenchman's path "like hunting dogs," and execute him. Canids again represent death as the pursuer (146). The Frenchman follows Frederic Henry dropping out of the incompetent Italian army in *A Farewell to Arms,* and the pursuing Russians who execute him take up the role of the carabinieri who carry out executions at the bridge over the Tagliamento River. Considering the general chaos of war, not to mention the particular horrors of chaos, incompetence, and tragedy depicted in Hemingway's fiction set in the Spanish Civil War, the Frenchman is one of Hemingway's few portraits of sane participants. Even later, in depicting the horrors faced by the narrator and his party, the description is derived from what the Frenchman must have experienced before he decided to walk away:

> We had been all that morning in the place the middle aged Frenchman had walked out of. We had been there in the dust, the smoke, the noise, the receiving of wounds, the death, the fear of death, the bravery, the cowardice, the insanity and failure of an unsuccessful attack. We had been there on that plowed field men could not cross and live. You dropped and lay flat; making a mound to shield your head; working your chin into the dirt; waiting for the order to go up that slope no man could go up and live. (146–47)

After a brief discussion with the narrator regarding discipline in war, the Extremaduran tells the story of the terrified boy Paco, who had his hand amputated after a self-inflicted wound but who soon admitted his failing: "Paco said, 'That was a cowardly and foolish thing. I am sorry that I did that thing. But I try to be useful with one hand. I will do what I can with one hand for the Cause'" (149). Paco is later brought back to the front, to the place where he had wounded himself, by two Russians who brutally execute him without warning in front of the Extremaduran's company.

The Extremaduran describes the same sort of uniformed authority who shot the Frenchman: "When such people with the leather coats and pistols come it is always a bad omen in a war, as is the arrival of people with map cases and field glasses" (149). These are the gendarmes who chase the deserter in the Gauertal, who arrest Jean Valjean, the MPs who chase Harry and the Armenian woman; they are the Versailles troops who slaughter the Communards (**IM 4.5**), the Mountie who pursues Jack Westondale, King George's redcoats, Max and Al, the game wardens of "The Last Good Country," and so many other of the agents of murderous uniformed authority who have pursued men on trail discussed so far. They are Harry's bicycle policemen. They are compared to canids in their pursuit, like Harry's hyena, the hallucinated wolf of "A Pursuit Race," and the wolves of medieval battlefields. They are minions of the *Nada,* who hand out death to the unarmed and defenseless without exposing themselves to danger. The offense is compounded in "Under the Ridge" by the fact that those who carry out the executions are Russians, guests of Spain, and neither of the two they kill are Russians.

Thus, the Extremaduran's reaction suggests that the Russians have overstepped their bounds as guests, especially in their execution of Paco, a Spaniard and not much more than a child. The Extremaduran does, finally, come to an uneasy truce with the narrator:

> "It is for this that I now hate Russians as well as all other foreigners," said the Extremaduran. "We give ourselves no illusions about foreigners. If you are a foreigner, I am sorry. But for myself now, I can make no exceptions. You have eaten bread and drunk wine with us. Now I think you should go." (150)

The Extremaduran is aware that the bonding behavior (eating the same bread, drinking the same wine, and telling stories) will never work for him, and the narrator understands:

> "I understand your hatred," I said.
>
> "Good," he said and put out his hand. "I do not refuse to shake hands. And that you, personally, have much luck."
>
> "Equally to you," I said. "Personally and as a Spaniard." (150)

The ceremony of incorporation is thus highly qualified in a civil war. The Russians are the villains because they have presumptuously assumed the role of executioners and battle police in someone else's civil war. The result is that the narrator visits a group, drinks the wine, eats the bread, shares stories, shakes hands, wishes luck, and departs without becoming part of the group. The conditions of civil war have decisively and irrevocably eroded hospitality.

"BLACK ASS AT THE CROSS ROADS"

Scholars, critics, and biographers have said little about "Black Ass at the Cross Roads," a World War II story. Smith refers to the story as a "sketch" and lumps it with other stories unworthy of discussion (396). Oliver, remarkably, deems the story "[u]nfinished" (26). As usual, Flora's comments show insight, comparing and contrasting the story with chapter 3 of *In Our Time,* also about the deaths of German soldiers shot from ambush, though in World War I (*Ernest Hemingway* 102–04).

In "Black Ass at the Cross Roads," the pursued are retreating Germans. The narrator seems to be a participant, as opposed to Henry Emmunds's role as observer in the Chicote's stories. Through the lens of archetypal interpretation, this story too stands up on its own and without psychobiographical connections. The narrator has been ordered to (or has chosen to) carry out ambushes with French irregulars on the German troops retreating through France during the later stages of the war. The ambushes, carried out at a rural crossroads, are successful in killing a number of Germans but leave a bad taste, a depression—or whatever other negative feelings the phrase *black ass* covers.

Killing enemy in combat proves different emotionally from ambushing retreating troops, few of whom offer resistance. The first group, staff car occupants, are shot at close range, and their car crashes. Four bicyclists are similarly shot from ambush at "too intimate" a close range (582). The German rear guard arrives in a half-track, which carries a load of explosives. When the irregulars hit it with a bazooka round, the resulting explosion, disturbingly, rains body parts down on the narrator and on the French.

This horror recalls "A Natural History of the Dead," which begins by treating the horror of bodies, both human and animal, shattered by war. An ironic distance is initially created by black humor, but the story ends with the poignant scene of conflict over how to treat the mortally wounded. The question of the use of morphine comes up in that final scene, which prefigures the final italicized memory of "The Snows of Kilimanjaro," in which Harry gives all of his morphine tablets to the obviously mortally wounded Williamson (**IM V**). In both stories, Hemingway focuses on the moral dilemma that confronts the host figure.

The stragglers, also on bicycles, fall in a singularly undramatic fashion, though one of them is a teenager who is wounded severely. The tenderness with which the narrator and the irregulars care for him provides an effective gauge of how emotionally grueling the entire ambush episode has been for them all. Neither patriotic duty nor the comradeship of arms nor revenge for the atrocities of war nor the knowledge that they were eliminating Germans they would otherwise have to fight at a later date seem to cover the black ass emotional price of the ambushes, especially given their usual attitude toward German prisoners: "German prisoners who had been taken by irregulars were often as cooperative as head waiters or minor diplomats. In general we regarded them as perverted boy scouts. This is another way of saying they were splendid soldiers. We were not splendid soldiers. We were specialists in a dirty trade. In French we said, *'un métier très sale'* [a very dirty business]" (581).

They would have preferred to have taken prisoners, but the Germans do not surrender, nor do they ask for hospitality. Neither do the irregulars afford them the option to surrender. The circumstances do not permit treating them as men on trail—as Harry is able to treat the Gauertal deserter. Harry is not a combatant. The Germans, especially the rear guard, are too well armed and would (and do) fight rather than surrender. But their position as retreating, defeated enemy puts them all too close to man-on-trail status—and thus marginally worthy of hospitality, making their killings tragic and distasteful, much like Barker's killing of the Austrians on leave of "The Snows of Kilimanjaro" (**IM 1.5**). Their close proximity to possible prisoner status (as close as they can expect to come to hospitality, given the combat conditions) gives the story a further tragic quality. Far from an incomplete tale, "Black Ass at the Crossroads" follows the classic short-story pattern of pointing all details of character, setting, and conflict to the production of a single stunning effect, in this case the "black ass" emotional devastation of carrying out combat deaths of ambiguous necessity. In an America that is currently experiencing an average of twenty-two suicides of combat veterans per day, this clearly complete story may offer some insight into some of the psychic costs paid by those who have so courageously volunteered to do our killing for us, often in the situations of ambiguous necessity and morality that armed conflict inevitably presents. It is a story for "our time."

"A ROOM ON THE GARDEN SIDE"

"A Room on the Garden Side," finally published in 2018, appears to be a second story based on the same American narrator's experiences with the same French irregulars as in "Black Ass at the Cross Roads." The names "Claude," "Marcel," "Red," and "Onésime," for example, appear in both stories. Further, at the conclusion of "Black Ass," Claude stays beside the wounded teenage German soldier until he dies. In "Garden Side," the narrator hopes that the signs of aging he sees in the irregulars will not last but doubts whether that will be the case with Claude, an apparent reference to Claude's "black ass" over the young German soldier's death. With "Black Ass" depicting the moral and physical horrors of war and "Garden Side" depicting a respite from those horrors, it makes sense to assume that the stories take place in that order, at least until evidence to the contrary appears. Three other stories involving these characters have yet to be published, though two are scheduled to be published, along with "A Room on the Garden Side," in "The Hemingway Library" edition of *For Whom the Bell Tolls* in the summer of 2019, too late, alas, to be included in this discussion.

Not at all surprisingly, the story takes place at a hotel, the Paris Ritz, and includes a host, Charles Ritz (1891–1976), referred to as the "Patron." He offers civilized hospitality in the form of books, champagne, conversation about writers (Proust, Hugo, Dumas, and Baudelaire). Music occurs in the form of a ribald soldiers' song, begun by Onie and finished with a communal chorus.

As the war winds down, elements of civilization return. The irregulars develop a taste for champagne, actually drunk from glasses. The narrator reads poetry (Baudelaire's *Les Fleurs du Mal*) and books on fishing. War maps no longer needed cover a bed on which weapons rest. They have just come from the very dirty business of "Black Ass at the Cross Roads," but the narrator twice mentions that the weapons are being cleaned, perhaps even cleansed.

Paris represents the traditions of hospitality of all the best of civilization, the Paris Ritz represents Paris, and Charley Ritz represents the Ritz. The narrator and his band of irregulars have enjoyed the traditions of hospitality embodied in the Ritz, traditions that are part of what they are fighting for; as early as "Che Ti Dice La Patria" Hemingway exposed the traditions of hospitality so characteristically perverted by the fascists. Stopping too long to enjoy the Ritz and all it represents would constitute a dereliction of duty, as emphasized by the story's truly magnificent final words. The narrator, preparing to take a last walk through the town before moving out in the morning, understands that "the town would never look the same again unless you left it when you should" (10). Further enjoying the hospitality of the Ritz would be an indulgence without properly securing it first. They must earn their return trip, an idea similar to what Hemingway said of Paris in the closing lines of *A Moveable Feast:* "Paris was always worth it and you received return for whatever you brought to it" (211). Or hospitality repaid.

Other Posthumously Published Works

As does *A Farewell to Arms,* the first paragraph of *Islands in the Stream* begins with a description of a house, Thomas Hudson's house in Bimini, and the storms it has withstood, thus establishing its credibility as a place of hospitality. At the end of part 1, "Bimini," Hudson suffers the deaths of all three of his sons. As in *A Farewell to Arms,* the loss of the people with whom one carves out some meaning from the chaos results in loss of identity and purpose. The opening of part 1, "Cuba," begins with Hudson's relationship with his cats, a loving but poor substitute for his family. At the Floridita, he hits bottom, drinking frozen daiquiris as if he were a character from *The Sun Also Rises* and keeping company with Honest Lil the whore. Neither she nor the cats can take the place of what he has lost. His road to recovery begins when his ex-wife enters the Floridita, and they spend a few hours before she must catch a flight. Part 3, "At Sea," is largely bereft of the usual locales of hospitality, but his fishing boat, on a civilian submarine-hunting patrol and outfitted with weapons and a crew of friends, becomes a substitute home with a substitute family. He establishes new, purposeful relationships with the members of his crew, roughhewn characters though they are, and begins to create a new meaning for his life.

The characters in *The Garden of Eden* (1986) do not even seem to have homes other than the hotels at which they stay. Not surprisingly, the very first sentence of the novel mentions the hotel at which David and Catherine are staying. More so than in any other work of Hemingway's intercourse seems to be used to indicate rites of passage.

"THE LAST GOOD COUNTRY"

While there is no proof positive that Hemingway read any of the Windemere stories, it is perfectly clear that they were readily available to him from a very young age and at a place where, free of schoolwork, he could read at his leisure. It is also clear that the man-on-trail and hospitality themes occur with regularity in the Windemere volumes. Further, in 1915, at about the time he might have read these stories, Ernest illegally shot a heron, was pursued by a game warden, and briefly spent time on the run before surrendering and pleading guilty (see Baker, *A Life Story,* 20–21). This episode later became the basis for "The Last Good Country," which includes many of the elements of the hospitality and man-on-trail plots discussed in this study: the man on trail (Nick Adams), pursuers (game wardens, who exploit the locals' hospitality in a manner reminiscent of Penelope's suitors), a character (Littless, Nick's younger sister) who offers hospitality (food, drink, shelter, rest, advice, storytelling), and characters who delay or resist the pursuers. Most of these elements do not exist in the biographical accounts, indicating that much of Hemingway's invention here consists of the addition of the standard archetypes of hospitality and of the less recognized man on trail. Flora notes the importance of food: "The presentation and sharing of food have been important motifs in many of the Nick Adams stories. That careful attention be paid to food in 'The Last Good Country' seems inevitable" (*Hemingway's Nick Adams* 272).

Hemingway's choice of the books Nick and Littless take with them appropriately includes hospitality and man-on-trail themes. Stevenson's *Kidnapped* features Alan Breck Stewart, quite clearly a pursued man on trail. Stewart was a survivor of the Battle of Culloden, the climactic defeat of Bonnie Prince Charley's rebellion (1745) against the British throne; after the defeat the fictional Stewart remained a fundraiser and loyal operative of the defeated Jacobites, whom the crown relentlessly pursued. They also read from Emily Brontë's

Wuthering Heights, which Hemingway listed as one of his favorite books as early as his *Esquire* letters (*By-Line,* 186). Heathcliff, while not pursued by anyone like Inspector Javert, lived as an orphan on the back streets of Liverpool. He enters the story literally from the trail, brought home by old Mr. Earnshaw on horseback and wrapped in a cloak, his emergence from which is a kind of birth. The conflict that follows rages over hospitality; after the death of Old Mr. Earnshaw, Catherine, Heathcliff's adopted sister, falls in love with him, and Hindley, his jealous adopted brother, hates and torments him. Briefly experiencing life on the lam and reading stories of hospitality for the pursued man at about the same time may have helped to fix the elements of this plot in Hemingway's mind.

While he used hospitality plot elements with consummate creativity in "The Snows of Kilimanjaro," he returned to them again in "The Last Good Country" in the 1950s, when he struggled creatively, producing massive amounts of material but completing and publishing little. Frieda Fordham, in commenting on Carl Jung's psychology, summarizes one of his key insights: "Because myths are a direct expression of the collective unconscious, they are found in similar forms among all peoples and in all ages, and when man loses his capacity for mythmaking, he loses touch with the creative forces of his being" (27). Thus, Hemingway—after his nearly fatal plane crashes and beset by the multitude of difficulties of all sorts that would ultimately prove his undoing—returned gamely to the bedrock of myth in "The Last Good Country." He sketched out the man-on-trail plot with a few minimalist touches in "The Snows of Kilimanjaro," most notably in the Gauertal incident; moving in the opposite direction in the 1950s, trying to find his way again, he employed a maximal number of man-on-trail and hospitality plot elements in "The Last Good Country." He was back on trail.

Comparison table 9: The Spanish Civil War stories

Title of story	"The Denunciation"	"The Butterfly and the Tank"	"Night before Battle"	"Under the Ridge"	*For Whom the Bell Tolls*
Man on trail / fate	Luis Delgado / Arrested and executed	Pedro, the flit gun man, "One of only four men in civilian clothes in the place" (103) / shot in Chicote's	–	The Frenchman / killed; and Paco / executed by the Russians	Robert Jordan / killed in combat
Place(s) of hospitality	Chicote's	Chicote's	Chicote's	An area near the fighting but sheltered from fire by a ridge	Pilar's cave
Host(s)	The waiters at Chicote's	—	—	—	Pilar
Betrayer(s) of hospitality	Old Waiter, Henry Emmunds (narrator)	Nervous patrons	—	Russian battle police	Pablo, who steals Jordan's equipment and attempts to subvert his mission
Elements of hospitality extended or denied	Gin and Schweppes Indian tonic water	Waiters take offense at Pedro's joking squirts	Shared meal	The Extremaduran who hates foreigners: "You have eaten bread and drunk wine with us. Now I think you should go" (150).	Food, wine, whiskey (gift to Jordan from Sordo), intercourse, shelter
Uniformed authority / agents of death	Pepé at Seguridad / six agents with submachine guns, two in plainclothes	"three men in uniform" oust the harmless Pedro before he is shot by some of the same (104)	—	"people with the leather coats and the pistols" (149)	Fascist troops

Chapter 9

THE FIGURE IN THE CARPET

The Man-on-Trail and Hospitality Plots in "The Snows of Kilimanjaro"

> "What is it, Harry?" she asked him.
> "Nothing," he said.

The figure in the carpet of "The Snows of Kilimanjaro" is composed of multiple strands of woven plot lines involving hospitality: the man on trail, the host/hostess, the place of hospitality, the betrayal of hospitality, and social bonding at the place of hospitality. Application of the traditional host/guest/double/brother/*philoxenia* archetypes, as well as other archetypes associated with the man on trail established here, illuminates both the basic narrative segments and the italicized reminiscences of "The Snows of Kilimanjaro." It is time to return to the original list of Harry's memories. Some have already been extensively examined, and some will now be seen in the clearer light of ancient archetypes.

"The Snows of Kilimanjaro" also has narrative sections and an introductory epigraph, which must not be neglected. Indeed, each italicized memory bears connections to the adjacent narrative sections. The story begins and ends with narrative, and each of the five groups of italicized memories is placed after a narrative segment, technically totaling six narrative segments and five italicized memories. However, Hemingway inserted a line break into the second narrative segment and two line breaks into the final segment, realistically bringing the narrative segments to nine. Each narrative segment will be referred to here as **Narrative** and will be numbered **I, II.A, II.B III**, et cetera.

Epigraph: Mount Kilimanjaro and the Leopard Carcass

The epigraph, to a slight degree, and **Narrative I** provide the scene and establish a mood, leading to the memories in **IM I**. All, except waiting for the train at Karagatch, have to do with snow. The epigraph clearly identifies the top of Kilimanjaro as a beautiful place of peace and calm, the "House of God," like the "good place" where Nick Adams makes his camp in "Big Two-Hearted River."

The leopard is another matter, as interpretations of its function have varied according to interpretive agendas. Hemingway's epigram tells us, "No one has explained what the leopard was seeking at that altitude." No one has ever opined that he was seeking God, peace and solitude, or the good place. He was not. As philosophers are wont to remind us, all creatures act according to their own natures. The nature of a predator is to hunt, to travel on trail stalking game. Harry, like the leopard, dies on trail, as analysis of his death scene will show.

***Narrative I**: Exposition and Quarreling*

1. Harry's situation is revealed as Harry and Helen quarrel.

In the first of the story's many flight references, Harry mentions having closely observed the flight of the gathering vultures, in case he might have the opportunity to use a description of their flight in his writing. He also tells Helen, "[Y]ou can shoot me" and later uses the phrase "For Christ's sake," paralleling the wounded Williamson's plea in **IM V**: "Shoot me, Harry. For Christ sake, shoot me" (4, 24).

***Italicized Memory I**: Memories of snow in war and peace*

1. Waiting for the Orient Express in Thrace after the Greek retreat / The secretaries sent by Nansen die in the snow.
2. The deserter-in-the-Gauertal incident.

IM I.2 develops the man-on-trail archetype. Appropriately, in the very first of his reminiscences he recalls himself as a traveler: he carries a pack and waits at the Karagatch station for a train after his experiences in the Greco-Turkish War. Immediately following is the story of travelers who, like the leopard, die in the snow. As Harry has learned of the tragedy of Nansen's refugees, his willingness to help the deserter who appears at his hut—as a man on trail, with his bloody feet—is no surprise. Like the leopard and the secretaries, the deserter faces the possibility of death by hypothermia.

A literary forbearer of the Nansen secretaries episode is Bret Harte's "The Outcasts of Poker Flat." Each involves a group of people forced out of a community and into the snowy mountains where they die of hypothermia. The similarities between the two tales have been overlooked, probably because of the difference in authorial style—Harry's told objectively and Harte's told with his characteristic rank sentimentality.

3. Skiing in Schrunz, breathtakingly described.

Harry remembers "the noiseless rush the speed made as you dropped down like a bird," another of the story's many references to flight. As the critics have noted, Harry's speed down the mountain contrasts with the impeded flight of the secretaries who die in the snow. Further, paralleling the "noiseless rush" down the mountain, Harry (near the end of **Narrative II.B**) feels his first realization of his impending death, which comes upon him "with a rush" (15).

4. Snowbound at the Madlener-haus. Herr Lent, arguably the proprietor, loses everything gambling / Thoughts on gambling.

The story of Herr Lent, a professional host, is tragic in every way. It is similar to incident **III.3**, in which another professional host, the proprietor of the Triberg Hotel, commits suicide after he loses his capital in the postwar inflation. The parallel suggests that Herr Lent may have committed suicide as well.

5. Barker, the aviator, machine-gunning the leave train of Austrian officers.

As the secretaries are travelers betrayed, so are the Austrian officers on the leave train, on Christmas Day as in the Gauertal episode—which actually qualifies them as pilgrims as their journey has a religious significance; they are gunned down by a pilot named Barker whose own brother officer says to his face, "You bloody murderous bastard" (8). The name "Barker" characterizes him as an animal, a canid in particular, someone less than civilized.[1] Marion Montgomery perceptively points out that both Barker and the hyena are "scavengers" who prey on "helpless game" (147).

The use of the adjective *bloody* suggests a British voice condemning Barker—although Harry uses the word elsewhere in the narrative segments (5, 24). Further, Harry's being in the same officers' mess with Barker, an aviator, suggests that Harry may have served as an aviator as well. One must suppose that aviation units, stationed near airfields, might not always mess with troops from infantry, artillery, or mechanized units. This suggests Harry could have been part of the aviation unit, perhaps a British one; otherwise, some other reason is needed to justify Harry and Barker eating in the same mess. The mess, of course, is where those in the military share food and, therefore, hospitality and comradeship. The condemnation of Barker is that much more bitter, coming as it does in a place dedicated to hospitality and brotherhood of arms.

In **IM I.3**, Harry thinks of skiing as a flight as he recalls "the noiseless rush the speed made as you dropped down like a bird" (7). In the dialogue with Helen that opens the story, Harry mentions observing the flight of the vultures closing in on his camp, perhaps an interest sparked by aviation experience. Aviation experience would add another dimension to Harry's death flight, taking him back to his youth and what he believed was his more authentic involvement in life. The same holds for the memory of flight in **IM 3.4,** in which he remembers what may have been a ritual of incorporation—and, therefore, of hospitality—having shared a glass of wine with the taxi-driver husband of the manager of the bal musette, the latter before a day of taxi-driving and the former before he "had to take an early flight" (20). Once again, Harry remembers a more authentic involvement in humanity than that found in the life he now lives among the rich, and he has another memory of aviation.

Two other references suggest that Harry was an aviator. As he nears death on his cot, he is "lifted" (*lift,* of course, being a key aviation term) and finds release: "And then, while they lifted the cot, suddenly it was all right and the weight went from his chest" (25). Finally, during Compton's plane's takeoff with Harry tucked inside, the engine's "clatter moved into the old familiar roar" (26). The roar would naturally be familiar to a former aviator.

6. After the war, skiing, hunting, and discussing the war with Hans, an Austrian officer.

The very next episode establishes a spirit of potential but now lost brotherhood with the slaughtered Austrian officers: "*Those were the same Austrians they killed then that he skied with later. No not the same*" (8). But they might well have been, had Barker not slaughtered them. That is the point. They are men on trail; they are brothers; they are slaughtered. Harry joins in the condemnation. The distaste for what Barker has done bears similarity to the distaste depicted by the narrator of "Black Ass at the Cross Roads." Harry's identification, and indeed the author's and the readers', with the traveler is a reaction to an archetype, an ancient archetype, whose emotional force trumps the rational and bypasses the pursued man's status as outside the law or even as enemy combatant. The vulnerability of the man on trail brings out this response in us because we are all pursued by death, just as Harry is stalked by the scavenging hyena, the vultures, the bicycle policemen, the MPs, the Turkish army, and the *Nada.*

7. Winters in the Voralberg and the Arlberg, the fox seller, kirsch, skiing. And arriving at an inn.

The first of these two memories begins with Hans, an enemy combatant who had fought as a member of the Kaiser-Jägers, an old and elite Austrian light infantry unit originally consisting of hunters, sharpshooters, scouts, et cetera. Fittingly, *jäger* means *hunter* in German. In her insightful examination of foodways in Hemingway—focusing on "Big Two-Hearted River," "Ten Indians," and *For Whom the Bell Tolls*—Hilary Kovar Justice comments on Hemingway's treatment in *For Whom the Bell Tolls* of the "distortion" of the role of hunting brought about by civil war:

> In the novel . . . Hemingway splits "gathering" from "hunting" and locates "trapping" somewhere between. . . . He then establishes, at length, the trauma of civilization in the distortion of hunting (in the first conversation between Anselmo and Pablo) [*For Whom the Bell Tolls* 15], in Pilar's struggle to maintain hospitality (in the scenes at the cave), and in the complete inversion of agriculture (in the history of Maria's body and the story of Pilar's village). Only one food system, gathering, remains untroubled by war. . . . Such food is not produced by man, but by grace. (26)

The history of the Kaiser-Jägers extends, under varying names and designations, back as far as the eighteenth century. Nevertheless, Hemingway no doubt saw the irony of the civilized role of the hunter corrupted by its military application. This corruption is indicated in *For Whom the Bell Tolls* by Pablo's increasing anxiety over being regarded as prey, and in "The Snows of Kilimanjaro" by Barker's destruction of harmless "prey" rather than active combatants. After the war, Harry and Hans, men who fought on opposite sides, by hunting together work to return this traditional civilized activity to its proper function in a world groping its way back to civilized behavior.

Harry and Hans hunt as they discuss engagements in which they might well have fought on opposite sides. Notably, Harry had not written of "*Pasubio and of the attack on Pertica and Asalone . . . Nor of Monte Corno, nor the Siete Commum, nor of Arsiedo*" (8).[2] The placement of the last three engagements in a separate sentence (actually a sentence fragment—an incomplete thought for uncompleted stories) suggests that he may not have discussed them with Hans, as though he had some other reason, such as having actually experienced them, to write about them. Naturally, he regrets not having written about any of those engagements. The seventh and final memory is of the joys of peace in the mountains of Austria: the skiing and the accordion music and warmth of an inn—a place of welcoming hospitality redolent of the bonding elements of music and wine—in the Austrian mountains. Neither the intellectual discussions of the various engagements of the war nor the enjoyments of the good life and hospitality in the Vorarlberg and the Arlberg will be possible for the Austrian officers—men on trail—whom Barker slaughtered.

Overall, **IM I** establishes Harry as a man on trail—as he once again tries to become one in Africa—and binds together the snow references with themes of men and women on trail and affected by the snow. He appears with his pack waiting for transport and later offers the deserter hospitality. Like the secretaries, whom death pursues (and catches), the deserter is pursued by the gendarmes. If caught, he might well face execution. Snow impedes both the secretaries and the deserter, a contrast to the speed Harry achieves skiing down the mountain during peacetime. The Austrian officers whom Barker slaughters are also men on trail. Harry's peacetime enjoyment of the snow is highlighted by his friendship with Hans and his enjoyment of skiing. The speed that enables Barker to make his kills ironically parallels the peacetime speed of Harry skiing. The italicized memory ends with Harry arriving at a sensuously described place of hospitality, a mountain inn, the sort of spot that the secretaries and the Austrian officers never reach.

***Narrative II.A**: Harry and Helen Quarrel*

Waking up from his reverie, Harry asks Helen where they stayed in Paris. She names two expensive hotels: the Crillon and Pavillon Henri-Quatre in St. Germain. Significantly, he cannot remember the Paris hotels he has stayed in most recently, though he has just had clear memories of the Madlener-haus as well as other places of hospitality from the years before he met Helen. This short segment ends in a quarrel as Harry goads Helen until she cries and then insincerely protests his love for her.

Places of hospitality play an important role in the story. Eight hotels are mentioned: the Madlener-haus in the Voralberg province of Austria (7); an unnamed alpine inn in the Voralberg or the Arlberg (8); the Paris Crillon (8); the St-Germain Pavillon Henri-Quatre (8); the Régence in Paris (15); the Pera Palace in Constantinople (16), often used by passengers on the Orient Express, which appears in Harry's first memory (**IM I.1**) and on which he apparently traveled to and from Anatolia; the Hotel in Triberg (19); and the hotel in Paris where French poet Paul Verlaine died. Other places of hospitality play roles in the story: drinking spots—the "weinstube in Schrunz" (7) and the café where Harry sees Tristan Tzara and an American poet; the military mess where the Barker episode takes place (8); drinking spots in or around the Place Contrescarpe, the poor neighborhood where he began his career; the Café des Amateurs (20), where the poor escaped their troubles; the bal musette (20), which offered the questionable hospitality of prostitutes; the zinc bar at which he would drink a glass of wine before catching a flight; the club where he wrote the ill-fated letter to his first love, later seen by his wife; and Taxim's, an expensive restaurant in Constantinople that he passes by but does not patronize (15). The list of places where Harry stops, sleeps, eats, dances, or drinks forms a social and emotional biography.

And at the time of Harry's truest emotional bonding with a neighborhood, Place Contrescarpe, where he began his writing career in earnest, there are also the greatest number of references to persons associated with hospitality: the concierge who sleeps with the trooper; the concierge who sleeps with a policeman; Marie, Harry's *femme de menage;* the manager of the bal musette; and her husband, with whom Harry drinks white wine before his flights. These are in contrast to the rich, whom Harry refers to as Helen's "goddamned Old Westbury, Saratoga, Palm Beach people," those who "were all much more comfortable when he did not work" (6, 10).

Narrative II.B: *Helen Hunts and the Quarrel Ends with Drinks*

At five and a half pages, this is the longest unbroken narrative section.

That same evening, Helen goes out to hunt to supply the camp with meat. A considerate hostess, she hunts far enough away to avoid disturbing the game around the camp, which she knows Harry enjoys observing. Harry's decline as a writer, Helen's past life, and the start of their relationship are established. Helen returns from a successful hunt, and as she and Harry rebond over drinks—which she, not Harry, orders, suggesting compromise on her part—and over civil conversation, the hyena passes by the camp, reminding Harry that death is near and that he is the pursued. As in "A Clean, Well-Lighted Place" nothingness becomes part of the story. Earlier in this section:

> His personal boy was sitting by the bed.
> "Memsahib's gone to shoot," the boy said. "Does Bwana want?"
> "Nothing." (10)

As part of **Narrative II**, this follows **IM I**, stories not of his childhood but of his youth; they are personal, which is emphasized by the reference to "personal boy." In his mind, Harry comes to a more charitable reevaluation of Helen and how she has treated him. Without knowing his thoughts, she validates this through the bonding ritual of drinking. At this point, death makes its presence felt again.

> She was a fine woman, marvelous really. And just then it occurred to him that he was going to die.
>
> It came with a rush; not as a rush of water nor of wind; but of a sudden evil-smelling emptiness and the odd thing was that the hyena slipped lightly along the edge of it.
>
> "What is it, Harry?" she asked him.
>
> "Nothing," he said. (15)

As in other tales, the pursuer of the man on trail, in this case the hyena, is a canid or has a canid quality and represents death and the nothingness that follows. The hostess has done all she can, but she cannot enable him to continue on the trail. He must go on in his mind and find any possible redemption alone.

This use of *nothing* parallels that in chapter 21 of *A Farewell to Arms*. Just prior to revealing her pregnancy, Catherine and Frederic engage in this exchange:

> She seemed upset and taut.
>
> "What's the matter, Catherine?"
>
> "Nothing. Nothing's the matter."
>
> "Yes, there is."
>
> "No nothing. Really nothing."
>
> "I know there is. Tell me, darling. You can tell me."
>
> "It's nothing." (119)

She refers to "nothing" in a biblical three lines of dialogue although Hemingway has her use the word five times, just in case the reader might have not have noticed it. Obviously, on the most superficial level, her reticence expresses the not unusual reluctance of a woman to inform her lover of her pregnancy. At this point, it is important to remember that Hemingway also wrote—in the not too distant future—"A Clean, Well-Lighted Place," a story that offers a depiction of existential dread as well as an antidote to it. A reversal of the words reveals the true dread that Catherine feels: The "matter" "really" is "nothing." It is the nothing of Sartre's *Being and Nothingness*. On an existential plane, the meaning of life is not determined a priori but in human interactions, which Frederic and Catherine have established meaningfully. The tragedy of *A Farewell to Arms* is that Frederic comes to this understanding only through the process of losing the person with whom he has established a meaning. In that sense, he loses the part of himself that she had become.

This construction of life's meaning in the identification with one's love is what attracted Hemingway to the tumultuous love of Catherine and Heathcliff in Emily Brontë's *Wuthering Heights.* (Hemingway listed it as one of his favorite books. See *By-Line* 186.) As Catherine Earnshaw tells Nelly Dean in chapter 9: "Nelly, I *am* Heathcliff—he's always, always on my mind—not as a pleasure, any more than I am always pleasant myself—but, as my own being—so, don't talk of our separation again." (70). In chapter 15, Heathcliff says to her, "Catherine, you know that I could as soon forget you, as my existence" (136). That same night Catherine Earnshaw, like Catherine Barkley, dies shortly after childbirth.

In her focus on the nothing, Catherine Barkley reveals her own existential perception of the *Nada*—based only partly on the bitter experience of losing her former love. Frederic Henry finally arrives at a full understanding at the novel's conclusion.

Thoughts of the stories about the American west Harry has failed to write come to him at the end of **IM.4** along with another reference to the "nothing":

> *He knew at least twenty good stories from out there and he had never written one. Why?*
>
> "You tell them why," he said.
> "Why what, dear?"
> "Why nothing." (23)

Nothing indeed. Actually, in "deed," in his writing, he has done "nothing." And he faces what Jung called the "monstrousness" of the universe, the nothing, the *Nada.* Harry, like Catherine Barkley, has responded to a biblical three questions with five *nothings*. He must make his own peace with them and find his own redemption. In Gloria Dussinger's words "selfhood is the process of controlling nothingness" (161n12).

***Italicized Memory II**: The Letter and Anatolia*

1. Quarreling with and losing the love of his life, following women who looked like her, writing her a letter asking her to write back / Picking up a woman to dance with, leaving her to pick up an Armenian woman / Vicious street fight with a British gunner over the Armenian woman / Escaping from the MPs and having sex with the Armenian woman.

IM II: Harry is an actor in some of the events of **IM I**—the Gauertal incident, skiing in Schrunz, gambling at the Madlener-haus, hunting with Hans, skiing in the Voralberg, and stopping at an inn after skiing. He is a spectator of the conversation between Nansen and the secretaries and of the Barker mess incident. **IM II**, taking another direction, forms an entire and coherent story, one in which Harry is an active participant throughout. The quarrel with Helen ended, Harry reflects on the quarrels of his past relationships. His breakup with his first love, "*the first one, the one who left him,*" the one to whom he writes the letter, is narrated (15). The content of the letter is summarized in three consecutive sentences, each beginning with "How." He writes of seeing a woman who could have been her "*outside the* Regence," another place of hospitality and of following women who looked like her (15). The third "How" sentence evokes "The Sea Change": "*How what she had done could never matter since he could not cure himself of loving her*" (15). The nonspecific reference to "*what she had done*" seems to echo the situation depicted in "The Sea Change," in which Phil, the protagonist, accepts his lover's lesbian affair, which is never specifically mentioned. Similarly, Phil, the protagonist of "The Sea Change" also seems to have been a writer: "'No,' she said. 'We're made up of all sorts of things. You've known that. You've used it well enough'" (58). The place where he would have used that insight would have been in his writing. Biographers have not documented a lover Hemingway lost to a lesbian paramour, so in both cases, the incident must be credited to Hemingway's own invention.

Of all the nationalities and ethnicities of Europe and the Levant, Hemingway picked an Armenian woman for Harry to have intercourse with. A likely refugee of the Armenian holocaust perpetrated by the Turks in Eastern Anatolia in 1915, she qualifies as a woman on trail. It is easy to imagine her as having been a refugee and using sex as an escape from memories of horrors she may have seen or experienced—and which Hemingway wrote movingly of in his fiction, his journalism, and even his poetry. The list of crimes against humanity the Turks perpetrated on the Armenians featured, among other acts, mass hangings and drownings, beheadings, and even crucifixions. Her dancing with him, "*her belly against him so hot it almost scalded*"; her fleshiness—"*over-ripe . . . big-breasted and needed no pillow under her buttocks*"; and her passionate promiscuity—she is a "slut," not a prostitute—all are consistent with using physical overindulgence as a means of repressing emotions, in this case the trauma of witnessing and escaping genocide. Their intercourse—described as having been more than satisfactory to both—is a rite of bonding and incorporation, especially considering he is on his way to observe a clash between the Greeks and Turks—where, in the next paragraph, he will see "*things he could never think of and later still . . . much worse*" (16). In this regard, the Armenian woman fulfills the archetypal roles of threshold guardian and initiator, in this case the threshold of the horrors of war that Harry is about to experience. Arnold Van Gennep supports this view: "Coitus as the final act in initiation ceremonies I interpret also as a rite of incorporation" (170). The bonding is with the poor, a probable refugee, and thus reminiscent of his bonding with the poor in the Paris neighborhood where he started his career.

Hemingway was certainly aware of the Armenian holocaust, as his poem "They All Made Peace—What Is Peace" reveals in its bitterly satirical treatment of world leaders who fail to address the issue: "All of the turks are gentlemen and Ismet Pasha is a little / deaf. But the Armenians. How about the Armenians? / Well the Armenians" (ll. 1–3).

After a fistfight with a British soldier over her, Harry and the woman escape in a taxi, reminiscent of Jake and Brett's final scene in *The Sun Also Rises,* in which uniformed authority, in the form of a policeman, halts their progress. In light of the recurring images of uniformed authority found throughout Hemingway's works, as well as in other man-on-trail plots by other authors, Jake's sardonic reply to Brett's statement that they might have "had such a damned good time" (198) may be seen as a comment on the inevitability of death's pursuit rather than on Jake and Brett's ostensible inability to have lived together happily (198). Becoming a couple on trail and fleeing the MPs—the man-on-trail plot's recurring image of uniformed authority and death—Harry and the Armenian woman share one night of frantic passion almost as hopeless as the love of Jake and Brett.

2. Leaving for Anatolia the next night / newly arrived incompetent Constantine Greek officers perpetrate a friendly-fire incident, bringing a British observer to tears.

3. The Turkish troops' attack on the bizarrely attired Greek Evzone troops and sights of horror / Running in the retreat with the British observer / An American

poet in a café talking with Tristan Tzara / His current wife sees and asks about the newly arrived letter from his former love, requested in incident **II.1**.

The bizarrely attired Greek Evzone troops, depicted as cannon fodder, contrast with the many other instances of uniformed authority prominent in various iterations of the man-on-trail plots. There is a strange connection between the Evzones and Hemingway's other African stories of this period, *Green Hills of Africa* and "The Short Happy Life of Francis Macomber." The Mannlicher-Schoenauer used by both the character P. O. M. and somewhat more famously by Margaret Macomber was also a standard issue weapon for the Greek Evzone troops of the Greco-Turkish War period (*Green Hills* 40; Calabi, Helsley, and Sanger 85, 86; Knupp 70).

His flight with the British observer parallels his fight with the British subaltern a short time before. He and the Armenian woman then run away as uniformed authority, in the form of the MPs, is on the way. Pursued, he is a man on trail engaged in desperate flight in both instances, running from the MPs and running with the defeated Greeks.

The sights of horror that Harry has witnessed and later cannot stand to think of or bear to hear reference to are paralleled in Helen's inability to look at the dead Harry's leg. The effects of these sights on Harry are also parallels to Nick Adams's traumatic experiences *In Our Time* and in other stories as well. Both men experience the traumatic stress of war and seek out the means of coping with their memories of it.

The affectatious Tristan Tzara (with his monocle and headache) enjoying the hospitality of a café contrasts with the scenes of horror Harry has just witnessed in Anatolia.[3]

4. Remembering the changes he had seen in the world and realizing his duty to write about them.

Harry's inability to write may well have been the result of the horrors he has witnessed, and his easy life with Helen may have been his way of repressing his memories of those horrors. Helen, too, has experienced loss. Her first husband has died, and her daughter has been killed in a plane crash. Harry, then, may be seen as being used by both Helen and the Armenian woman to achieve their own goals of repressing traumatic memories.

Narrative III: *Bonding over Libations*

Roughly a page long, the next narrative section takes place just a little later, after Helen's bath. As Helen shared a whiskey soda with Harry in the previous segment, despite her misgivings about alcohol's possible negative effects on Harry, so now Harry partakes of the broth—made from the gazelle shot on Helen's hunt—that Helen politely asks him to drink. As Helen had misgivings about the whiskey, Harry nearly gags on the broth but does not reject Helen's act of hospitality. Thus, they have bonded twice over libations. As Harry has sexual thoughts about Helen, he feels death pass by closely once again. He wants to write. At this point, he asks Helen whether she can take dictation. Significantly, she cannot. While she provides everything a hostess might and more, writing is something Harry, like every other writer, must do alone. Hemingway's Nobel Prize acceptance speech includes a relevant observation: "Writing, at its best, is a lonely life" (134).

Italicized Memory III: *Bonding and Paris in Harry's Writing Voice*

Places of hospitality constitute the focus of **IM III**: his grandfather's house, the Hotel in Triberg, and the Place Contrescarpe neighborhood where he began his career. His grandfather's log house burns down and the proprietor of the hotel hangs himself, both tragic events related to places of hospitality.

IM III is different from the others because it is in Harry's writing voice.[4] The others, to employ Lamb's useful terminology, are focalized as memories: Group **I**: "*Now in his mind he saw* . . ." (*Art Matters* 78–112). The next sentence begins "*That was one of the things he had saved to write* . . ." (6). This focalization continues in several places in **IM I. IM II.1** begins, "*He thought about alone in Constantinople that time* . . ." (15). The second paragraph, **IM II.2**, begins, "*That same night he left for Anatolia and he remembered,* . . ." (16). The final paragraph begins, "*He remembered the good times with them all* . . ." (17). **IM IV.1** begins, "*No, he had never written about Paris*" (22). **IV.2** begins, "*What about the ranch* . . ." (22), in the third person but still a presentation of Harry's thoughts. **IM V** begins, "*He remembered long ago when Williamson, the bombing officer,* . . ." (23).

The narrative immediately preceding **IM III** takes a different approach from all the others, continuing focalization of Harry's thoughts in the second and third person: "There wasn't time of course, although it seemed as though it telescoped so that you might put it all into one paragraph if you could get it right" (18). But when **IM III.1** begins, the readers get their one encounter with Harry the writer: "*There was a log house . . . There was a bell . . . Behind the house were fields . . . A line of lombardy poplars. . . .*" **IM III.2**: "*In the Black Forest after the war we rented a trout stream*" (19). **IM III.3**: "*The other way was to climb . . .*" and "*There were birches along the stream. . . .*" The voice of Harry the writer blinks out for only the beginning of one sentence: "*You could dictate that, but you could not dictate . . . ,*" which is followed by a catalog of things remembered and presented in the same Hemingwayesque style as the rest of **IM III**.

The style of the **IM III** paragraphs is not a fictionalized one crafted from whole cloth to represent how Harry might have written but rather is typical of the Hemingway style.[5] Beginning the first two sentences, the expletive adverb constructions with the usual accompanying forms of the verb "to be" (There was/were), for example, recall similar constructions from the opening page of *A Farewell to Arms:* "there were pebbles and boulders"; "there were many orchards"; "There was fighting"; "there was not the feeling"; "There was much traffic" (3). Hemingway's characteristic use of second person also appears: "*and you asked grandfather if you could have them to play with*" (19). Hemingway's characteristic repetition is also evident in the following words: fields, poplars, house, road, log house, burned, guns, lake, barrels, deer foot/feet, ashes, all repeated in the first paragraph of Group **III**. In **IM III,** the reader thus encounters what must be regarded as the voice of Harry the writer. It also supports Flora's contention that there is redemption in Harry's attempt to write (*Ernest Hemingway* 88).

1. The burning of his grandfather's house, including the loss of his grandfather's guns.[6]

For a child, a grandparents' residence is a place of often wonderful hospitality. Once again, the place of hospitality comes to a tragic end, in this case by fire but still reminiscent of the losses suffered by the proprietors of Madlenerhaus and the Hotel in Triberg.

2. Postwar trout fishing in the Black Forest and the first way of walking to the trout stream.

3. The second way of walking to the trout stream / Suicide of the Triberg Hotel's proprietor.

The hotel proprietor is a provider of hospitality whose suicide by hanging is caused by postwar inflation and parallels the tragedy of Herr Lent (**IM I.4**) and perhaps also that of Harry's grandfather.

4. Paris: poor neighbors at Place Contrescarpe: Flower sellers / Children in

the street / The Café des Amateurs and the bal musette / Concierge has affair with an army officer / The tenant whose husband is a bicycle racer / Sharing a glass of wine with the husband of the woman who ran the bal musette.

In these memories, Harry recalls his early career as a poor, struggling writer. He lives among the poor, and the many references to wine and spirits signify an authentic and ritualistic bonding with both the good and bad of the neighborhood.[7] Before leaving on an apparent journalism assignment, he shares a glass of wine with the taxi-driver husband of the manager of the bal musette they lived above. The bal musette also suggests the bonding implied by music and dancing (echoing the accordion music of the alpine inn at the end of **IM I.7**). Sharing a glass of wine marks a ritual of incorporation and parallels his sharing of libations with Helen, which signify his rebonding with her. He knows and understands the people of his neighborhood, as revealed in his rendering of the drunkards and the *sportifs*. Several other references to wine in this memory further establish Harry as authentically involved in this neighborhood beyond the simple sharing of the suffering of poverty. At the Place Contrescarpe, he remembers the "*old men and the women, always drunk on wine and bad marc*" (20). In that neighborhood where "*he had written the start of all that he was to do,*" he lived "*across the street from . . . a wine co-operative*" (20). The man who sold "*wood and coal . . . sold wine too, bad wine.*" Harry remembers "*the green painted co-operative where they bought their wine; good wine and cheap*" (21). The wine (actually referenced in the italicized memory on the sights from Harry's Paris apartment, **IM III.6**) establishes the authenticity of his belonging in that neighborhood, as he knows who sells the good wine and who the bad. The good wine being from a cooperative implies a community-based institution rather than a sole proprietorship capitalistic enterprise. Harry's memories of the poor are, by contrast, more convincing and true than the vague plans he later formed to write about the rich—of which he was never really a part but by his own admission merely "a spy in their country" (10). In **Narrative II.1** he had to ask Helen which of the luxury hotels they had stayed at in Paris; his inability to remember them indicates that he never truly incorporated into that class of people.

5. The drunkards and the *sportifs*, descendants of the Communards, whose ancestors had been slaughtered / Streets of Paris; apartment where he lived and started his writing career / The hotel where Verlaine died / Harry's writing room.

The drunkards and *sportifs*, in whose neighborhood—the Place Contrescarpe—Harry lived, were relatives and descendants of the Communards, Parisians who had participated in the commune of 1871 and were brutally and scandalously killed and persecuted after the breakup of the commune. The Versailles troops who perpetrate the persecution of the communards are depicted as typical—indeed, archetypal—uniformed authority who function as agents of death, the ubiquitous pursuer. But these troops do not engage in combat: they simply execute anyone who appears to be a worker. In this sense, they are scavengers—like the hyena, like Barker, like the carabinieri at the bridge, like the Russian goons in "Under the Ridge"—bringing death in an ugly and indiscriminate way and at no risk to themselves. Of the *sportif* class, we meet the wife of the bicycle racer who cries tears of joy when she learns that he has placed well in his first race.

Unlike his unshared memories of the rich, Harry's memories of the poor include characters, even one with a name. Marie, his *femme de menage,* comically complains of the hardships of the wife of the working man.

Paul Verlaine dies in a place of hospitality, a hotel room; however, his having lived in the neighborhood validates it as an appropriate place to begin a writing career. Further, Verlaine was part of the Communard movement of 1871, a time of his life marked by authentic involvement with community and family, a strong contrast to the dissipation of his years with Arthur Rimbaud and the "*ivresse*" of his last years (21).

6. Sights from his Paris apartment: the wood and coal dealer, the butcher shop, drunks.

7. The Republican Guard trooper sleeping with the concierge / Marie's protest of the eight-hour working day as promoting drunkenness of working-class men.

The "Boucherie Chevaline," a butcher shop specializing in horse meat, emphasizes the gap in wealth between Harry and Helen. While Helen had earlier devoted herself to her stables and horses, Harry had lived in a neighborhood in which horse meat was common.[8] Further, Hemingway, as he does so often and so well, describes food well enough to make the reader hungry: "[t]he golden horse's head outside the Boucherie Chevaline where the carcasses hung yellow gold and red in the open window" (21). There is a similar description of carcasses hanging in a butcher shop in the opening paragraph of Hemingway's "In Another Country." Harry's goading of Helen with his reference to what seems the source of Helen's money is also relevant here: "Your damned money was my armour. My Swift and my Armour" (9). Helen's understated reply—"Don't"—seems to indicate that Harry's barb was well aimed. The ranch of **Narrative IV.2** may well have been the property of Helen's family—thus explaining her interest in her stable of horses as well as Harry's dig about Swift and Armour, since meatpacking may have been the source of her family's wealth. Harry's inauthentic life among the rich is suggested by the highly processed meats of corporate America, as opposed to the simple carcasses hung in the butcher shops of Harry's Paris neighborhood.

The incident of the concierge and the trooper derives from an apparent affair Hemingway suggests he had when he lived in Paris, although the telling of it is pat enough to make one wonder whether it was fantasy. It has been published several times since his death.[9] The concierge having an affair with the Republican Guard trooper (**III.1**) and policeman sleeping with a concierge (**III.4**) are both disturbing images of a provider of hospitality linked to the death image of uniformed authority. That authority plays the role of pursuer in iterations of the man-on-trail plot in Hemingway's works and elsewhere—the redcoats of "Minions of the Moon," the night watch of "A Lodging for the Night," and the gendarmes of *Les Misérables,* to name just three examples. The trooper's helmet, with its prominently mentioned horsehair plume, thus emphasizes his uniform.

Further, the tales of drunks and the incident of Marie complaining that the newly shortened working day merely leads to more drunkenness among workingmen and more despair and suffering among their wives all validate Harry's understanding of and therefore his bonding with his neighbors—about whom he quite clearly had more to say than he did about the rich he eventually came to spend his time with who "were all much more comfortable when he did not work" (10).

In this sense, "The Snows of Kilimanjaro" (August 1936) further develops the themes of wealth and poverty that, not very surprisingly, Hemingway had already published in the stories that would become part of *To Have and Have Not* (October 1937), a novel whose main character is named Harry.

***Narrative IV**: Shared Libations*

The ritual of shared libations taken up in this very short narrative section serves as a coda to the bonding themes in **IM III.4–7**. Harry tells Helen the broth he nearly gagged on was "awfully good," but he politely declines her offer of more—with light humor and invoking the bonding power of music, Cole Porter in particular—and insists on a whiskey soda. Helen does not press the issue. Thus, after their quarreling, Helen has had whiskey soda with Harry, even requesting the drinks herself, and Harry has drunk Helen's proffered broth and politely complimented it (17). Helen returns the compliment when she tells Harry, "You know I like you to drink" (22). They have returned to civil discourse in their conversation and may be seen as rebonding over libations.

Death is not present, though it is characterized as something that passes by quietly on bicycles.[10] This sets up the final image of death as policemen on bicycles, a bird (suggesting the gathering vultures), or a hyena in **Narrative VI.A**.

Italicized Memory IV: *Memories of Ranch Life*

1. Introductory paragraph switching the scene from Paris to other memories.

2. Herding cattle at the ranch.

Harry's first memory is of being on trail himself, in the fall cattle roundup. In western parlance, when he participates in the cattle drive, he becomes a man on trail, though obviously in this instance there is no pursuit.

3. Incident of the half-wit chore boy.

The incident is a complete story of hospitality denied, derived from accounts of a real 1913 murder and from Prosper Mérimée's classic story of hospitality betrayed, "Mateo Falcone." Further, the old man whom the chore boy kills is partially devoured by the ranch dogs. Like the hyenas or the vultures around Harry's camp, they are scavengers who lurk around where death is near. And dogs, of course, are "barkers" and, thus, echo the combat scavenger Barker who kills the Austrian officers on leave (**IM I.5**) and the Versailles troops (**IM 3.5**) who indiscriminately slaughter anyone they could find who appeared to be a working man (**IM III.5**).

R. W. Stallman attempts to make his early (1961) interpretation of the narratives and italicized memories comprehensive: "What has not been noticed about 'The Snows of Kilimanjaro' is how it is designed. Scenes of external reality alternate with juxtaposed scenes of internal monologue, reminiscences of Harry's past life that Harry failed to utilize as a writer" (89). He goes on to say that "[t]hese cutbacks . . . relate thematically" (89). Good enough so far. But his interpretation of the italicized memories, based on the themes of betrayal and flight, falters fatally in dealing with several episodes. Those having to do with flight—the deserter (**I.2**), skiing (**I.3**, **6**, and **7**)—represent Harry "in flight from himself" (91). Harry does not flee in the episode of the deserter, either literally or metaphorically. The skiing episodes do not imply flight other than the reference to the flight of a bird; thus Stallman conflates the word's different meanings, one the act of flying and the other the act of fleeing. The gambling sequence (**I.4**) represents how "Harry, too has gambled on life and lost" (91).

Harry does not lose in the gambling episode—Herr Lent does. Those depicting betrayal represent "Harry betraying himself": the secretaries (**I.1**), the Barker episode (Stallman quoting the corrupt text naming the pilot Gardner instead of Barker), and Harry's infidelities (**II.1** and **3**). Stallman then determines that Harry "betrays" the chore boy (91, **IV.3**). Given the murder over some feed and the grotesque neglect of the corpse—appalling violations of hospitality, there is little doubt Harry acts properly. Harry's heroism in the memory of Williamson's death (**V**) does not receive mention.

The corpse of the old man is frozen when Harry arrives back at the ranch, paralleling the frozen carcass of the leopard on Mount Kilimanjaro, and perhaps even the secretaries who die in the snow (**IM I.1**). A frozen corpse also figures prominently in Hemingway's short story "An Alpine Idyll." One of the Windemere stories, "Mrs. Knollys" by J. S. of Dale [Frederic Jesup Stimson] concerns a corpse that emerges from a frozen glacier decades after the victim plunged into a crevasse; A. E. W. Mason's "The Crystal Trench," which uses the same plot device, is mentioned by Jake Barnes in chapter 12 of *The Sun Also Rises.*[11] The corpses emerging from the glaciers are, in a perverse way, dead men still on trail.

Narrative V: *The Rich and Poor Julian*

In this very brief narrative section, Harry finally realizes that he would not write about the rich, nor about Helen, as she is one of them. He scoffs at "poor Julian" and his writing about the rich. His last thoughts in this section are about death and pain, which leads him to his memory of Williamson, whose death was hideously painful.

Italicized Memory V: *Williamson*

1. Death of Williamson.

In **IM V**, the final episode of Harry's memories, Harry takes on a heroic role, giving his own morphine tablets to the dying Williamson, a brother officer grotesquely disembowelled by a combat wound. The Christlike nature of the sacrifice is emphasized by Williamson's mention of Christ and Harry's in **Narrative I**. In case the reader might miss the parallel, Hemingway calls attention to it by having both men requesting to be shot.

On his way to Calvary, Christ is a man on an especially grueling trail, driven by the uniformed authority of Roman soldiers. The legend of the wandering Jew is one of hospitality denied, and the legend of Veronica's veil is one of hospitality, succor actually, freely offered. Like Harry dying in Africa or like Christ, Williamson is a traveler caught traumatically between the land of life and the land of death. Williamson is the pursued. Harry is the host. Harry does right by his guest, generously giving him all of his own morphine tablets, just as Harry gave socks to the deserter in the Gauertal and just as St. Veronica offers succor to the suffering Christ.

The Williamson episode does not take place at Christmas, but note that Williamson says, "Shoot me, Harry. For Christ sake shoot me" (24). In addition, it is important to note that at the beginning of the story Harry uses very similar language. In response to Helen's request that Harry tell her what she might do for him, Harry replies: "You can take the leg off and that might stop it, though I doubt it. Or you can shoot me" (4). Not only does the "shoot me" request parallel Williamson's, but his comment about taking his leg off matches the easily repressed and forgotten dismemberment Williamson must undergo before he can be brought in out of the line of fire. Furthermore, a few lines later, Harry's "For Christ's sake" echoes Williamson's "For Christ sake." Williamson, who suffers truly hideous horror and agony in death—until Harry gives his all of his morphine tablets, thus becomes a foil to Harry, who suffers a painless death, as Harry indicates as early as the first line of the story. Jerry Herndon perceptively notes of the Williamson episode that "it is not surprising that his last meditation puts it all—all the pain and the questioning—into one paragraph," just as Harry had hoped he could (123; "The Snows" 18).

***Narrative VI.A**: Death in Different Forms*

Pursuant to their bonding over libations, Harry accepts Helen and the hospitality she has lovingly tried to build to support him: "The party's over and you are with your hostess now" (24). The hyena is heard outside the camp just as Harry begins to bicker again. He rewards his hostess with the soundest wisdom he has taken from his experience of death:

> Because, just then, death had come and rested its head on the foot of the cot and he could smell its breath.

> "Never believe any of that about a scythe and a skull," he told her. "It can be two bicycle policemen as easily, or be a bird.[12] Or it can have a wide snout like a hyena." (25)

Harry has not "spoiled" his death, "the one experience he had never had," as he had feared he might (18). He has been blessed with the rarest of opportunities, that of passing on to Helen the wisdom he has achieved in his own experience of death. As a former reporter, he makes the most of his final opportunity—reporting from death's door about the true nature of death, the ultimate journalistic scoop. Williamson's bad luck prevents his doing the same. His initial and no doubt hideous pain prevent him from expressing his experience of death, and his ingestion of Harry's morphine tablets eases his pain but only by easing him out of consciousness as well. This prepares the reader for Harry's last utterance, his observation about the true nature of death. Harry becomes the lucky recipient of grace, in the form of a painless death, one that enables him to make his final utterance a meaningful and even heroic act for Helen and himself.

In his last conscious spoken words, Harry treats death with an appropriate and heroic contempt:

> "Tell it to go away."
> It did not go away but moved a little closer.
> "You've got a hell of a breath," he told it. "You stinking bastard." (25)

The weight finally goes from his chest when his cot is "lifted," a fitting aeronautical term for a man who appears to be a former aviator (25). Harry has acted in an existential context, finding meaning in his own death through his final act of communicating with another human being regarding the knowledge of death he has come to understand.

Narrative VI.B: *Harry's Death Flight*

The role of the character Compton, the Charon-like figure who takes Harry on his last flight, is also illuminated by the analysis established thus far. The forms in which death has appeared or been represented by in the story are consistently repugnant and sinister: the hyena, the vultures, a foul-smelling rush, Barker, and uniformed authority in the form of gendarmes, MPs, the Versailles troops, and Russian and Italian battle police. And uniformed authority, as has been established here, has represented or carried out death in so many other literary plots throughout the ages. But Compton must rank as the least sinister Charon figure in literature. He has a certain English brusqueness, especially in his refusal of breakfast and then of tea—two offers of hospitality from Harry, who once again takes on the host's role. Death does not accept hospitality. However, Compton's clothing, "slacks, a tweed jacket and a brown felt hat" (26), the first thing about the man Hemingway describes, does not qualify in the least as a uniform, nor does it suggest that Compton represents in any way the uniformed authority that so often brings death, not only in "The Snows of Kilimanjaro" but in other Hemingway stories and in man-on-trail stories by other authors through the ages. In case the reader might have missed it, during Harry's flight Hemingway, with his characteristic repetition, again mentions "old Compie's tweed back and brown felt hat" (26–27). Compton is dressed and sounds like an English gentleman. It is thus a gentleman, nearly an angel, who takes Harry—perhaps once an aviator—on his last flight. Harry dies not just the good death; he dies the aviator's good death.

Hemingway's choice of the Puss Moth as the plane that Compie arrives in and that carries Harry away in the final flight sequence has received little analysis. Baker makes the obvious biographical connection that the Puss Moth was the model used to fly Hemingway to a hospital when during his African safari he suffered from amoebic dysentery ("The Slopes," 105). This connection has proven compelling to biographical critics who see it through the lens of Hemingway's mid-career self-evaluation.

The only interpretive comment found regarding the plane comes from Robert W. Lewis's *Hemingway on Love* and carries a sexual connotation that would seem to be a comment on Harry's alleged promiscuity: "The 'old cock' Harry is put in the Puss Moth, where there is, naturally, room for only one" (110; see P. Smith 359).

Beyond these considerations, however, the Puss Moth carries a significant suggestion of transformation, a key component of redemption. Joseph DeFalco sees Harry as transformed:

> Harry's situation at the literal level is a pathetic one, to be sure, but his mental journey, his recapitulation of his misspent life, purges him of his errant ways. Compie's entrance at the conclusion of the narrative indicates that a transformative process has taken place. Had the situation remained in the realm of the literal, death might have been depicted by the hyena symbol. As it turns out, the hyena is more of a comment on the world Harry has left than on Harry himself. Harry is thus more properly identified with the leopard. (210)

What might the leopard have to do with the Puss Moth? The suggestion of transformation is in Hemingway's choice of aircraft. The Puss Moth was a light, two- or three-seater, single-engine monoplane manufactured by the de Havilland Aircraft Company of Great Britain from 1929 through 1933.[13] De Havilland produced several lines of aircraft designated as moths; these were aircraft whose wings could be folded back to facilitate storage. Seen from above with wings folded, they resemble moths. Compie's plane was officially known as the DH.80A Puss Moth, and fewer than three hundred were manufactured. The moth, which begins life as a caterpillar until it molts and forms wings, is a natural symbol of transformation. However, in its caterpillar stage the puss moth distinguishes itself in two ways: first by its beautiful coat, which is said to resemble that of a cat, and second by the excruciatingly painful sting caused by the spines that form that beautiful coat. It is one of the world's more dangerous insects. The caterpillar is not unlike Harry, who attracted Helen by what he wrote but, while they are in Africa, makes her the victim of his uncharitable invective. This should be enough to sketch out a Harry-unredeemed interpretation, with Harry as a nasty caterpillar who never morphs into a moth.[14] However, it can also support the transformation interpretation, as Harry moves from the ground of the nasty caterpillar to the flight of the beautiful moth. One more consideration must be noted: a new model in the de Havilland line. In 1933, the Puss Moth was replaced by the DH.85, which was produced from 1933 to 1936. De Havilland designated the new model as—of all things—the Leopard Moth. In its caterpillar stage the leopard moth is not irritating or dangerous. In his death flight, Harry is thus equated with the leopard of the story's opening epigraph, thus making Harry's ending a transformative one, validating DeFalco's mythic interpretation.

Narrative VI.C*: Helen's Dream and Discovery of Harry's Death*

Harry's wife is named Helen. While the name suggests ideal beauty, as has been noted (Flora, *Ernest Hemingway* 87), Helen is also involved in the most notable violation of hospitality in western literature, Paris's abduction of Helen, the wife of his host Menelaus. It is this act, of course, that both causes the Trojan War and predetermines the Greeks' eventual victory, as it is Zeus, the father and most powerful of the gods, who enforces the laws of hospitality. While the name may indeed conjure visions of ideal beauty and may inspire analysis, violations of hospitality are at least equally important. Harry accepts Helen as his hostess: "The party's over and you are with your hostess now" (24). In

Harry's case, however, Helen acts as a proper hostess—this despite Harry's uncharitable verbal attacks—supporting him in his last struggle with the *Nada*, enabling him to come to terms with his own life and his own death, and creating the conditions under which he can at least envision his continuance on the trail, albeit not in this life.

Despite his desire to sleep outside, Helen has Harry carried into their tent and thus into the place of hospitality she has created. When death crouches on his chest, he is unable to speak to her to ask her to tell it to go away, nor is he able to insist that he remain outside the tent—and, therefore, outside her hospitality. Although when Harry is lifted into the tent, the weight of death is lifted, and he is once again brought back into her place of hospitality. "He could not speak to tell her to make it go away and it crouched now, heavier, so he could not breathe. And then, while they lifted the cot, suddenly it was all right and the weight went from his chest" (25). This moment is manifestly not his moment of death, for the next morning when Helen awakes to find him dead, she sees that "somehow he had gotten his leg out and it hung down alongside the cot"; the dressing has also come unraveled. Thus Harry lives long enough to get his leg off the cot (25).[15] Several connections can be made. First, the position of the leg might be a result of his positioning himself according to the posture he must assume in Compton's plane in his final, fantastic flight. Or it may be the result of his desire to return to his life on trail. As the leopard has died while acting according to his nature as a predator in following his prey, so Harry, the writer who has lived under the hospitality of the rich for too long, returns to acting according to his nature both as a writer, stalking stories, and as an aviator, taking flight. The unraveled dressing can also be seen as the beginning of the puss moth molting from nasty caterpillar into its beautiful moth stage. Harry takes his last step in returning to the trail as he lifts his leg off his cot. Either result works in Harry's favor. Even if he is repositioning himself according to the interior of the plane, he is returning to the trail, because flight constitutes a proper trail for the former aviator.

Harry is seen in a variety of roles throughout the italicized memories. He is a witness to men and women on trail who continue their journeys, such as the deserter, and who are betrayed, such as the Nansen secretaries and the Austrian officers. He is a man on trail during the Greek retreat and waiting for the train at Karagatch. As a man on trail or traveler, he visits notable places of hospitality and is accepted at them. He offers Williamson hospitality and receives it from the Armenian woman. He rightly (though sadly and painfully) turns the violator of hospitality—the chore boy—over to justice. He accepts the hospitality of and is initiated into the neighborhood of the Place Contrescarpe. It is no surprise that in his dream he offers Compton hospitality, in the form of breakfast and then tea. While on trail, he has seen horrors of war that he cannot think about or have mentioned. These horrors are only spoken of once, which is appropriate, as those who experience such are not wont to talk about them promiscuously or even repeatedly. His failing in matters of hospitality has been to have accepted the hospitality of the rich and to have drunk too much, the latter "a good man's failing," as the Irish say. On the whole, Harry has acted properly, even nobly, on the stage on which Hemingway has made him a player, the stage of hospitality. He simply does not fail in matters of hospitality, as guest, man on trail, host, initiate, or witness. Harry is the man on trail, and the man on trail is the figure in the carpet of "The Snows of Kilimanjaro."

Chapter 10

THE CASE FOR HARRY'S REDEMPTION

> [A]nd they gave him woolen socks and held the gendarmes talking until the tracks had drifted over. . . . [A]nd he gave him all his morphine tablets he had always saved to use himself.
>
> —"The Snows of Kilimanjaro"

The ultimate test of any discussion of "The Snows of Kilimanjaro" is whether it can explain one or both of the sphinxlike conundrums that every reader of the story must confront: the frozen leopard carcass at the beginning of the story and Harry's majestic flight to Kilimanjaro at the story's conclusion.

In his article "'The Snows of Kilimanjaro': An African Purge," Kenneth G. Johnston has stated the problem of the flight rather well: "It is an ending that cannot be supported by the narrative. Harry's few bitter regrets and remarks in his dying moments concerning his betrayal of craft and self do not atone for a wasted artistic life. Clearly, he has not earned the flight to Mount Kilimanjaro. Perhaps the imagined flight was intended to reveal Harry's final illusion, but since the writer is already dead, the reader is left to struggle with the logic" (225).

Critics have struggled with Hemingway's aesthetic logic. Even Earl Rovit, who looks at Harry's death flight as "Hemingway's trick on the reader" and who views Harry as "egocentric, hypocritical, and morally as well as physically rotten," somewhat sarcastically summarizes the redemptive view that "the story elevates him to the snow-capped summit and forces the reader to accept him as a superior man" because of his attitude toward death "and the fact that in the face of death, he practices his craft; *he writes*" (36, 37). Rovit, however, is troubled by the hyena observing and crying over Harry's death. He compares the reader, who accepts the "thoroughly upside-down world" of the corrupt Harry's death flight, to the observing and human-sounding hyena and by extension—Rovit demurring that he is not "pushing the metaphor too far," even though he is—to the other hyena described in *Green Hills of Africa* who, gutshot, comically tears out and devours its own intestines (37, 38).

Rovit's monolithic view of the italicized memories resulted in his overlooking the obvious: the Williamson story, as well as other similar situations in Hemingway's work. Like the picador horses of *Death in the Afternoon* and like the picador horse of chapter 10 of *In Our Time,* Williamson dies amid the horrors of disembowelment. Hemingway, always trying for something new and ever unwilling to repeat himself, does not treat even disembowelment monolithically. The gutshot hyena is treated in a comic mode, as a "dirty joke," although the laughter is consistently attributed to M'Cola, not the narrator (29). Note also what Hemingway writes of the picador horses: "In the tragedy of the bullfight the horse is the comic character. . . . You should be terrified and disgusted at these parodies of horses and what happens to them. . . . They are so unlike horses" (6).

Harry witnesses the disemboweled Williamson, a horrific incident of war. But Williamson is not a parody of a soldier; he is "a fat man, very brave and a good officer although addicted to fantastic shows" (24). Had he regarded the "fantastic shows" as comic, Hemingway would have obligated himself to provide an example, which he certainly does not. Further, the idea that the supposed human failing implied in the description of Williamson as "a fat man" or the supposed failing of his "fantastic shows" is weak. Williamson's "shows" are an understandable reaction to the unimaginable horrors of trench warfare. The idea that they make his manner of death appropriate is as grotesque as Williamson's death itself. Harry does not laugh, as does M'Cola at the hyena, nor does he simply ignore Williamson as Hemingway disregards the picador horses. Hemingway has Harry give Williamson "all his morphine tablets he had always saved to use himself," because Williamson, in essence a man on trail and Harry's guest, deserves the succor the tablets provide in his hour of death (24). Harry's heroic generosity in this instance (as in the Gauertal incident) provides sufficient justification for him to earn his own painless death. In fact, it is Harry's contemplation of and thankfulness for his own painless death that sparks his memory of Williamson's death. Critics who find betrayal in the Williamson incident are blinded by their own agendas. Harry commits no act (of commission or omission) in the Williamson episode that can in any way be regarded as an act of betrayal.

Joseph Flora, however, sincerely asserts Harry's redemption through writing: "A failure in so many ways, Harry nevertheless has hold of the redeeming idea. Writing is for him the ultimate pull toward life. Following his mental recapturing of his first marriage, he says, 'I want to write' . . . , and just before his death he has indeed been writing. How much we cannot say, but the idea redeems" (*Ernest Hemingway* 88). Clearly, what Harry has written will never see print, as Flora indicates: "His gift will never be shared with the world" (88). Art is long but not permanent. It is the connection with others of our kind, rather than a distant deity, that establishes our identity on the existential level. For a writer, it is his readers. For Harry, the only audience left is Helen—and, notably at the very end, he does not betray her.

After the Williamson memory, Harry has a pleasant conversation with Helen, realizing that "the party's over and you are with your hostess now" (24). Helen has, indeed, played the hostess as well as has the older waiter of "A Clean, Well-Lighted Place," and in recognition of that, he refrains from quarreling—at least until she missteps in flattering him:

> He had just felt death come by again.
>
> "You know the only thing I've never lost is curiosity," he said to her.
>
> "You've never lost anything. You're the most complete man I've ever known."
>
> "Christ," he said. "How little a woman knows. What is that? Your intuition?"
>
> Because, just then, death had come and rested its head on the foot of the cot and he could smell its breath. (25)

What Harry could detect was the evil-smelling emptiness of the *Nada*, and his petty quarreling stops for the final time. A similar confrontation with death occurs near the end of **Narrative III** during Harry's sexual thoughts about Helen: "[A]nd as he looked and saw her well known, pleasant smile, he felt death come again" (18). Writing was his way of dealing with the *Nada*, his own response to life's most significant existential question. We note a key passage in the Hemingway Nobel Prize acceptance statement: "For he [the writer] does his work alone and if he is a good enough writer he must face eternity, or the lack of it, each day" (134). Anyone who hears the audio recording of Hemingway reading those words cannot miss the pauses before and after and the chilling emphasis he places on the words *or the lack of it*. Hemingway had noted the evil-smelling emptiness. Whether he saw himself confronting eternity or the lack of it is a matter of some debate, but neither Hemingway's choice nor our own of how to regard that most difficult of existential questions is totally relevant to this story. What Hemingway actually did in relation to that existential question is completely clear: he wrote. That is how he faced that question every day. That is why Harry writes. Even Rovit (albeit begrudgingly and in an endnote) admits this: "Hemingway takes special care to emphasize that Harry is not just thinking of writing, but actually writing. 'I've been writing,' he said. 'But I got tired.' Immediately after that the death-hyena climbs on his chest" (178). Harry's final witnesses, Helen and the hyena, are not his only audience. In the final confrontation, whether it be with eternity or with the evil-smelling emptiness, the writer is also his own audience, and it is thus of importance to Harry that he writes.

Also of relevance to the idea of the redemption by writing theme is Gloria Dussinger's analysis. She concludes that during his death-dream Harry "record[s] faithfully and in precise detail the sensory impressions of his journey. The passage narrating the flight contains colors, textures, motions, temperatures conveyed in the incisive Hemingway prose style. It is the restoration of the seeing eye, which perceives the final flight with as much sensory accuracy as the flashbacks, that announces Harry's victory" (161).

Not surprisingly, Dussinger arrives at this conclusion after more analysis of the italicized memories than most other critics have been willing to offer. Treating **IM I** as a whole, she concludes that the "juncture of disparate topics mirrors the chaotic world of the war generation" (160). She determines that **IM II** "uncovers the real Harry; it deals with his loves and his wartime trauma" (161). Dussinger qualifies as one of the few who consider trauma, what is referred to today as post-traumatic stress disorder, as an aspect of Harry's character or motivation. The burning of his grandfather's house in **IM III** results in the loss of his grandfather's guns, thus introducing a castration theme that parallels the situation with Harry's gangrenous leg.[1] Of the Place Contrescarpe memories, she notes, preparatory to her conclusion, that "[t]he accuracy of the sense impressions signifies the rebirth of Harry's artistic integrity, for the Hemingway hero holds to the truth of the sensations, honesty perceived and recorded" (160).

I must, however, take exception with the remainder of her analysis of the italicized memories. Of **IM IV** she writes: "Additional proof of Harry's forsaking the lie can be found in the fourth flashback.[2] Here Harry names himself the betrayer, an admission he had skirted in the first series, pointing at Nansen and Barker instead" (161). First, there is the difference in motives: Nansen's are humanitarian, and Barker's are clearly self-aggrandizing and sinister.

Second, application of the guest/host and man-on-trail archetypes frees Harry of the charge of betrayal. The only betrayal Dussinger can be read as referring to "in the fourth flashback" is Harry's turning the chore boy over to the sheriff. (Dussinger never mentions the chore boy or any specific betrayal.) Note that it is neither "the law" nor "the police" but a person, a sheriff, to whom Harry hands the boy. The story takes place in an isolated (sixty miles to town) and primitive location. It evokes the primitive values of hospitality, just as does Mérimée's "Mateo Falcone." We have seen killers (Leggatt), enemy combatants (the deserter in the Gauertal, Priam), thieves (Renee from "Brother Sebastian's Friendship," Hardy's Timothy Summers, Hugo's Jean Valjean, Mérimée's Gianetto Sanpiero, London's Jack Westondale), a poacher (Nick Adams), and cutthroats (Richard Guy Isshaw) escape or come close to escaping because of the aid of their hosts or hostesses. But the chore boy was not a man on trail. He was the host. Harry did not give the order to prevent anyone from taking hay: "*About the half-wit chore boy who was left at the ranch that time and told not to let any one get any hay*" (22). Hemingway carefully slips into the passive voice here, not revealing who gave the order. He does not do so to make it look as if Harry is hiding behind the bureaucratic passive or avoiding responsibility, as Dussinger suggests he does in the Nansen and Barker episodes; more likely, he does so simply to avoid having to introduce another otherwise unnecessary character. The chore boy must be turned over to justice for the same reason that Fortunato Falcone is executed by his father: he has grossly violated the traditions of hospitality. That someone else ordered him to prevent the taking of hay or feed does not clear him of the charge of murder. It is his overreaction to the situation—shooting the old man (who had previously beaten him and who threatened to do so again) and leaving his frozen body on the ground for the dogs to partially devour—that compels Harry to turn him over. Leaving the body for the dogs is an appalling affront to humanity. The circumstances fail to sufficiently mitigate the chore boy's actions. If Harry acts otherwise, he becomes complicit in the violation of hospitality. In short, Harry acts properly. Had this not been the case, had Hemingway intended to depict Harry as the betrayer, he would not have included the detail of the dogs devouring part of the frozen corpse. And, clearly, the dogs who devour the body parallel the canid pursuers of so many other works previously discussed. He does not act unfeelingly, for he clearly depicts the boy's anguish at his arrest. Treating bodies of the dead with respect is primal, a tradition older than history, the honoring of which affirms our humanity.

Dussinger's analysis does not otherwise contradict mine up to this point although, to her credit, her analysis depends on a careful and chronological look at the actual content of the italicized memories, with one exception: inexplicably she omits all reference to Williamson (**IM V**) entirely. As once again Harry acts properly, even heroically, and in accordance with the laws of hospitality in his treatment of Williamson, this constitutes a significant omission.

Jerry A. Herndon's is another attempt at a comprehensive view of the italicized memories. In a methodical and thoughtful analysis, Herndon finds in each group of memories episodes of "pain and loss" (121). In the **IM I** group, he finds "the pain and losses he [Harry] has witnessed in the lives of others, even in the lives of nations" (121). In **IM II** he finds "personal losses" (122). In **IM III**, there is "a series of images of pain and loss" (123). In **IM IV** "Harry recalls the beauty of a ranch in Wyoming," the pain and loss seen in the suffering of the chore boy (123). Finally, in **IM V** Harry achieves his goal of expressing "the essence of life . . . 'all in one paragraph,'" as the Williamson episode "puts it all—all the pain and questioning—into one paragraph" (123). This sort of conclusion leads—not at all surprisingly—to Herndon's position that Harry has indeed redeemed himself as both an artist and as a man. As in Dussinger's analysis, but not the analyses of Friedman and Rovit, close attention to the details of Harry's memories inevitably leads to the conclusion that Harry has redeemed himself. Harry's memories are an integral part of the story. They are not Hemingway's garage sale of saved material that he ultimately decided not to use. "The Snows of Kilimanjaro" is not a dumping ground, and the contents of Harry's memories cannot convincingly be interpreted monolithically.

The second of the story's great conundrums is the leopard, which in the epigraph is linked inextricably to Mount Kilimanjaro. Also inextricably linked is the leopard at the beginning of Dante's *Commedia* to any subsequent literary reference to a leopard. Every leopard in literature does not echo Dante, but so famous is Dante's leopard that one must pause and consider. Such consideration also applies to Hemingway's leopard, another of the most famous leopards in literature; Dante's Paradise is reached only by ascending Mount Purgatory, just as the Masai *Ngàje Ngài*, the House of God, is found at the top of Mount Kilimanjaro. A critical commonplace regarding "The Snows of Kilimanjaro" is the Dantesque appropriateness of Harry's gangrene as emblematic of his desertion of his talent. Accordingly, one must ask whether the horridly dramatic and painful death of Williamson, the fat man "addicted to fantastic shows," is similarly emblematic and appropriate (24). The sanctimonious argument would be that the manner of his death is, in a Dantesque manner, appropriate punishment for his "fantastic shows." However, since it is clearly a fool's errand to try to out-Dante Dante in concocting the cruelly appropriate, the ever-competitive Hemingway, eager to do his round in the ring with Dante, counters by granting grace rather than inflicting epic punishment.[3] Therefore,

Hemingway has Harry give Williamson a pass, grace (under pressure, no less) in the form of his morphine tablets.

Harry has indeed neglected his talent, but he has been a righteous man in his treatment of archetypal travelers—both the deserter and Williamson (and has condemned the killing of other travelers—the secretaries in the snow and the Austrian officers on Christmas leave). He has obeyed the laws of Zeus, shown *philoxenia;* in the Christian tradition he has offered hospitality on Christmas Day and "for Christ sake." Hemingway grants him the grace of a pass to the top of Kilimanjaro, to *Ngàje Ngài,* to the House of God, because he has done the right thing in life, if not in art.

Hemingway depicts Harry as both a generous and even heroic host (to the deserter, to Williamson, and, even in his dream, to old Compton) and as man on trail (especially in the italicized memories that depict his journalistic coverage of the Greco-Turkish War). He has witnessed and been appalled by betrayals he has seen (of Nansen's secretaries and the Austrian officers) or those that were before his time (of the Communards of 1871). He has never been the household member eager to betray the guest, nor has he served as betrayer in the role of host. He has never taken on the part of uniformed authority in pursuit of the person on trail. To assume that Harry has betrayed the chore boy is to grossly misunderstand the ethics of hospitality and guest-host relations. Within those time-honored ethics, Harry has always acted properly. Further, the story never depicts him as responsible for the death of another human being, although some critics have taken him to task for his promiscuity. Harry has made love, not war, which many will argue is to his credit. The only violence Harry is depicted as committing is in the street fight with the British gunner subaltern—over who would spend the night with the Armenian woman. If causes such as this were all that humankind fought over, the world would be an incomparably better place.

A writer does not consign his character to a grotesque, Dantesque hell because he has deserted his art. He does so when his character has deserted humanity—which Harry has not done. The penalty for deserting his writing is inherent: his books are not published, and nobody reads them. For the critics, treating the italicized memories monolithically is a key element in denying that Harry achieves redemption. As Herndon's perceptive analysis asserts—after his detailed examination of Harry's memories—Harry has redeemed himself both aesthetically and morally.

Harry has earned his pass. He goes to Africa to "work the fat off his soul," and—like the leopard—dies on trail (11). Hemingway clearly states in his epigraph that the leopard's reason for climbing to such an altitude is unknown. His body, however, remains. Both leave mysteries behind—the leopard's reason for climbing so high and the books Harry might have written. Granted, Harry's body rots on the plain, but his death flight takes him to the mountain top, where the leopard is.

Hemingway must be a proper host to his character. Harry is Hemingway's double, "a character like me whose defects I know" ("The Art of the Short Story" 316). Harry is to Hemingway as Jack Westondale is to Malemute Kid, as Leggett is to Conrad's ship captain narrator, as Jean Valjean is to the bishop, as Villon is to the old Knight, as Priam is to Achilles, as the deserter, the slaughtered Austrian officers, and Williamson are to Harry. Harry is Hemingway's own man on trail, to whom he has shown *philoxenia* by granting him the beautiful death flight to the top of Mount Kilimanjaro.

And we, the readers, must each come to our own reactions to Harry, for it is in our hearts where Harry follows his trail. Do we play the role of host who takes in the traveler, or do we take on the role of the untrusting household member who, disregarding what Harry has been through, would slam the door in his face on the basis of his bickering with his wife? Let those who have not bickered throw the first stones.

Epilogue

HISTORICAL, BIOGRAPHICAL, CRITICAL

Historical

Various critics have given the specifics of hospitality scenes and plots, as well as the specifics of the hero's journey, detailed and thoughtful analysis. When applied to literary studies, Arnold Van Gennep's classification of the rites of passage into rites of separation, transformation, and incorporation can explain and justify otherwise mysterious specifics of some literary plots. Joseph Campbell's application of the monomyth provides, in its exegesis of the heroic journey, the most user-friendly plot construction guide in the history of literature. Steve Reece's outline and analysis of the component parts of the Homeric hospitality scene reveal the ancient roots of hospitality scenes. Scholars of the Milman Parry / Albert Lord school, as well as Julian Jaynes's theory of the bicameral nature of pre-Homeric and Homeric verse, reveal enough about the ancient plot elements to strongly suggest their genesis in the collective unconscious.

None of these, however, includes those elements of the man-on-trail archetype that make it a plot pattern with unique features, despite that it also includes elements of hospitality scenes, rites-of-passage plots, and heroic-journey plots. These elements bear repetition. The man-on-trail plot tends to be focalized through the perspective of the host as often as through the hero on his journey. The host accepts the man on trail intuitively and immediately. The importance of this element cannot be understated. The host acts instinctively rather than according to the dictates and/or requirements of his social group. His decision cannot be called irrational, because the host does not reject the rational. He simply bypasses it. The decision is a-rational. This a-rationality—found in works of literature from widely varying times and places—constitutes the strongest evidence that the host, the author, and the reader all react to the compelling power of the man-on-trail plot's origin as a set of primordial images from the collective unconscious of mankind and not to an origin in traditional or contemporary cultural practices.

Pursuit is also an element of the man-on-trail plot, though Campbell also quite emphatically includes it as a major element of his monomyth. The man-on-trail plot adds two heretofore largely unrecognized elements, one in how the tale is told and the other in its specific content. The first is a tendency to focalize through the host rather than through the guest/stranger/quest hero. The second consists of the related elements of delay or obstruction of pursuit by the host and of aid rendered to the stranger for the specific purpose of helping him or her escape pursuit. Once again, these elements have been shown to appear in works from sufficiently disparate times and places to suggest an ultimate origin in the collective unconscious.

This study thus suggests an answer to the problem Joseph DeFalco first stated: "How much of Hemingway's use of the journey artifice and other manifestations of psychological and mythological symbolism is conscious or unconscious is, of course, difficult if not impossible to ascertain" (18).

As a cursory review of Hemingway's oeuvre has shown, Hemingway has used elements of rite-of-passage, hospitality and man-on-trail plots with astonishing frequency, climaxing, but not ending, with "The Snows of Kilimanjaro." What work of literature mentions more places of hospitality per equivalent page? What author has set more stories in bars? The answer to that question may lead easily to a tabloid-worthy excursion through evidence of Hemingway's alcoholism. However, when his settings in hospitals, cafés, restaurants, boardinghouses, brothels, hotels, bal musettes, campsites, and transportation vehicles and stations are considered, it becomes clear that his imaginative life was animated by a search for hospitality on both literal and metaphorical levels and perhaps even on the psychological or spiritual levels. And biographers should consider this same focus on hospitality on the personal level as a key component of Hemingway's personality. Add to that the number of hospitality providers who play key roles in his stories—cooks, bartenders, hotel padrones and proprietors, waiters, waitresses, prostitutes, parents, nurses, and doctors—and the picture becomes even more compelling.

There is an old, perhaps apocryphal tale of a romance writer who published 118 romance novels of the girl-meets-boy, girl-loses-boy, girl-finds-boy-and-lives-happily-after variety. The joke, of course, was always that she did not write 118 novels. Rather she wrote the same novel 118 times. Ernest Hemingway quite consciously and proudly chose never to be that writer. He could have amassed a fortune writing sequels to *A Farewell to Arms.* He could have made enough money in a few years to retire and spend an extended retirement deep-sea fishing and drinking. He chose not to. In his Nobel Prize acceptance speech, he rejected such an approach consciously and specifically. Making the argument that any one of Hemingway's books or short stories is a retread of a previous one puts one on a fool's errand. Yet, the recurring archetypal plots, themes, and characters are revelatory. To his credit, he puts the same pieces together differently each time. The same parts appear in stories by Faulkner, Steinbeck, Joyce, London, Maupassant, Flaubert, Tolstoy, Pushkin, Twain, Crane, Shakespeare, and others Hemingway read on a regular basis, but never at the same level of concentration at which they appear in his own works. A writer as determined as Hemingway was to avoid repeating himself might have worked at a lower concentration of these elements. Certainly, as has been demonstrated, these elements appeared in his reading. He could have consciously derived these plot elements from his reading, or—more likely—encountering them in his reading may have permanently opened a metaphorical doorway through which they emerged from the collective unconscious and entered into his works without his being more than dimly aware of their predominance or their overall patterns of recurrence. There is no evidence to indicate that he owned copies of works either Maud Bodkin or Joseph Campbell, and at any rate most of his major works were published before Campbell's *The Hero with a Thousand Faces,* a book that informs DeFalco's pioneering analysis. At the same time, he wrote journalistic pieces on refugees on trail—"A Silent, Ghastly Procession," on the plight of the refugees of the Greco-Turkish War in 1922 and "Refugees from Thrace" (*By-Line* 51–52, 56–60). Man-on-trail elements—the Greek refugees and their pursuers, the Turks—are presented in the first of these; the second includes a description of Madame Marie's, the grotesque, lice- and mosquito-ridden excuse for hospitality in Adrianople. He never dignifies her establishment with terms like hotel or inn, simply referring to it as "Madame Marie's." The madame herself, slovenly and drunken, price gouges shamelessly. Loathsome as the accommodations are, they are still beyond the means of the refugees stumbling along in the rain. Both of these pieces appeared long before he had the opportunity to internalize through his reading the literary components, including many of the works discussed here, of the man-on-trail plot. The evidence thus seems to suggest that the answer to DeFalco's question lies more in the area of unconscious or intuitive adaptation of the archetypes than of conscious adaptation through literary or cultural conditions.

If what we have seen here constitutes the collective unconscious speaking to us through the various points of view of writers from many diverse times and places—Hemingway of course included, then we must consider what the messages of these archetypes reveal to us, for they may well speak to our time as well.

Starting at the beginning of Hemingway's career we see in *in our time* (and repeated in *In Our Time*) the tragic movement of refugees—entire peoples on trail. Perhaps the most famous image from Hemingway's treatment of this event is his presentation of the woman in labor—one of the most vulnerable moments a human being can face—in the back of a moving cart in a long column of Greek refugees in the rain along the Karagatch road, complete with pursuers, in this case the Turks. Its journalistic genesis in his first-hand reporting on the event ("A Silent, Ghastly Procession," *By-Line* 51–52) for *The Toronto Daily Star* (20 October 1922) resonates with the power of his understated and heart-rending description. That piece later supplied chapter 3 of *in our time.* In the Nansen episode of "The Snows of Kilimanjaro," Nansen's "exchange of populations" solution results in the similarly tragic outcome of the secretaries who die in the mountain snow. There are no specific pursuers, but the secretaries' fate is associated with bureaucratic indifference and incompetence. Hemingway's implied criticism of the entire situation is treated with extraordinary sensitivity in Charlton Heston's audio recording of "The Snows of Kilimanjaro"; Heston pronounces *exchange of populations* at a slightly slower rate and *populations* with slightly more emphasis on the first syllable than in everyday usage, giving the phrase an entirely appropriate tone of bureaucratic euphemism and complacency. Looking at these pieces from the perspective of our time, *exchange of populations* has apparently been drained of its euphemistic effect, possibly through usage, since euphemisms often suffer a short shelf life. It has been replaced by a fresh and temporarily sanitizing upgrade to *ethnic cleansing.* In earlier decades, Hitler euphemized mass murder as *the final solution.* Following the defeat of Nazism, the world adopted the terms *genocide* and *Holocaust,* words whose derivations resist euphemistic usage. The refugee crisis continues in various spots around the globe, most notably for this study in the eastern Mediterranean, where Hemingway decades earlier had so movingly described similarly inhuman slaughter.

National responses to the movement of refugee populations have often spurned the ancient traditions of hospitality. Around the world, refugees languish in camps for years. Opportunistic politicians demonize asylum-seekers as murderers, rapists, and drug dealers. Many come from nations where drug gangs react violently to the refusals of those who will not join their ranks and where drug cartels execute their competitors. The practice of hanging the beheaded bodies of victims from bridges is common among narco-terrorists. Upon arrival in the host country, refugees often experience the questionable hospitality of corporate, for-profit detention centers, sometimes euphemized as detention "facilities." Movements of strangers, refugees, men on trail, or anyone guilty of "otherness," have been, and are today, slowed by border guards and fences. Epic walls followed or are under proposal in places like East Berlin and the border between the United States and Mexico. Deadly force was employed, for example, at the Berlin Wall and still is used at the border between North and South Korea. These walls are not uniquely modern; they have precedents in such barriers as the Great Wall of China and Hadrian's Wall separating England and Scotland. Policies such as these represent a dark and sinister rabbit hole, our entry into which constitutes an unfortunate rite of passage. In particular, the passage is a rite of separation, which always requires leaving something behind. In these cases and at appalling risk, we leave behind the ancient traditions of hospitality and the portion of our humanity that is nurtured by those traditions.

Biographical

Archetypal figures sometimes appeared in Hemingway's life, and at times he became the archetypal host.

Two of Hemingway's contributions to *Esquire* record his experiences with men of archetypal qualities who passed through his life during his time in Key West and who have some relevance to ideas pursued in this study. Most writers—Hemingway certainly not excluded, as his sons lived to testify—prefer to work in a quiet environment. In "The Sights of Whitehead Street: A Key West Letter," Hemingway describes what the mythologists would call a "threshold guardian," an elderly, scary-looking man Hemingway hired to sit in front of the Whitehead Street house in the mornings while he worked (*By-Line* 192–97). The man's job was to either scare away the tourists who would infringe on Hemingway's writing time or to convince them that he was actually Hemingway.

Despite his frustrations with unwelcome visitors (see, for example, Baker, *A Life Story,* 283), Hemingway could be the most generous of hosts. "Monologue to the Maestro: A High Seas Letter," his October 1935 *Esquire* contribution, begins with a stranger at his door: "About a year and a half ago a young man came to the front door of the house in Key West and said that he had hitch-hiked down from upper Minnesota to ask your correspondent a few questions about writing" (*By-Line* 213–20). The young Arnold Samuelson wanted to be a writer and wanted to go to sea. Hemingway hired him as a deckhand and night watchman for the *Pilar,* even keeping hours free for him every day to work on his writing. Samuelson played the violin, and so earned the nickname Maestro. A profile of him and the time he spent with the Hemingways occupies a significant portion of Paul Hendrickson's *Hemingway's Boat* (2011). Samuelson never found success as a writer; however, his book *With Hemingway: A Year in Key West and Cuba* (1984) did find success, albeit sadly, three years after his death in 1981.

One of the more thoroughly researched and written niche biographies of Hemingway in recent years has been Paul Hendrickson's insightful *Hemingway's Boat: Everything He Loved in Life and Lost, 1934–1961* (2011). It is certainly longer and more substantive than many full-life biographies. Although many family members and friends appear in the book, Hendrickson devotes much of his considerable efforts to narrating and examining the roles of three significant people from Hemingway's life during this period: his son Gregory, Arnold Samuelson, and Walter Houk. Houk usually receives brief mention in Hemingway biographies, but Hendrickson's account is extensive and is the gold standard.

Hemingway met Houk in 1949, when he hired as a part-time secretary Houk's fiancé Juanita "Nita" Jensen, who worked at the American embassy in Cuba. Walter also worked at the embassy, as a diplomatic officer. The couple became social friends of the Hemingways and often accompanied Hemingway aboard the *Pilar.* He participated in their wedding ceremony, giving away the bride. Walter wrote a memoir in his later years, eventually donating it and other Hemingway materials to the Firestone Library at Princeton University.

Hendrickson narrates an event that lends some insight into one of Hemingway's personal offerings of hospitality, on the occasion of Walter and Nita announcing their wedding: "[T]he lovebirds drove out to the *finca* with their surprise news. Nita, who didn't quite have Hemingway twisted around her little finger, had said that evening: 'Papa, won't you please come? Papa, will you be one of our witnesses? Papa, would you give me away?' 'Done, daughter,' he'd answered. And almost in the next heartbeat: 'Would you like to have the reception here?'" (309).

He replies to the first request with a quickness that reveals not just his willingness but his enthusiasm. The immediacy of his offering his home for the reception is, as we have seen repeatedly, unfiltered and genuine. He not only sought and enjoyed hospitality, but he offered it spontaneously as well, bypassing consideration and acting instead on intuition.

Even on a less happy occasion, Hemingway maintained his generosity with his guests. The inspiration for the character of Renata in *Across the River and into the Trees* (1951) was a young Italian woman named Adriana Ivancich. Hemingway's romantic pursuit of her, fortunately for all involved, ended without success and is analyzed without fail and in detail by all full-life Hemingway biographies. For a time, Adriana's brother Gianfranco was a guest for an extended stay at the Finca Vigía. The tabloid view of his offer of hospitality is that he offered his home in order to ingratiate himself to the family and thus advance his romantic designs. Walter Houk narrates an incident involving Gianfranco that sheds quite a different light on the matter. This story is from an e-mail posted to the Hemingway listserv housed at the University of Michigan. "René" is René Villareal, Hemingway's majordomo and coauthor, with his son Raúl, of *Hemingway's Cuban Son: Reflections on the Writer by His Longtime Majordomo.*

Mr. Houk's story goes like this:

In 1950 the Hemingways were in Europe. As per usual René Villareal and Miss Nita Jensen, then the future Mrs. Walter Houk, were entrusted with the care of the finca. Hemingway had previously invited Gianfranco to treat it as his own home. Gianfranco did—to the annoyance of Nita and Raúl. He arrived late one night with a carload of boisterous cronies, who engaged in a food fight while cooking, stuck flowers in loaves of bread, and perpetrated other adolescent pranks. Nita wrote to Hemingway in Europe about the incident as well as other bad behavior, such as leaving furniture outside, neglecting to use ashtrays, and leaving food under the furniture. Mary wrote from Europe sympathizing with the staff.

Hemingway's response was clear: Gianfranco was a guest and should be treated respectfully all times. Have we not seen these characters before under different names? There is no suggestion of pursuit or delay thereof, so it forms a hospitality plot rather than a man-on-trail plot. Its characters, albeit in a more comic genre, parallel those of the episode of Jean Valjean's visit to the Bishop of Digne in Hugo's *Les Misérables.* Hemingway is the Bishop of Digne; Gianfranco, Jean Valjean; Mary, Nita; and Raúl, the staff not sure of how to treat the guest. Hemingway, every bit as assured and individuated as the Bishop of Digne, acts as decisively as he did in the Houk wedding episode. Although he acts in a letter rather than in person, he refuses completely, though politely, to validate Nita and Raúl's feelings. He speaks in the individuated voice of the true host.

Critical

Hemingway's recurring and persistent use of hospitality elements in his stories, novels, and even his nonfiction indicates that his access to the hospitality and man-on-trail series of archetypes must have been, at least to a degree, intuitive and drawn from the depths of the collective unconscious rather than taken completely from contemporary cultural traditions, customs, and mores. Had he been fully conscious of his predilection to include these archetypes, he would likely have curtailed their use. His reactions to the incidents in his life suggest the same predilection.

Regarding "The Snows of Kilimanjaro," whether or not one agrees with the analysis of Harry as redeemed, it is my hope that one thing should now be clear to all: monolithic analysis of Harry's memories—that is, analysis without due attention to the recurrent elements of plot, character, and setting in those memories and of how those memories interact with each other and with the overall narrative framework—can no longer purport to be complete, definitive, or even useful. A deep irony haunts the analyses of those critics who condemn Harry for not writing about his memories but who in their own analyses of "The Snows of Kilimanjaro" also fail to address the specifics of Harry's memories.

ACKNOWLEDGMENTS

My mother always kept our house supplied with books and passed on a love of reading. In the classes of Charles Cutshall, Ralph Smith, and Arthur Knight at California State College of Pennsylvania I had my first exposure to Hemingway. I first heard the word *archetype* there also, in Jack Goodstein's class in Victorian literature. Daniel E. Wilson, a student of Philip Young, advised my master's thesis on Hemingway there.

Irwin Steinberg introduced me to archetypal and mythic criticism during my time as a graduate student at Carnegie Mellon University. Sumner Ferris of California State College and Jan Cohn of Carnegie Mellon University—through their teaching and through their example—opened my eyes to the methods and the thrills of literary research. Pete Jones advised my doctoral thesis on California writers, one of whom was Jack London.

After I taught English literature for a couple of decades at Butler County Community College of Pennsylvania, my department dean, William Miller, and my academic vice president, Francie Spigelmyer, decided that I should teach American literature as well. In preparing for these courses, I reread after many years "The Snows of Kilimanjaro" and immediately saw the similarity between the deserter-in-the-Gauertal incident and Jack London's "To the Man on Trail." I presented those findings at the Hemingway Society Conference in Petoskey, Michigan, in 2012. The Butler County Community College Foundation financially supported my attendance at that conference, and Dean Miller financially supported my attendance at that conference and others.

At the Petoskey conference, I was pleasantly surprised by the positive reactions and encouragement from such notable Hemingway scholars and

Hemingway Society regulars as Fred Svoboda, Peter Hays, Joseph Flora, Boris Vedofsky, and Peter Krynicki.

My initial Petoskey presentation and my written submission to *The Hemingway Review* were read by Eric Pedersen, Joy Walsh, Greg Mason, Steve Josephs, Renee Anderson, and Scott Campbell, all of whom provided thoughtful feedback. Joy Walsh provided feedback on the development of this project as well. Ernest Hemingway Mainland, the owner and resident of Windemere, the Hemingway family cottage, generously opened the home to attendees of the 2012 Hemingway Society Conference in Petoskey. Susan Beegel, then editor of *The Hemingway Review,* saw the importance of the *Stories by English Authors* and *Stories by American Authors* volumes well before I did and encouraged me to write a second article on them for the *Review.* She was understanding when my article grew longer than she or I had anticipated.

Throughout my research on the conference presentation, on the *Hemingway Review* articles, and on this book, Butler County Community College librarian Jean Shumway performed amazing feats of research and acquired numerous interlibrary loans. At the 2018 Paris conference, Chris Warren of the Hemingway Society graciously informed me of the basic facts I needed to track down the murder on which the chore-boy incident is based. Thanks again to Jean Shumway for locating the original newspaper accounts of the murder and subsequent trial.

Former colleagues provided assistance. James Morrow of Butler County Community College explained to me the significance of the difference between the slow-twitch muscles of dogs and the fast-twitch muscles of cats Erika Nail helped me deal with some mysteries of the digital world. Mike Aikins told me to stop trying to write a book and just write it. Bill and Patty Weisberger supported me and never seemed to doubt that I could do this.

Paul H. and Philip G. gave me thoughtful and informed advice on sensitive issues.

Leah Warsing aided me in gaining access to databases.

Tom Adams and Daniel Homfelt of the Hemingway email list at the University of Michigan graciously produced copies of digital documents that disappeared from my files when I retired. William McFarland of the same group provided me with information from his copy of a rare facsimile of a Hemingway manuscript. The members of this group represent a huge body of knowledge and are pleased to have a forum in which to share it.

The Kent State University Press peer reviewers were especially helpful; they tended to both the forest and the trees. Both Kirk Curnutt and the second reader made me see my stylistic excesses, lapses of taste, inconsistencies, and plain old errors. They saved me from myself. Thanks to Kirk for recommending ways of broadening the appeal of the book to reach a wider audience. The second reader reminded me that Hemingway taught us that less can be more and that, therefore, some passages of analytical overkill should be deleted (and they were).

Will Underwood, my acquisitions editor, kept me calm through the entire unsettling process. His willingness to stage the peer reviews sequentially rather than simultaneously was enormously helpful to me. Erin Holman, my copy editor, saved me from at least one embarrassing error per page. Both were unfailingly positive and encouraging.

Julian Warsing handled the photographic portraiture assignment thoughtfully and professionally, making me look better than I usually look.

The physical appearance of the book was very important to me. The design choices made by Christine Brooks showed both creativity and a very quick understanding of the design features that I indicated were important to me. Mary Young managed the whole editorial process without drama. Overall, all of the KSUP personnel I came into contact with carried out their roles in an unfailingly professional manner. The questions I asked were always answered, and the replies were notably prompt.

My brothers and sisters, Daniel, Dale, Jill, and Nancy supported me throughout the process, as did my children, Daniel and Melissa, all matter-of-factly, as if they always knew.

The beautiful Raquel gave me *At the Hemingways* and her love.

The totality of the thanks I owe these individuals and groups for their contributions and support is humbling. Thank you, one and all. I hope your association with this book will make you proud.

The reader may find defects in this book. I own them.

I was able to reprint in lightly to heavily modified form my articles originally published in *The Hemingway Review.* For this I thank The Hemingway Foundation. All Rights Reserved. Copyright 2013 Volume 33, Number 1. Copyright 2014 Volume 33, Number 2.

I also thank The Hemingway Foundation for permission to quote lines from a poem by Ernest Hemingway, "They All Made Peace—What Is Peace." Ernest Hemingway, *Complete Poems,* edited by Nicholas Gerogiannis. Revised ed. University of Nebraska Press, 1992, p. 49. Copyright © 1979, 1992 by The Ernest Hemingway Foundation and Nicholas Gerogiannis.

I am grateful for permission to use quotations from the Oxford World's Classics translation of Prosper Mérimée's *Carmen,* copyright Nicholas Jotcham, 1989, reproduced with permission of the Licensor through PLSclear.

Material from "Under the Ridge" is reprinted with the permission of Scribner, a division of Simon & Schuster, Inc. All rights reserved. Copyright © 1936 by Ernest Hemingway; Copyright renewed © 1964 by Mary Hemingway.

Material from "The Snows of Kilimanjaro" is reprinted with the permission of Scribner, a division of Simon & Schuster, Inc. All rights reserved. Copyright © 1938 by Ernest Hemingway; Copyright renewed © 1966 by Mary Hemingway.

Material from "Under the Ridge" and "The Snows of Kilimanjaro" from The Complete Short Stories by Ernest Hemingway, published by Jonathan Cape, is reproduced by permission of The Random House Group Ltd. © 1992.

"Waitin' Around To Die" by Townes Van Zandt © 1968 Silver Dollar Music, Inc. (ASCAP) admin. by Wixen Music Publishing, Inc. All Rights Reserved. Used by Permission.

Appendix

EVENTS OF HARRY'S LIFE

A Speculative Chronology

Useful sources for constructing a chronology of Harry's life are "The Slopes of Kilimanjaro: A Biographical Perspective," by Carlos Baker, Hemingway's official biographer; the two *Texas Quarterly* articles coauthored by Robert Lewis and Max Westbrook; and Robert O. Stephens's discussion of "Snows" in his *Hemingway's Nonfiction* (273–82).

Baker asserts that though "the episodes Harry recalls ignore strict chronology . . . [,] if they are arranged in historical sequence, they provide a rough running account of scenes from the life of the author" (104). Note that Baker traces episodes in the story that parallel those from Hemingway's life; he does not commit the biographical fallacy of claiming that the order of events in Hemingway's life must perforce determine Harry's chronology. Accordingly, Baker's research is helpful in determining the order of historical events as well as events Hemingway invented. Westbrook (in "The Stewardship of Ernest Hemingway," part 3 of "The Texas Manuscript") makes similar confirmations using parallels to *A Moveable Feast.* Stephens finds that Hemingway actually did write about much of what Harry failed to—more often in his nonfiction than in his fiction and after as well as before "Snows."

From Childhood to Early Adulthood

Baker explains that the log house of **III.1** belongs to Hemingway's Grandfather Bacon and is located near Petoskey, Michigan. However, while Grandfather Bacon's log house was in Michigan, Harry's grandfather's house could easily be in Wyoming—which would make Harry's chronology more manageable. If one assumes that Harry is but a few years older than Hemingway, then all of **IV** (herding cattle and the chore-boy incident) might well take place as Harry comes to manhood in Wyoming before serving in World War 1. The chore-boy incident takes place during bitter winter weather, a season Hemingway did not spend in Wyoming. Baker regards the chore-boy incident as Hemingway's invention (it is actually based on a real 1913 murder and on my reading of "Mateo Falcone"; see chapter 6, pages 107–14).

The incidents at the ranch are otherwise difficult to situate. They could have occurred before World War I, especially if we accept that Harry is older than Hemingway by a few years; the difficulty with such a placement is the high degree of responsibility Harry shows in dealing with the murder committed by the chore boy. If, however, it is placed after the war, it is still difficult to fit in. Do we assume that his grandparents have died and that Harry has inherited the ranch? Does he then leave to participate in World War I?

World War I

Baker follows these with the episodes from World War I: fighting on the Austrian front (which Harry discusses with Hans in **I.6**) and Williamson's death (**V**), both of which Hemingway seems to have invented. Baker does not include the Barker episode (**1.5**), which also seems to have been invented.

Living in Place Contrescarpe and visiting the Black Forest

Baker writes that the Parisian "cityscape" (**III.6**) is described as it appeared from the flat where Ernest and Hadley lived in 1922–23. This would also include everything about Place Contrescarpe (**III.4–7**), as well as the fishing trip to the Black Forest described in **III.2–3**—the rented trout stream and the suicide of the proprietor of the Triberg Hotel.

During this period (fall 1922) both Hemingway and Harry cover the Greco-Turkish War. Hemingway's *Toronto Star* articles on the refugees of this conflict were published in October and November 1922. This includes virtually all of **II.1–4**, which forms a complete and linear narrative.

At this point, problems arise in attempting to equate the domestic lives of Hemingway and Harry. Unlike Harry, Hemingway had children; thus, he returned to North America where his first son was born. Baker notes that Hemingway did not use the apartment Ernest and Hadley lived in on the rue Notre Dame des Champs in "Snows" because he had already done so in *Green Hills of Africa.* He points out, however, that it was during their tenure there, during the winters of 1924–25 and 1925–26 that they stayed in "a village called Schruns in the Austrian Voralberg" (137). The Herr Lent episode (**I.4**) is based on one of Hemingway's experiences from this period. The parallels between Hemingway's life and the life of Harry, his character, break down seriously at this point: "How many years had he lived in the Voralberg and the Arlberg? It was four." (8). Thus, Harry might have lived in the Voralberg and the Arlberg from about 1924 to 1927.

Adulthood

When Harry witnesses the events of the Greco-Turkish War (1919–22), he seems to do so as a journalist rather than as a combatant. Since so many critics have commented on the autobiographical elements of "The Snows of Kilimanjaro," should we simply follow the settings in the order in which Hemingway encountered them? This theory is complicated by Harry's having stayed in places where Hemingway never did: the Gauertal, the Voralberg, and the Arlberg, for example. Harry has also been to Africa before, a period of his life also difficult to place (10).

Postwar Living in Austria for Four Years

The exact order of events is unclear.

1. The deserter-in-the-Gauertal.
2. Skiing in Schrunz.
3. Discussing the war, after the war, with Hans, an Austrian soldier.
4. Four years in the Voralberg and the Arlberg; the fox seller; kirsch; and skiing.
5. Postwar trout fishing in the Black Forest.
6. Two ways of walking to the trout stream.
7. Suicide of the Triberg Hotel's proprietor.

Paris

The order of events is unclear.

1. Paris: neighbors at Place Contrescarpe.

2. The drunkards and the *sportifs*, descendants of the Communards; streets of Paris; apartment where he lived and started his writing career.

3. Sights from his Paris apartment.

4. Policeman sleeping with the concierge; Marie's protest of the eight-hour working day as promoting drunkenness of working-class men.

5. Quarreling with and losing the love of his life, following women who looked like her, writing her a letter asking her to write back.

6. Sees an American poet in a café talking with Tristan Tzara.

7. His current wife sees and asks about the newly arrived letter from his former love, requested in the fifth incident.

Greco-Turkish War (1921–22)

Events 1–6 seem to take place between the fifth and sixth events of the Paris section.

1. Picking up a woman, then leaving her to pick up an Armenian woman.

2. Vicious street fight with a Brit gunner over the Armenian woman.

3. Escaping from the MPs and having sex with the Armenian woman.

4. Leaving for Anatolia the next night; newly arrived incompetent Constantine officers perpetrate a friendly-fire incident.

5. The attack of the Turks on the bizarrely attired Greek Evzone troops and sights of horror.

6. October 1922: Waiting for the Orient Express in Thrace after the Greek retreat.

7. The secretaries whom Nansen sent die in the snow.

Africa

"Africa was where he had been happiest in the good time of his life, so he had come out here to start again" (10). It is difficult to locate this time in his life.

1. Marriage to Helen and life among the rich.

2. Safari in Africa.

NOTES

Introduction

1. See Hamilton (175–76). Jung heavily revised *Psychology of the Unconscious.* It is accessible currently as volume 5 of his collected works and retitled *Symbols of Transformation.*

2. See Trogdon, *Lousy Racket* (260), for more detailed data on numbers printed of each title.

3. Subsequent to "Snows," Hemingway employed italics in a recalled memory passage in chapter 21 of *To Have and Have Not.* (Thanks go to Kirk Curnutt for reminding me of this.)

4. Harding notes the similarity of "Snows" to *In Our Time* (28). Santangelo contrasts the interchapters of *In Our Time* with Harry's memories (254–56).

5. The first small-press volume was *Three Stories and Ten Poems,* which is more of a random collection rather than the unified whole that *in our time* clearly is. The spring 1923 "Exiles" edition of *The Little Review, Three Stories and Ten Poems,* and the 1924 *in our time* are available on the internet. The latter two were printed in facsimile editions in small numbers in the 1970s. Prior to their appearance online, and even afterward, they have been accessed because readers have tracked them down, not because they have appeared on bookstore shelves. Hemingway himself had problems accessing copies of the 1924 *in our time.*

The number of copies of *in our time* is usually given as 170, which is demonstrably incorrect. Three hundred copies were printed, but 130 included a printing error in which the frontispiece portrait of Hemingway was marred by the watermark visible over Hemingway's face. See Grissom, who reports that the exact number of damaged copies that survive is unknown (29). The Le Bruit du temps 2011 reprint of the Éditions Gallimard 1999 French/English edition includes an image of the damaged frontispiece, clear visual evidence of the survival of at least one damaged copy.

6. From the extremely rare 1923 text printed in *The Little Review,* to the 1924 *in our time,* to the 1925 Boni & Liveright *In Our Time,* and finally to the edition of the 1930

Scribner's *In Our Time,* variations in the texts occur, some significant, some not (see Cohen; Grissom).

7. Hemingway's epigraph lists the height as 19,710 feet. The *Encyclopedia Britannica* gives it as 19,340 feet. See also Helama (119). Current online sources list the height as 19,341 feet, for a difference of 369 feet, more than the length of an American football field—including the end zones! Early measurements of the mountain's height were made in meters, opening up the possibility that the incorrect measurement might have been the result of an error in mathematics by either Hemingway or the source he used; such an error, however, seems unlikely, as the first measurement—of 6010 meters, published in 1891 by Hans Meyer—corresponds roughly to Hemingway's 19,710 feet. A more accurate measurement of 5930 meters, which Fritz Klute made in 1921 and Clement Gillman used in 1923, might well have been available to Hemingway or to fact-checkers at Scribner's (3). Hemingway might have consulted an outdated source or intentionally used an inaccurate figure. For discussion of Hemingway's possibly intentional inaccuracies, see chapter 9, note 2. This note would not have been possible without the thoughtful input of Samuli Helama, geographer and Hemingway scholar.

8. In 1952 Philip Young, preceded Rovit in presenting the Bierce thesis, noting that Hemingway included "An Occurrence" in his *Men at War* (1942). Crane (1969) and Habibi (2002) also develop the Bierce comparison. In addition, Young (1952; 1966) proposes Stephen Crane's *The Red Badge of Courage* as the model for Hemingway's other African story, "The Short Happy Life of Francis Macomber"; Young had no way of knowing about the Windemere volumes (See chapter 2 in this volume), from which H. Rider Haggard's "Long Odds" emerges as a likely source as well. Allan Quatermain, that tale's narrator, says: "I was beginning to get excited now, for, as you know, there is nothing in experience to warm up your nerves like a lion at close quarters, unless it is a wounded buffalo" (*Stories by English Authors: Africa* 47).

9. Jung defined *archetype* fairly consistently, with minor changes in emphasis depending on the context of individual works. In *Symbols of Transformation,* he uses categorization as a technique of definition, classifying *archetype* as a "functional disposition," rather than a hereditary idea: "[I]t is not a question of a specifically racial hereditary, but of a universally human characteristic. Nor is it a question of *inherited ideas,* but of a functional disposition to produce the same or very similar ideas. This disposition I later called the *archetype*" (102).

10. The stories based on his reading of Jung include "Like Argus of the Ancient Times," "The Water Baby," "Shin Bones," "The Bones of Kahelili," and "The Tears of Ah Kim." For analysis see Labor (57–59) and McClintock.

11. Hemingway actually owned three copies of *The Golden Bough: A Study in Magic and Religion* (Brasch and Sigman, items 2351–53). His son Gregory reports that Hemingway carried a copy of it in a book bag on the *Pilar* during his submarine patrols in the Caribbean during World War II (109).

12. The first edition of Thrall and Hibbard's *A Handbook to Literature* (1936) does not include an entry for *archetype.* The 1960 revised edition, by Thrall, Hibbard, and Holman includes the definition for the first time. Subsequent editions (third through the twelfth [of 2012]) by Harmon include the same definition with the Frye quote but with other occasional very minor revisions.

13. Various critics have employed varied terminology for these italicized memories, such as cutbacks, flashbacks (Georgoudaki 261), mental flashbacks (Meyers 121), italicized reminiscences/recalls (Friedman 279), internal monologues (Stallman 89), memories (Montgomery 148), italicized reflections (147), stream of consciousness monologues (Baker, "The Slopes" 104), meditations (Herndon 122), and vignettes (Harding 28; Rovit 36).

1. *The Man on Trail*

1. See Hays, "Hemingway and London," for an overview of London's influence on Hemingway.

2. One other minor piece of evidence that suggests Hemingway's familiarity with "To the Man on Trail" is in the opening line of "After the Storm," which also includes in its opening sentence a reference to making punch: "It wasn't about anything, something about making punch" (3).

3. Plimpton apparently refers to Gregor Mendel (1822–1884), one of the founding figures of the science of genetics.

4. Earlier in the story, the captain had looked at the sea as his judge: "In this breathless pause at the threshold of a long passage we seemed to be measuring our fitness for a long and arduous enterprise, the appointed task of both our existences [his and the ship's] to be carried out, far from all human eyes, with only sky and sea for spectators and judges" (92). Similarly, after Malemute Kid has explained to his fellows everything Jack Westondale has done and before he makes his final toast, he "glanced round the circle of his judges" (297). And, annoyingly, typing "the man on trail" into a word-processing program, typically results in the spelling and grammar check underlining *trail* and suggesting *trial* as a substitute. These are indeed men and women on trial as well as on trail.

5. The awkward lengths the narrator goes to in avoiding actually speaking an outright lie during this scene recalls the final scene of *Heart of Darkness*, in which Marlow goes through similarly awkward lengths to avoid telling Mr. Kurtz's "intended" the monstrous truth about the moral degeneration Mr. Kurtz underwent in the wilderness.

6. Conrad may be seen as staging the same synchronicity in "The Secret Sharer." Leggatt, a brother or double, appears as the host/narrator—on his first night as captain of a ship—must himself be reborn in his new role.

2. *The Books at Windemere*

1. What follows is clearly a stretch, so the reader's indulgence is requested. If one looks at the photographs of the young Hemingway in outdoor activities in Michigan included in Federspiel's *Picturing Hemingway's Michigan*, it seems possible that he may have been photographed with volumes of this size in his pockets. Note for example the photographs on pages 154 (right jacket pocket), 156 (right trouser pocket), and 166 (right and left breast pockets under his sweater).

2. One wonders whether, if by chance the young Hemingway did read this story, it influenced his treatment of gender issues—androgyny of dress and appearance—in *The Garden of Eden.* Much has been written about gender issues in Hemingway's works, for example, *Hemingway's Genders* by Comley and Scholes. Primary evidence in many such works are early childhood photographs of Hemingway dressed as a girl by his mother. Such a photograph appears on the cover of *Hemingway's Quarrel with Androgyny* by Mark Spilka. Criticism too often looks to biographical source material in its analysis of Hemingway and not often enough to literary sources, though to their credit, the authors mentioned do not neglect literary sources. Along with Frederic's "Brother Sebastian's Friendship" from the Windemere stories, also of interest on the theme of gender disguise is R. K. Douglas's "A Chinese Girl Graduate," in the volume *The Orient* in the *Stories by English Authors* collection.

3. *Elements of the Man-on-Trail Plot*

1. Two other London Klondike stories, "Love of Life" and "To Build a Fire," share narrative features with "The Snows of Kilimanjaro." Both are tales of men isolated by extreme geography and stalked by death, the protagonist of "Love of Life" struggling across the Canadian Barrens and the protagonist of "To Build a Fire" trying to survive the "white silence" of an arctic cold spell. The latter is accompanied by a wolf dog, and the former is stalked by a wolf, parallels to Harry's hyena. In a third London story, "The Law of Life," an old man, blind and decrepit, is left behind by his tribe members as they depart from their isolated camp, leaving him with only a fire and a few sticks to keep it burning. He feels death approach in the form of a wolf pack, which he first senses when he hears their howls and then with greater terror when feels "[a] cold muzzle thrust against his cheek," similar to death climbing onto Harry's cot in the form of a hyena (48). Death is also associated with canines in two stories from Hemingway's juvenilia. In "Judgment of Manitou," which certainly has the feel of London influence, wolves bring death, and in "Sepi Jingan" a dog saves his master by ripping out the throat of his would-be assailant.

2. As Joseph Flora has noted, "From first to last, Hemingway used placement of his stories to emphasize meanings" (*Hemingway's Nick Adams* 252n). "A Clean, Well-Lighted Place" is also the first story to follow "The Snows of Kilimanjaro" in *The Snows of Kilimanjaro and Other Stories.* Published in January 1961, at a time when Hemingway was confronting his own death, which would occur six months later, the volume is dominated by the subject of death. Besides the two stories mentioned in the text, "A Day's Wait" and "The Killers" deal with characters' knowledge of death. "A Way You'll Never Be" includes a battlefield covered with corpses, and both "In Another Country" and "The Short Happy Life of Francis Macomber" end with deaths.

3. A similar image of uniformed authority representing death occurs in *A Farewell to Arms* in chapter 30, when Frederic Henry is arrested by the carabinieri as he attempts to cross the bridge over the Tagliamento River during the retreat from Caporetto. Henry describes them as having "that beautiful detachment and devotion to stern justice of men dealing in death without being in any danger of it" (194). In that regard, they are much

like the Barker episode (**IM I.5**) in "Snows," in which the helpless Austrian officers on leave are slaughtered. Further, since they place themselves at a bridge, a passage to safety for desperate men on trail, they pervert myth as well as justice.

4. *The Race Was the Artist*

1. Parry defines the *ornamental adjective* as "one which mentions some characteristic of an object without regard or reference to the special condition of that object in the narrative" ("Comparative" 426). Incidentally, the same sort of ornamental adjective still occurs in blues, which has some of the characteristics of oral-formulaic poetry, though its genre is usually lyric rather than narrative. One notes, for example, that Robert Johnson's now famous "Cross Road Blues" (take 1), recorded in 1936, uses the lyric "Risin' sun goin' down" Apparently "risin'" is such a common ornamental adjective for modifying the sun that it applies even when the sun is setting.

2. The term *Phoenician alphabet* may not necessarily be accepted by linguists, who may prefer terms such as *unvocalized syllabary* (see Havelock 59).

3. In his *Germania,* the Roman historian Tacitus hints at a similar function of communal poetry among the late first century Germanic tribes: "In the traditional songs which form their only record of the past the Germans celebrate . . . " (102).

5. *Divinity and Divine Agents on Earth*

1. Accounts of the first murderer come from Sumeria, Babylon, and Egypt, from which the biblical account may have been adapted. The adaptation probably resulted in the many logical questions that arise from the muddled biblical tale. The original myth probably derived from the transition from hunter/gatherer cultures to agrarian cultures, with Abel representing the hunter gatherer and Cain the new agrarian. This being the origin, the original sources do not significantly affect our understanding of the man-on-trail plot/myth/archetype.

6. *Guests Betrayed and Hosts Repaid*

1. The two letters are included in *Selected Letters* (201, 301). The Perkins letter is in the *Letters of Ernest Hemingway,* vol. 3, *1926–1929,* (64), and the Wister letter is in vol. 4, *1929–1931* (51). The *Letters* may yet reveal other references to Mérimée and may give some context to Hemingway's reference to Mérimée in his letter to Owen Wister. If the two writers had been discussing Mérimée, it might well be revealing to learn which one initiated the discussion.

2. Maxwell Smith notes that Pierre Richard has suggested that the influence of "Mateo Falcone" can be seen in Balzac's "The Vendetta" (1830), Daudet's "The Child Spy" (1873), and Maupassant's "Two Friends" (1882) (100).

3. Hemingway could well have used, for example *oats, feed,* or *fodder* just as easily as *hay.* This reference to hay suggests a marker leading back to Mérimée as his source, as might his use of *socks* lead back to the gift socks reference in London's "To the Man on Trail." The question of whether these references were conscious or not remains open.

4. There is some controversy over the translation of the word indicating Rahab's profession. It may also be taken to mean *food merchant* or *innkeeper. Harlot,* of course, offers more opportunity for pious moralizing.

7. Poetic Expressions and Popular Music

1. Robert Lewis outlines a case for Helen being Harry's mistress rather than his wife (*Hemingway on Love* 103–05). As early as 1950, Engstrom refers to Helen as Harry's "wealthy mistress" (203).

2. As "The Snows of Kilimanjaro" is best analyzed with minimal leaning on biographical detail, so too are Johnson's lyrics, which also stand by themselves. Johnson's unoriginal publicity stunt of promoting himself as having sold his soul at a crossroads at midnight to sinister forces of darkness in exchange for certain guitar-playing skills has produced reams of commentary, most of which is blather and twaddle without the slightest merit. It is important to remember that there are no literal sinister forces of darkness that will engage in such deals. One notes, for example, the Latin spell that Dr. Faustus recites in Christopher Marlowe's *The Tragical History of Doctor Faustus.* Write out a contract in blood and recite that spell at midnight on Friday the thirteenth (or every other single night or noon of the year) at the crossroads of your choice. Mephistopheles will not appear. (I guarantee it.) One can sell one's soul figuratively but not literally.

3. LaVere's transcription titles the song "Hellhound on My Trail"; the original 1937 release of the song, on a 78 rpm vinyl record on the Vocalion label, used the title "HELL HOUND ON MY TRAIL."

8. Hospitality in Other Hemingway Stories

1. Miklós Horthy (1868–1957) was a Hungarian military and political figure. His record on human rights remains questionable.

2. For an insightful discussion of the parallels and contrasts between "The Short Happy Life of Francis Macomber" and "The Snows of Kilimanjaro," see Flora's *Ernest Hemingway: A Study of the Short Fiction* (74–88).

3. Narration of the five first-person Spanish Civil War stories, despite the nomenclature in the texts, is treated here as focalized by a single individual. The narrator of "The Denunciation" appears to be named "Henry Emmunds." In "The Butterfly and the Tank," the narrator has no name. He is referred to as "Henry" in "Night before Battle" and unnamed in "Under the Ridge" He is "Ed" in "Landscape with Figures." Flora and Josephs, nodding to previous commentators, note the similarity of initials shared by Henry Emmunds, Edwin Henry, and Ernest Hemingway. His/their reasons for being

in Spain are also identical: They are part of a film crew documenting the conflict, as was Hemingway himself. Flora (*Ernest Hemingway* 91) includes helpful commentary on the confusion surrounding the names. Josephs observes that "Edwin Henry and Henry Emmunds, E. H. and H. E., are obviously heads and tails of the same coin" (318). The commentaries by Josephs and Flora seem to concur. Josephs also mentions Martin Light's essay "Of Wasteful Deaths: Hemingway's Stories about the Spanish War." Light recounts Hemingway's reluctance to see the three Chicote's stories reprinted in the 1958 collection *The Armchair Esquire,* claiming that he did not want them in book form without further revision, which would have afforded him the opportunity to fine-tune the names and bring more consistency. He did permit the inclusion in *The Armchair Esquire* of "The Butterfly and the Tank," which does not name the narrator. Steinbeck's praise of the story may have affected his decision to allow the reprint (Baker, *A Life Story* 337). An analogous situation is that of Raymond Chandler, who initially gave his famous private eye the names Carmody and John Dalmas, among others, when he published his early stories in pulp fiction periodicals; for his novels, which cannibalized material from those pulp stories, he finally settled on Philip Marlowe (and the rest is literary and cinematic history!).

9. *The Figure in the Carpet*

1. Regarding the Barker episode, Lewis and Westbrook point out that several editions change the name of Barker to either "Gardner" or "Johnson," "suggesting that different publishers are making an inconsequential change to identify their printing, or that Scribner's itself is so identifying reprints" ("The Snows" 69). Volumes in my personal Hemingway collection confirm this: "Gardner" was used in *The Fifth Column and the First Forty-nine Stories* (Collier, 1938, 155); "Johnson" is used in *"The Snows of Kilimanjaro" and Other Stories* (Penguin 1963, 12) and in *The Essential Hemingway* (Penguin, 1964, 447). Given the canine associations of the name Barker and of the hyena, this change seems much more than "inconsequential." "Textual vandalism" might more accurately describe the changes.

2. Massimo Bacigalupo points out that in this passage "Asalone" is a misspelling of "Asolone"; "Siete Commum," a misspelling of "Sette Comuni"; and "Arsiedo," a misspelling of "Arsiero." Both Arsiero and Monte Corno are mentioned in an early 1920s Hemingway poem "39 [Arsiero, Asiago . . .]" (49). See also Lewis and Westbrook ("The Snows" 93–95). A facsimile of a handwritten working draft of the poem is included in *Complete Poems.* In the draft in Hemingway's handwriting, "Arsiero" is quite clearly spelled correctly, which poses some questions. Are these printers' errors? Are they Hemingway's? Are they errors planted in the story to indicate a type of rottenness, a metaphorical rottenness of memory parallel to Harry's literal physical decay? That possibility can bring a wide variety of the story's content into question: Are the parallels between the chore-boy episode and "Mateo Falcone" Hemingway's borrowings from Prosper Mérimée? Or is it Hemingway's point that has Harry deluded himself into believing Mérimée's characters and plot line are actually his own?

Was Hemingway at this point in his career experimenting with implanted errors? (Keep in mind the gross error in the height of Mount Kilimanjaro in the story's opening epigraph.) In the often quoted Huck Finn passage from *Green Hills of Africa* (1935), for example, there are so many errors concentrated in one spot, the reader is truly compelled to consider whether they have been planted there: "All American literature comes from one book by Mark Twain called *Huckleberry Finn.* If you read it you must stop where the Nigger Jim is stolen from the boys" (22).

First, while it may well be "called" *Huckleberry Finn* or, more commonly but just as incorrectly, *The Adventures of Huckleberry Finn,* the real title, as Philip Young so perceptively noted and reminded the Hemingway community of, is *Adventures of Huckleberry Finn* (*Reconsideration,* 212n). Second, the phrase "Nigger Jim" is never used in the novel. Third, why the definite article in "*the* Nigger Jim"? How is Kandinsky—an auditor, not a reader—to tell the difference between "the Nigger Jim" and the even more racially insensitive "the nigger, Jim"? Finally the most egregious of the errors: "stolen from the boys." Jim is never stolen from "the boys." He is stolen from Huck in chapter 31; Tom Sawyer does not reappear in the novel until chapter 33. This latter fact Hemingway knew well, as the comments he made in a 2 January 1926 letter to Ernest Walsh make clear: "The story stops when Jim, the nigger, is captured and Huck finds himself alone and his nigger gone. That's the real end." The key phrase here is "finds himself alone." Then on the *very next page* in *Green Hills of Africa* Hemingway takes his contemporaries to task for writing "slop" in order to maintain their lifestyles. This character is not Ernest Hemingway; this is the racially unenlightened, pompous, drunken protagonist of a fictionalized memoir, albeit a protagonist dressed in Hemingway's clothes. It seems that implanted errors might be a part of that characterization. And by extension, the reader must wonder whether the errors of spelling, concentrated in one spot, function similarly in "The Snows of Kilimanjaro."

3. Kenneth Johnston's "The Silly Wasters" nicely traces Hemingway's contempt for both Tristan Tzara and the American poet.

4. Paul Smith's claim that of the italicized passages "the first four . . . were clearly remembered and not written" is questionable (358).

5. Jennifer Riddle Harding's interpretation must be noted here: "The vignettes contain several plots that might have formed whole stories, as well as details and settings that could have graced the fiction he might have written. But the stories are communicated to us not by Harry, but by a narrator who shares credit for bringing them into existence" (30). Although this analysis of the Hemingwayesque style of the memories regarding Harry's life in Paris (**IM III**) does seem to support Harding's point, some other factors must be considered. First, Harding does not account for the shift in narrative voice in **IM III**. Second, and in accord with Harding's assertion that "the narrator seems to be endorsing these stories as Harry's 'masterpieces that might have been,'" Hemingway was obligated to focalize the text in a classic and immortal style. What literary style and voice other than his very own could Ernest Miller Hemingway possibly have chosen? If he had parodied Faulkner, Dos Passos, Fitzgerald, Steinbeck, or Wolfe, would he not have just confused the matter completely? The only way Heming-

way could make Harry sound convincingly talented would be to make him sound like Hemingway himself, which he did.

6. This would seem to be, and might actually be, a memory of the same ranch treated later (**IM IV.2** and **3**). However, the log cabin with the white chinked mortar and the bell on a pole was inspired by a cabin Hemingway had known during his summers in Michigan. Michael Federspiel includes a photo of the cabin in *Picturing Hemingway's Michigan* (101). This raises some questions. Has Hemingway transferred the cabin further west? Or must we assume that Harry's grandfather's house is in Michigan and the scenes at the ranch have nothing to do with his grandfather's house but are set on a different ranch in the west?

7. Van Gennep identifies "libations" as "rites of incorporation" (24).

8. See Paul Hendrickson's discussion of Hemingway's brief relationship with Helen Hay Whitney, a wealthy heiress and horsewoman, who may have insulted Hemingway in conversation (77–84). Hemingway may have based the character of Helen, also a horsewoman, partially on her, as response to her possibly having referred to his books as "potboilers" (84). This may have been his retaliation against Whitney, who, as "the First Lady of the American Turf," would not have relished the reference to horse meat (81).

9. The account of the concierge, the trooper, and Hemingway first appeared as "An African Journal, Part 2: Miss Mary's Lion" in a *Sports Illustrated* article on 3 January 1972 (31). It subsequently appeared in 1974 in *The Enduring Hemingway* (578–79), in 1999 in *True at First Light* (147–48), and in 2005 in *Under Kilimanjaro* (177–78).

10. See Peter Hays's discussion of the association of bicycle policemen with death in both "The Snows of Kilimanjaro" and Faulkner's *Light in August* ("Hemingway, Faulkner").

11. "Mrs. Knollys" appears in *Stories by American Authors*, vol. 2 under the pen name of J. S. of Dale and in Brander Matthews's *The Short Story: Specimens Illustrating Its Development* under the author's real name, Frederic J. Stimson. "Mrs. Knollys" was first published in 1883 and "The Crystal Trench" in Mason's collection *The Four Corners of the World* in 1917. The plots are similar enough that a couple of contemporary reviewers made plagiarism accusations. In both plots, young men fall into the glacier and their wives, never remarrying, wait patiently for the bodies to eventually emerge. In "Mrs. Knollys" the elderly and faithful—even after death—widow is eventually buried next to her husband. "The Crystal Trench," however, ends in a more macabre fashion, with the faithful widow finding proof, in the form of a locket on his corpse, that her husband had been carrying on an affair at the time he died. In the Mason story, the body disintegrates upon emergence, very much in the manner of the final sentence of Poe's "The Facts in the Case of M. Valdemar." The faithful husband's body is interred with that of his widow, but the unfaithful husband's body immediately succumbs to corruption and disintegration. And, of course, Hemingway's Harry succumbs to corruption even before he dies. "The Crystal Trench" thus may have exerted an influence on Hemingway in more than one of his works.

12. Hemingway seems to have had a particular dislike of bicycle police. In his 17 November 1929 letter to Waldo Pierce, he remarks, regarding a German Lugar pistol

that belonged to Pierce, "I would like to have one when the revolution comes to pick off bicycle Cops with."

13. Baker mistakenly describes the Puss Moth as a "biplane" ("The Slopes" 105).

14. There are two insects designated as puss moths, the English/European puss moth (*Cerura vinula*) and the American puss moth (*Megalopyge opercularis*). Each is known by a variety of other common names. While the European puss moth does not have the painful spines of its American relative, it can still defend itself with a formic acid spray if threatened.

15. Albert Kolb, for example, seems to regard this, incorrectly, as the moment of death: "Apparently Harry's soul is free at the moment he is lifted by the bearers" (265). Similarly, Keneth Kinnamon states, "Death comes that evening as his wife instructs the servants to carry his cot into their tent" (284). This is not so, as it does not account for Harry's moving his leg.

10. The Case for Harry's Redemption

1. Sometimes a leg is just a leg.

2. Dussinger's terminology is confusing. "Between the first and second sets of flashbacks"; "The second set of recollections"; "The third group of reminiscences"; "Additional proof . . . can be found in the fourth flashback" (160–61). One can only assume that the "fourth flashback" refers to the chore-boy incident and that sometimes "flashback" sometimes means "group of flashbacks" and at other times means "flashback within an italicized section of flashbacks."

3. Note the comment from Hemingway's *Across the River and into the Trees* on Dante's sense of justice:

> "You sound like Dante," she [Renata] said sleepily.
>
> "I am Mister Dante," he [Cantwell] said. "For the moment."
>
> And for a while he was and he drew all the circles. They were as unjust as Dante's but he drew them. (246)

WORKS CITED

Some bibliographic documents are notable. Paul Smith's chapter on "Snows" from his *A Reader's Guide to the Short Stories of Ernest Hemingway* (1989) surveys and comments on criticism and scholarship through the mid-1980s (349–61). Kelli A. Larson's "On Safari with Hemingway: Tracking the Most Recent Scholarship" (in Mandel, *Hemingway and Africa*) is a chronologically arranged annotated bibliography of publications—on Hemingway's African works, not just "Snows"—from 1989 to 2010. The "Comprehensive Checklist" in *The Short Stories of Ernest Hemingway: Critical Essays* (1975) edited by Jackson Benson remains useful.

Anderson, David. "Analogues of the Deserter-in-the-Gauertal Incident: *Philoxenia* in 'The Snows of Kilimanjaro.'" *The Hemingway Review*, vol. 33, no. 1, Fall 2013, pp. 15–26.

———. "Hemingway's Early Education in the Short Story: A Bibliographic Essay on Brander Matthews and Twenty Volumes of Stories at Windemere." *The Hemingway Review*, vol. 33, no. 2, Spring 2014, pp. 48–65.

"Archetype." *A Handbook to Literature*, edited by William Harmon, Pearson, 2011.

Armes, William Dallam, editor. *Old English Ballads and Folk Songs*. Macmillan, 1915.

Bacigalupo, Massimo. "Italy in Hemingway's Forty-Nine Stories: With Index." *Rivista di Studi Americani*, vol. 11, 2000, pp. 29–45.

Baker, Carlos. *Ernest Hemingway: A Life Story*. New York: Scribner's, 1969.

———. "The Slopes of Kilimanjaro: A Biographical Perspective." 1967. Trudeau, *Short Story Criticism*, vol. 25, pp. 102–05.

"Battle of Brunanburh." Translated by Alfred, Lord Tennyson. *Ballads and Other Poems*. 1880. Available online at Russell Taylor, *Words*, https://www.telelib.com/authors/T/TennysonAlfred/verse/ballads/brunanburh.html.

"The Battle of Maldon." Hamer, pp. 48–69.

Benson, Jackson J., editor. "A Comprehensive Checklist of Hemingway Short Fiction Criticism, Explication, and Commentary." *The Short Stories of Ernest Hemingway: Critical Essays*. Duke UP, 1975, pp. 311–75.

Beowulf. Beowulf and Judith, edited by Elliott Van Kirk Dobbie, vol. 4 of *The Anglo-Saxon Poetic Records*. Columbia University Press, 1953, pp. 3–98.

Blume, Lesley M. M. *Everybody Behaves Badly: The True Story Behind Hemingway's Masterpiece* The Sun Also Rises. Houghton Mifflin Harcourt, 2016.

Bodkin, Maud, *Archetypal Patterns in Poetry: Psychological Studies of Imagination*. Oxford UP, 1934.

Brasch, James D. and Joseph Sigman. *Hemingway's Library: A Composite Record*. 1981. John F. Kennedy Library, 2000.

Browning, Robert. "Childe Roland to the Dark Tower Came." *Poems of Robert Browning*, edited by Donald Smalley, Houghton Mifflin, 1956, pp. 162–68.

Bruccoli, Matthew J., ed. *Hemingway and the Mechanism of Fame*. U of South Carolina P, 2006.

Calabi, Silvio, Steve Helsley, and Roger Sanger. *Hemingway's Guns*. Shooting Sportsman, 2010.

Campbell, Joseph. *The Hero with a Thousand Faces*. 1949. Princeton UP, 1968.

Child, Francis James, editor. *The English and Scottish Popular Ballads*, vol. 3 of 5. 1885. Dover, 1965.

Childs, Barney. "Hemingway and the Leopard of Kilimanjaro," *American Notes and Queries*, vol. 2, no. 1, September 1963, pp. 2–3.

"Clarks Fork Rancher Shot on Kitchen Ranch." *Park County Enterprise* (Cody, Wyoming), 4 April 1913.

Cohen, Milton A. *Hemingway's Laboratory: The Paris* in our time. U of Alabama P, 2005.

Coleridge, Samuel Taylor. "The Rime of the Ancient Mariner." 1798. *The Norton Anthology of Poetry*, edited by Arthur M. Eastman, et al., Norton, 1970, pp. 597–610.

Conrad, Joseph. *Heart of Darkness*. 1899. Doubleday, Page & Company, 1923.

———. "The Secret Sharer." *'Twixt Land and Sea*. Doubleday, Page & Company, 1924, pp. 91–143.

Crane, John Kenny. "Crossing the Bar Twice: Post-Mortem Consciousness in Bierce, Hemingway, and Golding." 1969. *Short Story Criticism*, vol. 169, edited by Lawrence J. Trudeau, Gale, 2012, pp. 4–11.

DeFalco, Joseph. *The Hero in Hemingway's Short Stories*. U of Pittsburgh P, 1963.

Downing, Michael. "The Use of Stereotype and Archetype in *Ma Rainey's Black Bottom*." *August Wilson's Pittsburgh Cycle: Critical Perspectives on the Plays*, edited by Sandra Shannon, McFarland, 2016, pp. 76–87.

Doyle, Sir Arthur Conan, "Silver Blaze." 1892. *The Annotated Sherlock Holmes*, vol. 2 of 2, edited by William S. Baring-Gould, Clarkson N. Potter, 1967, pp. 261–81.

Dussinger, Gloria R. "'The Snows of Kilimanjaro': Harry's Second Chance." 1967. Howell, pp. 158–61.

Dylan, Bob. "Shelter from the Storm." *Lyrics, 1962–1985*. Knopf, 1985.

Eagleton, Terry. *Literary Theory: An Introduction*. University of Minnesota Press, 1983.

Edwards, Mark W. "Homer and Oral Tradition: The Type-Scene." *Oral Tradition*, vol. 7, no. 2, 1992, pp. 284–330.

Engstrom, Alfred G. "Dante, Flaubert, and "The Snows of Kilimanjaro."" *Modern Language Notes*, vol. 65, March 1950, pp. 203–05.

Evans, Oliver. "'The Snows of Kilimanjaro': A Revaluation." 1961. Howell, pp. 150–57.

Federspiel, Michael R. *Picturing Hemingway's Michigan.* Wayne State UP, 2010.

Flora, Joseph. *Ernest Hemingway: A Study of the Short Fiction.* Twayne–Simon & Schuster Macmillan, 1989.

———. *Hemingway's Nick Adams.* Louisiana State UP, 1982.

Fordham, Frieda. *An Introduction to Jung's Psychology.* Penguin, 1966.

Frederic, Harold. "Brother Sebastian's Friendship." *Stories by American Authors,* vol. 6, pp. 145–64.

Friedman, Norman. "Harry or Ernest? The Unresolved Ambiguity in 'The Snows of Kilimanjaro.'" 1997. Trudeau, *Short Story Criticism,* vol. 212, 278–84.

Fruscione, Joseph. *Faulkner and Hemingway: Biography of a Literary Rivalry.* Ohio State UP, 2012.

Frye, Northrup. *Anatomy of Criticism: Four Essays.* Princeton UP, 1957.

Georgoudaki, Ekaterini. "Some Comments on 'The Snows of Kilimanjaro.'" 1973. Trudeau, *Short Story Criticism,* vol. 212, pp. 261–64.

Gillman, C[lement], "An Ascent of Kilimanjaro." *The Geographical Journal,* vol. 66, no. 1, January 1923, pp. 1–21.

Ginsberg, Allen. *Howl and Other Poems.* City Lights Books, 1956, pp. 9–20.

Gordon, R. K., trans. *Anglo-Saxon Poetry.* Dent, 1967.

Grebstein, Sheldon Norman. *Hemingway's Craft.* Southern Illinois UP, 1973.

———, editor. *Perspectives in Contemporary Criticism: A Collection of Recent Essays by American, English, and European Literary Critics.* Harper & Row, 1968.

Greene, Philip. *To Have and Have Another: A Hemingway Cocktail Companion.* Perigee-Penguin, 2012.

Grissom, Edgar A. *Ernest Hemingway: A Descriptive Bibliography.* Oak Knoll P, 2011.

Habibi, Don Asher. "The Experience of a Lifetime: Philosophical Reflections on a Narrative Device of Ambrose Bierce." 2002. *Short Story Criticism,* vol. 124, edited by Jelena O. Krstovic, Gale, 2010, pp. 48–62.

Haggard, H. Rider. "Long Odds." *Stories by English Authors: Africa* pp. 33–55.

Haley, James L. *Wolf: The Lives of Jack London.* Perseus / Basic Books, 2010.

Hamer, Richard, editor. *A Choice of Anglo-Saxon Verse,* Faber & Faber, 1970.

Hamilton, David Mike. *"The Tools of My Trade": The Annotated Books in Jack London's Library.* U of Washington P, 1986.

Harding, Jennifer Riddle. "'He Had Never Written a Word of That': Regret and Counterfactuals in Hemingway's 'The Snows of Kilimanjaro.'" *The Hemingway Review,* vol. 30, no. 2, Spring 2011, pp. 21–35.

Hardy, Thomas. "The Three Strangers." *Stories by English Authors: England.* pp. 121–57.

Harte, Bret. "The Luck of Roaring Camp." *Selected,* pp. 1–12.

———. "The Outcasts of Poker Flat." *Selected,* pp. 12–24.

———. *Selected Western Stories and Poems.* Walter J. Black-Classics Club, 1932, pp. 1–12.

Havelock, Eric A. *The Muse Learns to Write: Reflections on Orality and Literacy from Antiquity to the Present.* Yale UP, 1986.

Hays, Peter. "Hemingway and London." *The Hemingway Review,* vol. 3, no. 2, Spring 1984, 54–56.

———. "Hemingway, Faulkner, and a Bicycle Built for Death." *NMAL: Notes on Modern American Literature,* vol. 5, no. 4, 1981, item 28.

Helama, Samuli. "Ernest Hemingway's Description of the Mountaintop in 'The Snows of Kilimanjaro' and Climate Change Research." *The Hemingway Review,* vol. 34, no. 2, Spring 2015, pp. 118–23.
Hemingway, Ernest. *Across the River and into the Trees.* Scribner's, 1951.
———. "After the Storm." *Winner Take Nothing,* pp. 3–13.
———. "An Alpine Idyll." *Men without Women,* pp. 187–97.
———. "The Art of the Short Story." *Ernest Hemingway: A Literary Reference,* edited by Robert W. Trogdon. Carroll & Graf, 1999, pp. 310–21.
———. "The Battler." *In Our Time,* pp. 65–79.
———. "Big Two-Hearted River. *In Our Time,* pp. 177–212.
———. "Black Ass at the Crossroads." *The Complete Short Stories,* pp. 579–89.
———. "The Butterfly and the Tank." *The Fifth Column and Four Stories of the Spanish Civil War,* pp. 101–09.
———. *By-Line: Ernest Hemingway: Selected Articles and Dispatches of Four Decades,* edited by William White, Scribner's, 1967.
———. "Cat in the Rain." *In Our Time,* pp. 117–22.
———. "Che Ti Dice La Patria." *Men without Women,* pp. 97–114.
———. "A Clean, Well-Lighted Place." *Winner Take Nothing,* pp. 15–24.
———. *Complete Poems,* edited by Nicholas Gerogiannis. Revised ed. U of Nebraska P, 1992.
———. *The Collected Stories,* edited by James Fenton, Everyman's Library, 1995.
———. *The Complete Short Stories of Ernest Hemingway: The Finca Vigía Edition.* Scribner's, 1987.
———. "Cross-Country Snow." *In Our Time,* pp. 139–47.
———. "A Day's Wait." *Winner Take Nothing,* pp. 127–34.
———. *Death in the Afternoon.* Scribner's, 1932.
———. "The Denunciation." *The Fifth Column and Four Stories of the Spanish Civil War,* pp. 89–100.
———. *The Enduring Hemingway: An Anthology of a Lifetime in Literature,* edited by Charles Scribner Jr., Scribner's, 1974.
——— *Ernest Hemingway: Selected Letters 1917–1961,* edited by Carlos Baker, Scribner's, 1981.
———. *A Farewell to Arms: The Hemingway Library Edition,* edited by Séan Hemingway, Scribner, 2012.
———. *The Fifth Column and Four Stories of the Spanish Civil War.* Scribner's, 1969
———. *For Whom the Bell Tolls.* Scribner's, 1940.
———. "The Gambler, the Nun, and the Radio." *Winner Take Nothing,* pp. 189–221.
———. "God Rest You Merry, Gentlemen." *Winner Take Nothing,* pp. 41–50.
———. "The Good Lion." *The Complete Short Stories,* pp. 482–84.
———. "Great News from the Mainland." *The Complete Short Stories,* 602–04.
———. *Green Hills of Africa: The Hemingway Library Edition,* edited by Séan Hemingway, Scribner's, 2015.
———. "Hills Like White Elephants." *Men without Women,* pp. 69–77.
———. "Homage to Switzerland." *Winner Take Nothing,* pp. 103–26.

———. "In Another Country." *Men without Women*, pp. 58–68.
———. "Indian Camp." *In Our Time*, pp. 15–21.
———. *in our time / de nos jours*. 1999. Le Bruit du temps, 2011.
———. *In Our Time*. Scribner's, 1953.
———. *Islands in the Stream*. Scribner's, 1970.
———. "Judgment of Manitou." *The Collected Stories*, pp. 745–46.
———. "The Killers." *Men without Women*, pp. 78–96.
———. "The Last Good Country." *The Nick Adams Stories*, pp. 70–134.
———. *The Letters of Ernest Hemingway*, vol. 1, *1907–1922*, edited by Sandra Spanier and Robert W. Trogdon, Cambridge UP, 2011.
———. *The Letters of Ernest Hemingway*, vol. 2, *1923–1925*, edited by Sandra Spanier, Albert J. DeFazio III, Cambridge UP, 2013.
———. *The Letters of Ernest Hemingway*, vol. 3, *1926–1929*, edited by Rena Sanderson, Sandra Spanier, and Robert W. Trogdon, Cambridge UP, 2015.
———. *The Letters of Ernest Hemingway*, vol. 4, *1929–1931*, edited by Sandra Spanier and Miriam B. Mandel, Cambridge UP, 2018.
———. "The Light of the World." *Winner Take Nothing*, pp. 25–39.
———. "A Man of the World." *The Complete Short Stories*, pp. 492–95.
———. *Men without Women*. Scribner's, 1927.
———. "Monologue to the Maestro: A High Seas Letter." *By-Line*, pp. 213–20.
———. *A Moveable Feast*. Scribner's, 1964.
———. *A Moveable Feast: The Restored Edition*, edited by Seán Hemingway, Scribner, 2009.
———. "A Natural History of the Dead." *Winner Take Nothing*, pp. 135–53.
———. *The Nick Adams Stories*. Scribner's, 1972.
———. "Night before Battle." *The Fifth Column and Four Stories of the Spanish Civil War*, pp. 110–39.
———. Nobel Prize acceptance statement. Bruccoli, *Mechanism*, pp. 134–35.
———. "Nobody Ever Dies." *The Complete Short Stories*, pp. 470–81.
———. "Now I Lay Me." *Men without Women*, pp. 218–32.
———. "On the Quai at Smyrna." *In Our Time*, pp. 9–12.
———. "On Writing." *The Nick Adams Stories*, pp. 233–41.
———. "One Trip Across." *The Complete Short Stories*, pp. 381–409.
———. "Out of Season." *In Our Time*, pp. 125–35.
———. "A Pursuit Race." *Men without Women*, pp. 198–206.
———. "Refugees from Thrace." *By-Line*, pp. 56–60.
———. "The Revolutionist." *In Our Time*, pp. 105–06.
———. "A Room on the Garden Side." *The Strand Magazine*, no. 60, 2018, pp. 6–10.
———. "The Sea Change." *Winner Take Nothing*, pp. 51–60.
———. "Sepi Jingan." *The Collected Stories*, pp. 750–52.
———. "The Short Happy Life of Francis Macomber." *The Snows of Kilimanjaro" and Other Stories*, Scribner's, 1964, pp. 3–28.
———. *The Short Stories of Ernest Hemingway: The Hemingway Library Edition*, edited by Séan Hemingway, Scribner's, 2017.

———. "The Sights of Whitehead Street." *By-Line*, pp. 192–97.
———. "A Silent, Ghastly Procession." *By-Line*, pp. 51–52.
———. "The Snows of Kilimanjaro." *The Essential Hemingway*, Penguin 1964, pp. 443–63.
———. "The Snows of Kilimanjaro." *The Fifth Column and the First Forty-nine Stories*. Collier, 1938, pp. 150–75.
———. "The Snows of Kilimanjaro." *"The Snows of Kilimanjaro" and Other Stories*. Scribner's, 1961, 3–28.
———. "The Snows of Kilimanjaro." *"The Snows of Kilimanjaro and Other Stories."* Penguin, 1963, pp. 7–33.
———. "The Snows of Kilimanjaro," performed by Charlton Heston. Caedmon Audio CD, 2007.
———. "Soldier's Home." *In Our Time*, pp. 89–101.
———. *The Sun Also Rises: The Hemingway Library Edition*, edited by Seán Hemingway, Scribner's, 2014.
———. "Ten Indians." *Men without Women*, pp. 168–77.
———. "They All Made Peace—What Is Peace?" *Complete Poems*, pp. 63–64.
———. 39 ["Arsiero, Asiago . . ."], *Complete Poems*, p. 49.
———. "Today Is Friday." *Men without Women*, pp. 207–13.
———. *To Have and Have Not*. Scribner's, 1937.
———. "The Tradesman's Return." *The Complete Short Stories of Ernest Hemingway: The Finca Vigía Edition*, pp. 410–19.
———. *True at First Light*, edited by Patrick Hemingway, Scribner, 1999.
———. *Under Kilimanjaro*. Kent State UP, 2005.
———. "Under the Ridge." *The Fifth Column and Four Stories of the Spanish Civil War*, pp. 140–51.
———. "A Very Short Story." *In Our Time*, pp. 83–85.
———. "A Way You'll Never Be." *Winner Take Nothing*, pp. 61–85.
———. "Who Murdered the Vets? A First-Hand Report on the Florida Hurricane." Bruccoli, *Mechanism*, pp. 43–48.
———. "Wine of Wyoming." *Winner Take Nothing*, pp. 155–86.
———. *Winner Take Nothing*. Scribner's, 1933.
Hemingway, Gregory. *Papa: A Personal Memoir*. 1976. Pocket Books, 1977.
Hendrickson, Paul. *Hemingway's Boat: Everything He Loved in Life and Lost, 1934–1961*. Knopf, 2011.
Herndon, Jerry A. "'The Snows of Kilimanjaro': Another Look at Theme and Point of View." 1986. Trudeau, *Short Story Criticism*, vol. 25, pp. 121–28.
Homer. *The Iliad of Homer*. Translated by Samuel Butler. 1898. Dover, 1999.
———. *The Odyssey of Homer*. Translated by Robert Fagles. Penguin, 1996.
Hotchner, A. E. *Papa Hemingway: A Personal Memoir*. Random House, 1966.
Houk, Walter. "[M]ore on Gianfranco." Received by heming-l@mtu.edu, 28 March 2012.
Howell, John, editor. *Hemingway's African Stories: The Stories, Their Sources, Their Critics*. Scribner's, 1969.
Hugo, Victor. *Les Misérables*. 1862. Translated by Charles E. Wilbour. Modern Library, 1992.

Hurley, C. Harold. "'Pen,' 'Pencil,' and 'Penis' in Ernest Hemingway's 'The Snows of Kilimanjaro.'" *The Explicator,* vol. 72, no. 1, 2014, pp. 39–40.

Hyde, Lewis. *The Gift: Creativity and the Artist in the Modern World.* Vintage-Random, 2007.

———. *Trickster Makes This World: Mischief, Myth and Art.* Farrar, Straus & Giroux, 1998.

James, Henry. "The Figure in the Carpet." *The Complete Tales of Henry James,* vol. 9 of 12, *1892–1898,* edited by Leon Edel, Lippincott, 1964, pp. 273–315.

Jaynes, Julian. *The Origin of Consciousness in the Breakdown of the Bicameral Mind.* Houghton Mifflin, 1990.

Johnson, Robert. *The Complete Recordings,* edited by Steve LeVere, CBS Records, 1990.

Johnston, Kenneth G. "The Silly Wasters: Tzara and the Poet in 'The Snows of Kilimanjaro.'" *The Hemingway Review,* vol. 8, no. 1, 1988, pp. 50–57.

———. "'The Snows of Kilimanjaro': An African Purge." *Studies in Short Fiction,* vol. 21, no. 3, 1984, pp. 223–27.

———. "The Songs in Hemingway's 'The Snows . . . '" *American Notes & Queries,* vol. 23, November–December 1984, pp. 46–48.

Josephs, Allen. "Hemingway's Spanish Civil War Stories, or the Spanish Civil War as Reality." *Hemingway's Neglected Short Fiction: New Perspectives,* edited By Susan F. Beegel, U of Alabama P, 1992, pp. 313–27.

"Joshua's Conquest of Jericho." *Men at War,* edited by Ernest Hemingway, Bramhall House, 1942, pp. 894–98.

J. S. of Dale [Frederic Jesup Stimson]. "Mrs. Knollys." *Stories by American Authors,* vol. 2 of 10. Scribner's, 1896, pp. 70–91.

Jung, C[arl] G[ustav]. *The Archetypes and the Collective Unconscious.* Translated by R. F. C. Hull. Princeton UP, 1980.

———. *The Basic Writings of C. G. Jung,* edited by Violet Staub de Laszlo, Modern Library, 1993.

———. "Concerning Rebirth." *Four Archetypes: Mother Rebirth Spirit Trickster.* Translated by R. F. C. Hull. Princeton UP, 1973, pp. 45–81.

———. "Introduction to the Religious and Psychological Problems of Alchemy." *The Basic Writings of C. G. Jung,* pp. 537–81.

———. "On the Relation of Analytical Psychology to Poetry." *The Portable Jung,* edited by Joseph Campbell, Penguin, 1971, pp. 301–22.

———. From *Psychological Types. The Basic Writings of C. G. Jung,* pp. 230–357.

———. *Symbols of Transformation.* Translated by R. F. C. Hull. 2nd ed., Princeton UP, 1967.

———. "On the Psychology of the Trickster-Figure." *Four Archetypes: Mother Rebirth Spirit Trickster.* Translated by R. F. C. Hull. Princeton UP, 1970, pp. 135–52.

Justice, Hilary Kovar. "The Consolation of Critique: Food, Culture, and Civilization in Ernest Hemingway." *The Hemingway Review,* vol. 32, no. 1, Fall 2012, pp. 16–38.

———. "'Somewhat Rough Withal': Hemingway's Personal Copy of *Old English Ballads* (English I, Oak Park High School)." *The Hemingway Review,* vol. 33, no. 2, Spring 2014, pp. 126–35.

Kinnamon, Keneth. "The Politics of 'The Snows of Kilimanjaro.'" Trudeau, *Short Story Criticism,* vol. 212, pp. 284–91.

Kolb, Albert. "Symbolic Structure in Hemingway's 'The Snows of Kilimanjaro.'" 1976. Trudeau, *Short Story Criticism,* vol. 212, pp. 264–66.
Knupp, Jeremiah. "In Pursuit of a 'Really Good Rifle': The 1903 Mannlicher-Schoenauer Carbine." *American Rifleman,* May 2016, pp. 68–72.
Labor, Earl. *Jack London.* Twayne, 1974.
Lamb, Robert Paul. *Art Matters: Hemingway, Craft, and the Creation of the Modern Short Story.* Louisiana State UP, 2010.
Larson, Kelli A. "On Safari with Hemingway: Tracking the Most Recent Scholarship." Mandel, pp. 323–83.
Lawrence, D. H. *Studies in Classic American Literature.* 1923. Viking, 1961. Lewis, D. B. Wyndham. *Francois Villon: A Documented Survey.* Literary Guild of America, 1928.
Lewis, Robert W. *Hemingway on Love.* U of Texas P, 1965.
Lewis, Robert W. and Max Westbrook. "'The Snows of Kilimanjaro': Collated and Annotated." *Texas Quarterly,* vol. 13, Summer 1970, pp. 64–143.
———. "The Texas Manuscript of 'The Snows of Kilimanjaro.'" *Texas Quarterly,* vol. 9, Winter 1966, 66–101.
Light, Martin. "Of Wasteful Deaths: Hemingway's Stories about the Spanish War." *The Short Stories of Ernest Hemingway: Critical Essays,* edited by Jackson J. Benson, Duke UP, 1975, pp. 64–77.
London, Jack. *Jack London: Novels and Stories.* Library of America, 1982.
———. *Jack London on the Road: The Tramp Diary and Other Hobo Writings,* edited by Richard W. Etulain, Utah State UP, 1979.
———. "The Law of Life." *Children of the Frost.* Regent, 1902, pp. 35–49.
———. "Love of Life." *Novels and Stories,* pp. 418–37.
———. *The Road.* 1907. Peregrine, 1970.
———. "To Build a Fire." *Lost Face.* Macmillan, 1910, pp. 61–98.
———. "To the Man on Trail." *The Son of the Wolf: Tales of the Far North.* Grosset & Dunlap, 1900, pp. 102–18.
Lord, Albert B. *The Singer of Tales.* 2nd ed., edited by Stephen Mitchell and Gregory Nagy, Harvard UP, 2000.
Luttrell, Marcus with Patrick Robinson. *Lone Survivor: The Eyewitness Account of Operation Redwing and the Lost Heroes of Seal Team 10.* Little, Brown, 2007.
Mason, A. E. W. "The Crystal Trench." *The Four Corners of the World.* Hodder and Stoughton, [1917], pp. 30–47.
McClintock, James I. "Jack London's Use of Carl Jung's *Psychology of the Unconscious.*" *Jack London: Essays in Criticism,* edited by Ray Wilson Ownbey, Peregrine Smith, 1978, pp. 43–53.
Magill, Frank and Dayton Kohler, editors. *Carmen. Masterplots: Digests of World Literature.* Curtis Books, 1960.
Mandel, Miriam B., editor. *Hemingway and Africa.* Camden House, 2011.
Matthews, Brander, editor. *The Short-Story: Specimens Illustrating Its Development.* American Book Company, 1907.
Mellow, James R. *Hemingway: A Life without Consequences.* Perseus, 1992.
Mérimée, Prosper. *Carmen and Other Stories.* Translated by Nicholas Jotcham. Oxford UP, 2008.

———. "Mateo Falcone." Matthews, pp. 137–55.

Meyers, Jeffrey. "Tolstoy and Hemingway: 'The Death of Ivan Ilych' and 'The Snows of Kilimanjaro.'" 1985. Trudeau, *Short Story Criticism,* vol. 25, pp. 117–21.

Miller, Madelaine Hemingway. *Ernie: Hemingway's Sister "Sunny" Remembers.* 1975. Thunder Bay Press, 1999.

Montgomery, Marion. "The Leopard and the Hyena: Symbol and Meaning in "The Snows of Kilimanjaro.'" 1976. Howell, pp. 145–49.

"Not Guilty Is the Verdict." *Northern Wyoming Herald* (Cody, Wyoming), 21 November 1913, 1.

O'Donnell, Thomas F., Stanton Garner, and Robert H. Woodward. *A Bibliography of Writings by and about Harold Frederic.* G. K. Hall, 1975.

Oldsey, Bern. "The Snows of Ernest Hemingway." *Ernest Hemingway: A Collection of Criticism,* edited by Arthur Waldhorn, McGraw-Hill, 1973, pp. 56–82.

Oliphant, Ashley. *Hemingway and Bimini: The Birth of Sport Fishing at "The End of the World."* Pineapple P, 2017.

Oliphant, Laurence. "The Brigand's Bride." *Stories by English Authors: Italy,* pp. 101–36.

Oliver, Charles M. *Ernest Hemingway: A to Z.* Checkmark–Facts on File, 1999.

Ovid. "The Story of Baucis and Philemon." *Metamorphoses.* Translated by Rolfe Humphries. Indiana UP, 1955, pp. 200–04.

———. [Publius Ovidius Naso]. *Metamorphoses. The Classics Page.* Latin Library. n.d. http://www.thelatinlibrary.com/ovid.html.

Parry, Adam. Introduction to *Making of Homeric Verse,* by Milman Parry, pp. ix–lxii.

Parry, Milman. "A Comparative Study of Diction as One of the Elements of Style in Early Greek Epic Poetry." 1923. Parry, *Making of Homeric Verse,* pp. 421–38.

———. "The Homeric Metaphor as a Traditional Poetic Device." 1931. Parry, *Making of Homeric Verse,* p. 419.

———. *The Making of Homeric Verse: The Collected Papers of Milman Parry,* edited by Adam Parry, Oxford UP, 1987.

———. "Studies in the Epic Technique of Oral Verse-Making." 1930. Parry, *Making of Homeric Verse,* pp. 268–364.

———. "Traditional Metaphor in Homer." 1933. Parry, *Making of Homeric Verse,* pp. 365–75.

Plath, James. "Barking at Death: Hemingway, Africa, and the Stages of Dying." Mandel, pp. 299–319.

Plimpton, George. "The Art of Fiction: Ernest Hemingway," in *Conversations with Ernest Hemingway,* edited by Matthew J. Bruccoli, U of Mississippi P, 1986, pp. 109–29.

Pound, Ezra. "The Tree." *Selected Poems of Ezra Pound.* New Directions, 1957, pp. 6–7.

Pushkin, Alexandr Sergeyevitch. "The Captain's Daughter." 1836. *The Complete Prose Tales of Alexandr Sergeyevitch Pushkin.* Translated by Gillon R. Aitken. Norton, 1996, pp. 335–475.

"Quarrel Ended by a Bullet." *The Northern Wyoming Herald* (Cody, Wyoming), 1 April 1913, 1, 5.

Reece, Steve. *The Stranger's Welcome: Oral Theory and the Aesthetics of the Homeric Hospitality Scene.* U of Michigan P, 1993.

Reynolds, Michael S. *Hemingway's Reading, 1910–1940: An Inventory.* Princeton UP, 1981.

Reynolds, Nicholas. *Writer, Sailor, Soldier, Spy: Ernest Hemingway's Secret Adventures, 1935–1961.* William Morrow, 2017.
"Robin Hood and Little John." Child 3:133–36.
Robinson, F[rederick] W[illiam]. "Minions of the Moon." *Stories by English Authors: England,* pp. 23–55.
"Rodoschek [sic] Bound Over." *Park County Enterprise* (Cody, Wyoming), 12 April 1913, pp. 1, 5.
Rovit, Earl. *Ernest Hemingway.* Grosset & Dunlap, 1963.
Rushdie, Salman. "The Prophet's Hair." *East, West.* Vintage-Random, 1996, pp. 33–58.
Sanford, Marcelline Hemingway. *At the Hemingways: With Fifty Years of Correspondence between Ernest and Marcelline Hemingway.* U of Idaho P, 1999.
Santangelo, Gennaro. "The Dark Snows of Kilimanjaro." Benson, pp. 251–61.
Scott, Wilbur, editor. *Five Approaches of Literary Criticism: An Arrangement of Contemporary Critical Essays.* Collier, 1962.
Segal, Robert A., editor. *Jung on Mythology.* Princeton UP, 1998.
Smith, Maxwell A. *Prosper Mérimée.* Twayne, 1972.
Smith, Paul. *A Reader's Guide to the Short Stories of Ernest Hemingway.* G. K. Hall, 1989.
Stallman, R. W. "A New Reading of 'The Snows of Kilimanjaro.' 1961. Trudeau, *Short Story Criticism,* vol. 25, pp. 89–92.
Stephens, Robert O. *Hemingway's Nonfiction: The Public Voice.* U of North Carolina P, 1968.
Stevenson, Robert Louis. "François Villon, Student, Poet, and Housebreaker." 1872. *The Works of Robert Louis Stevenson,* vol. 3 of 20, edited by Edmund Gosse. Cassell, 1906, pp. 137–79.
———. *Kidnapped.* 1886. Penguin Classics, 2007.
———. "A Lodging for the Night." *Stories by English Authors: France,* pp. 9–41.
Stories by American Authors. 10 vols. Scribner's, 1896.
Stories by English Authors. 10 vols. Scribner's, 1896.
Stowe, Harriet Beecher. *Uncle Tom's Cabin; or, Life among the Lowly.* 1852. *Harriet Beecher Stowe: Three Novels.* Library of America, 1982, pp. 7–519.
Tacitus [Cornelius Tacitus]. *The Agricola and the Germania.* Translated by H. Mattingly and S. A. Handford. Penguin, 1970.
Tolstoy, Leo. "What Men Live By." 1885. *What Men Live by and Other Stories.* Translated by Ronald Wicks. Penguin, 1993, pp. 123–44.
Trilling, Lionel, editor. *Literary Criticism: An Introductory Reader.* Holt, Rinehart & Winston, 1970.
Trogdon, Robert W. *The Lousy Racket: Hemingway, Scribners and the Business of Literature.* Kent State UP, 2007.
Trudeau, Lawrence J., editor. *Short Story Criticism,* vol. 25. Gale, 1997.
———. *Short Story Criticism,* vol. 212. Gale, 2015.
Twain, Mark, *Adventures of Huckleberry Finn: Centennial Facsimile Edition.* Harper & Row, 1987.
Van Gennep, Arnold. *The Rites of Passage.* Translated by Monika B. Vizedom and Gabrielle L. Caffee. U of Chicago P, 1960.

Van Zandt, Townes. "Waitin' Around to Die." 1968. *For the Sake of the Song.* Fat Possum, 2007.

Villarreal, René and Raúl Villarreal. *Hemingway's Cuban Son: Reflections on the Writer by His Longtime Majordomo.* Kent State UP, 2009.

"The Wanderer." Hamer, pp. 172–79.

Weinstein, Arnold. *Morning, Noon, and Night: Finding the Meaning of Life's Stages Through Books.* Random House, 2011.

White, C. H. "The Village Convict." *Stories by American Authors,* vol. 6, pp. 5–30.

Whitman, Walt. "Song of Myself, 10." *Complete Poetry and Selected Prose.* Houghton Mifflin, 1959, pp. 25–68.

"Will Soon Face a Jury of His Peers." *Northern Wyoming Herald* (Cody, Wyoming), 7 November 1913, 1.

Willcock, Malcolm M. *A Companion to the Iliad.* U of Chicago P, 1976.

Young, Philip. *Ernest Hemingway.* Rinehart, 1952.

———. *Ernest Hemingway: A Reconsideration.* Revised. Harbinger–Harcourt, Brace & World, 1966.

INDEX